Journal of
British Cinema and
Television

Volume 9.3 · 2012

Film in Britain in the New Millennium

Issue Editors

John Hill
and
Julian Petley

Edinburgh University Press

Subscription rates for 2012

Four issues per year, published in January, April, August and December

		UK	Rest of World	N. America
Institutions	Print and online	£160.00	£175.00	$315.00
	Online	£141.50	£141.50	$254.50
	Back issues/ single copies	£35.50	£42.00	$75.50
Individuals	Print	£58.00	£64.00	$115.00
	Online	£58.00	£58.00	$104.50
	Print and online	£72.50	£80.00	$144.00
	Back issues/ single copies	£15.00	£17.00	$30.00

How to order

Subscriptions can be accepted for complete volumes only. Print prices include packing and airmail for subscribers in North America and surface postage for subscribers in the Rest of the World. Volumes back to the year 2000 (where applicable) are included in online prices. Print back volumes will be charged at the current volume subscription rate.

All orders must be accompanied by the correct payment. You can pay by cheque in Pound Sterling or US Dollars, bank transfer, Direct Debit or Credit/Debit Card. The individual rate applies only when a subscription is paid for with a personal cheque, credit card or bank transfer.

To order using the online subscription form, please visit www.eupjournals.com/page/jbctv/subscribe

Alternatively you may place your order by telephone on +44 (0)131 650 6207, fax on +44 (0)131 662 3286 or email to journals@eup.ed.ac.uk using your Visa or Mastercard credit card. Don't forget to include the expiry date of your card, the security number (three digits on the reverse of the card) and the address that the card is registered to.

Please make your cheque payable to Edinburgh University Press Ltd. Sterling cheques must be drawn on a UK bank account.

If you would like to pay by bank transfer or Direct Debit, contact us at journals@eup.ed.ac.uk and we will provide instructions.

Advertising

Advertisements are welcomed and rates are available on request, or by consulting our website at www.eupjournals.com. Advertisers should send their enquiries to the Journals Marketing Manager at the address above.

Contents

Introduction

John Hill and Julian Petley

In the first policy document to emanate from the newly established Film Council, launched in 2000, the organisation's first chair, Alan Parker, observed that 'sometimes with the UK film industry it's hard to know if we're waving or drowning' (2000: 1). Although he was subsequently to call for a 'radical reinvention' (Parker 2002) of the industry as the solution to this situation, it is fair to say that some ten years later the UK film industry continued to demonstrate a familiar mix of both strengths and weaknesses. Partly as result of the availability of tax incentives and other forms of public support, the level of UK feature production rose significantly higher than in the preceding two decades, totalling over 180 in 2003. However, although cinema admissions also rose slightly over the same period, reaching a 30-year high in 2002, Hollywood films continued to dominate the UK cinema box office while the majority of 'independent' British films struggled to obtain an adequate release. Indeed, as Sean Perkins' contribution to this issue indicates, the most commercially successful 'British' films of the decade – such as *Casino Royale* (2006), *Mamma Mia!* (2008) and the *Harry Potter* films – all depended upon the financial involvement of the US studios. To this extent, it is probably misleading to talk of a unified UK film industry given the range of film-making practices, funding levels and exhibition outlets of which it is composed.

Given this diversity it is also difficult to sum up the film-making activities of the decade in terms of clear trends. It was, of course, the decade of 'New Labour', first elected in 1997 and remaining

Journal of British Cinema and Television 9.3 (2012): 305–309
DOI: 10.3366/jbctv.2012.0092
© Edinburgh University Press
www.eupjournals.com/jbctv

in office until 2011. In contrast to the preceding Conservative administrations, the New Labour government was much more at home with representatives of the arts and media, whom they initially courted with some zeal. However, whereas it has been common to attempt to read British cinema of the 1980s in terms of the impact of the political project of Thatcherism, it has, a few films apart, been less usual to associate British films of the 2000s with New Labour ideology, partly due to the supposed 'pragmatism' (and absence of an alternative) with which the Labour government sought to invest its policies. The rhetoric of the 'creative industries', and its association with a post-industrial 'knowledge economy', did, however, encourage the government to provide extra assistance to the film industry, particularly in the form of tax reliefs that helped to swell the production figures during the early years of the decade and to encourage investment in UK studios. The UK Film Council itself was also a New Labour creation that subsequently fell victim to the cuts embarked upon by the succeeding Coalition government. Given its explicit combination of economic and socio-cultural goals, the UKFC might be said to have embodied elements of New Labour's conception of a 'third way'. However, as various contributors to this issue note, these goals did not always sit easily together and there were inevitably tensions between the promotion of the UK as a 'creative hub', fuelled by inward investment, and the cultivation of more culturally diverse and artistically challenging forms of indigenous film-making.

The politics of implementing tax relief also led, under pressure from the European Commission, to a revision of official definitions of what constituted a 'British film'. In some ways, this was a curious development. Film production has always been embedded in networks of international relations, but the vagaries of raising production finance, the growing dependence of 'national' films upon international audiences, and the increased 'globalisation' and 'hybridity' of 'national' and regional cultures have rendered any simple idea of 'British cinema' increasingly problematic. This is even more so given the impact of political devolution within the UK (encouraged by the Labour administration) and the semi-autonomous role that arts and film agencies have exercised in Scotland, Wales and Northern Ireland. Although devolution has encouraged a degree of resurgence of nationalism in both Scotland and Wales, this has not necessarily rested upon exclusivist ideologies, and both Jonathan Murray and Kate Woodward suggest how the cinemas of Scotland and Wales have engaged in a variety of transnational relationships and exchanges that complicate not only conventional notions of 'British' cinema but 'Scottish' and 'Welsh' cinema as well.

However, if the 'Britishness' of British cinema is no longer to be taken for granted (if, indeed, it ever could be), the idea of 'cinema' itself has also been undergoing change. Originally this issue was going to be entitled 'Cinema and Television in Britain in the New Millennium'. However, with one exception (which will be published in the next issue) the planned and hoped-for articles on television never materialised, and so initially we decided simply to drop the word 'television' from the title. But then we realised that this gave rather a misleading impression of the contents of the issue, which is by no means concerned only with the kinds of films which, traditionally, are shown first in cinemas. Indeed, many of the films discussed by Amy Sargeant are shown in gallery spaces, while a number of the horror movies mentioned by Johnny Walker went straight to DVD, a destination which is no longer regarded automatically as marking them out as flops unworthy of cinema exhibition.

As Sean Perkins indicates, in Britain, as elsewhere, even films which are first screened in cinemas are increasingly watched in locations other than cinemas. And despite the rise of the new media, television still remains the most popular venue for viewing films. The television companies, particularly Channel 4 and the BBC, also continue to be a major source of creative input and financial investment for British film-making. Channel 4's attempt to move in a more commercial direction ended in disaster following the box-office failures of *Lucky Break* (2001) and *Charlotte Gray* (2001). Ironically, however, the return to a more modest model of funding has not only led to the production of some of the most interesting British films of the last few years, such as *This Is England* (2006), *Hunger* (2008) and *Submarine* (2010), but also generated the most commercially successful, 'independent', 'British' film of the decade, *Slumdog Millionaire* (2008). While, as Charlotte Brunsdon points out, film and television are often defined against each other, the existence of a certain kind of British film-making practice continues to depend upon the patronage of television for which it, in turn, provides a degree of cachet and, perhaps ironically, a form of 'differentiation' from the norms of 'ordinary television'.

More generally, the rapid development of digital technologies has also transformed how films are made, shown and preserved. This has partly created an economic problem for the industry, insofar as the old models of revenue generation are now becoming severely strained, but it has also created new possibilities for low-budget production and distribution. Indeed, one of the most striking trends of the last few years has been the increasing number of low-budget films being made in the UK alongside the more headline-grabbing, big-budget studio films. Although digital technology has opened up a variety of aesthetic possibilities for film-making, it does not, as Sarah Street indicates, lead in any particular direction, and the films adopting digital have ranged from art cinema and documentary to science fiction and horror. For all of these reasons, then, we decided on the title 'Film in Britain in the New Millennium'.

As the above considerations might suggest, the kinds of British films that have emerged in the last decade have been highly varied. According to UKFC statistics for UK 'independent' films in 2009, comedies accounted for 18 per cent of cinema releases, documentary accounted for 13 per cent, horror accounted for 11 per cent and thrillers 9 per cent (with the amorphous category of 'drama' accounting for a further 26 per cent) (2010: 29). Given this range, it is hard to invest British film-making in the 2000s with a clear aesthetic identity although in terms of critical profile the long-standing British film-making traditions of costume drama and social realism (discussed by Claire Monk) have continued to prove resilient (if not numerically the most dominant). In the wake of the success of the Working Title films of the late 1990s and early 2000s, such as *Notting Hill* (1999) and *Bridget Jones's Diary* (2001), the pursuit of commercially successful British comedies has been a constant. However, as Johnny Walker points out, the same period has also witnessed the revival of the British horror film which in the past has functioned as a kind of alter ego to more critically respectable forms of British film-making. In terms of its adaption to low budgets and, in some cases, digital technology, the horror film might also be said to bear some similarity to the emergence of a new kind of 'artist's film', discussed by Amy Sargeant, involving a degree of cross-over between the cinema and the art gallery. Although very different in approach and style, the emergence of new forms of both genre and art cinema might also be said to exhibit a more general trend within British film-making (beginning in the 1980s) towards the crossing of artistic boundaries and the mixing of generic and stylistic elements.

Given the range of political, industrial, technological and artistic developments during the first decade of the new millennium, this special issue on film in Britain is necessarily selective in focus and emphasis. However, in pulling together analysis of and argument about all of these aspects, it seeks to place the past decade of British film-making in historical perspective and to identify some of the key terms in which future debate might be conducted.

References

Parker, Alan (2000), 'Foreword', *Towards a Sustainable UK Film Industry*, London: Film Council.

Parker, Alan (2002), *Building a Sustainable UK Film Industry: A Presentation to the UK Film Industry*, London: Film Council.

UK Film Council (2010), *Statistical Yearbook 10*, London: UKFC.

John Hill is Professor of Media at Royal Holloway, University of London. His most recent books are *Cinema and Northern Ireland* (2006) and *Ken Loach: The Politics of Film and Television* (2011). He was also a founding director of the UK Film Council and chair of the Specialised Distribution and Exhibition Committee that formulated a strategy in support of the distribution and exhibition of non-mainstream films through the establishment of a digital screen network and the Prints and Advertising (P&A) Fund.

Julian Petley is Professor of Screen Media and Journalism in the School of Arts at Brunel University. His latest book is *Film and Video Censorship in Modern Britain* (Edinburgh University Press, 2011) and he is currently writing a book on David Cronenberg's *Crash* for the BFI/Palgrave series *Controversies*, of which he is co-editor.

Film in the UK, 2001–10: A Statistical Overview

Sean Perkins

Introduction

It is 66 years since the peak of British cinema-going, when 1.6 billion tickets were sold – the equivalent of approximately 36 cinema visits per person per year. Of course, back in 1946 the cinema was the only place in which the British public could watch feature films. Television was still in its infancy (the limited London service was reintroduced that year following its wartime hiatus) and the first trials of videotape recording at the BBC were another six years away. Both television and the VCR had a huge impact on cinema-going in the years that followed, and yet the level of feature film consumption per capita is now much higher than it was in cinema's heyday.

In 2010, UK audiences watched feature films on 4.6 billion occasions, the equivalent of approximately 81 films per person (BFI 2011a). The technological shifts of the last ten years mean that UK audiences are now faced with a far more complex multi-platform world of digital film consumption and they can experience film through DVD and Blu-ray, on free-to-air and pay television, online, on mobile devices and of course at the cinema, which remains the crucial first step in the life cycle of a film. Of the 81 films watched annually per person, 64 are on TV, thirteen on DVD/Blu-ray, three at the cinema and only one through the nascent video-on-demand (VoD) platforms.

Film is both a vital cultural activity for the people of the UK and an industry with a highly skilled workforce that contributes significantly to the British economy. This article assesses the transformation in

Journal of British Cinema and Television 9.3 (2012): 310–332
DOI: 10.3366/jbctv.2012.0093
© Edinburgh University Press
www.eupjournals.com/jbctv

the UK film industry across the ten-year period 2001–10 as digital technologies radically altered the ways in which films are produced and consumed.

The UK film economy

The UK's film sectors (production, distribution and exhibition) showed strong growth over the period 2001–9, with total industry turnover doubling from £3.5 billion to £7 billion (Office for National Statistics (ONS) 2009, 2010). Film distribution represented 39% of the total industry turnover in 2009, followed by film production (25%) and film exhibition (19%). The film, video and TV post-production sector accounted for 16% of film and video industry turnover.

The contribution which an industry makes to UK Gross Domestic Product (GDP) is measured by its Gross Value Added (GVA). 'Value added' is industry turnover minus the cost of inputs brought from other industries and the main components are wages and salaries, interest and company profits. Value added is therefore a measure of the industry's ability to generate income for its workers, company owners and investors.

There are several ways of measuring the contribution of film to UK GDP. On the narrowest measure, the direct contribution to GDP by film exhibition, distribution and production, the ONS estimate for 2009 was £3.3 billion (0.3% of the UK's total GDP). This was up from £1.6 billion in 2001 (ONS 2009, 2010). Film distribution accounted for 46.8% of GVA in 2009, followed by the production sector (19.3%), post-production (18.6%) and exhibition (14.9%).

However, the impact of the film industry on the economy is wider than simply the narrow definition of direct contribution to GDP. Oxford Economics (2010) focused on the 'core' UK film industry – which includes companies and individuals involved in all film production in the UK plus distribution and exhibition activities associated only with UK-made films. Taking into account the wider impact of the film industry – through a range of direct and indirect multipliers such as companies supplying the film industry, connections with other creative industries, promoting British cultural life, attracting tourists to the UK and generating sales of other merchandise – it was calculated that the core UK film industry contributed £4.6 billion to GDP in 2009.

The film and video industries employ a high proportion of skilled people but it can be a volatile sector with unpredictable peaks and troughs in employment levels. According to the Labour Force Survey (LFS) conducted by the ONS, a total of 48,500 people worked in film and video production, distribution and exhibition in 2010. Over 30,500 (63%) were employed in film and video production, 11,200 (23%) in film exhibition and over 6,600 (14%) in distribution. The figures include workers whose main jobs are in film and those with second jobs in these sectors; they also include both full-time and part-time workers.

Because of changes to LFS estimates, employment figures across the decade are not directly comparable. Under the old classification, there were 47,000 people employed in the film and video industries in 2001 (66% in production, 25% in exhibition and 8% in distribution). Most people working in the film distribution and exhibition sectors were employees, but the film production sector had a higher proportion of freelance workers. In 2010, 60% of those engaged in film and video production, a total of 18,300 people, were self-employed. In 2001, the proportion of self-employed workers as measured under the old classification was 39% (British Film Institute (BFI) 2011a).

Two of the key strengths of the UK film industry are the depth of its production sector and its highly skilled workforce. In terms of geographical location the industry is well established in a number of key clusters – mainly in London and the South East where 68% of film companies are concentrated, but also in the North West, East, South West and Scotland. The number of companies involved in the film and video industries has grown rapidly in the last fifteen years, particularly in the production sector where the number of companies increased by 92% between 2001 and 2010. In 2010, there were nearly 5,000 film production companies (55% of the total number of film and video companies) and nearly 2,500 post-production companies (27%) in the UK. There were 395 film distributors (4.6% of the total) and 225 exhibitors (2.6%). The majority of companies were small (turnover under £250,000) but more than 70% of turnover was accounted for by the 185 companies with turnover over £5 million (BFI 2011a).

The UK film industry is a substantial exporter and makes a positive contribution to the UK balance of payments. In 2009, the most recent year for which data are available, the UK film industry earned £1,476 million in export income from film rights and inward investment in film production services. High-end production services are directly exported when overseas (particularly American) film productions use UK studios, locations and services such as visual effects and post-production. In 2009, the value of exported production services stood

Film in the UK, 2001–10

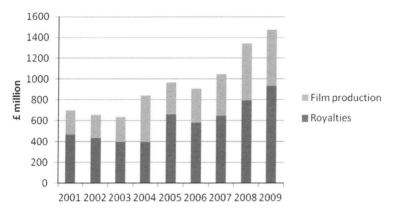

Fig. 1. Exports of the UK film industry, 2001–9. (Sources: ONS, BFI 2011a)

at £541 million with the remaining exports comprising £935 million and the industry achieved a trade surplus with the rest of the world of £929 million (Figure 1). Film exports in 2009 were 111% higher than in 2001 when the UK exported a total of £700 million made up of £468 million in royalties and £232 million in film production services.

According to a survey of global filmed entertainment markets by PricewaterhouseCoopers (2011), the UK is the third largest filmed entertainment market in the world, after the USA and Japan. The USA accounted for 41% of world 'filmed entertainment revenues' in 2010 which includes box-office receipts, home video (rental and retail) and online download and streaming revenues. It does not include television revenues other than pay-per-view. The next biggest individual territories after the UK were France, Canada, Australia, Germany and Italy. Although the Indian market is vast in terms of admissions, and although both India and China have huge populations and are growing fast economically, their filmed entertainment markets in US dollar terms still count below countries such as Australia and Italy.

Figure 2 shows the evolution of UK film revenues from 2001 to 2010, adjusted for inflation. After strong growth in the early part of the decade driven by the DVD market, aggregate film revenues have fallen since their peak in 2004. The theatrical market has grown, largely fuelled by ticket price inflation and 3D premium pricing while the physical video markets have declined markedly in value. The growth in digital multi-channel TV and pay-TV subscriptions driven by HD have helped to offset the decline in advertising revenues, but the VoD sector remains a very small element of the overall value chain for film.

313

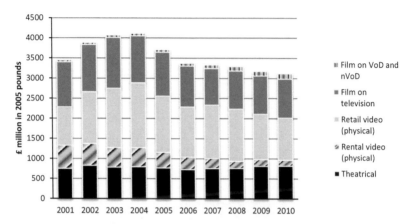

Fig. 2. Evolution of UK film revenues, 2001–10, expressed in 2005 pounds. (Source: BFI 2011a)

Film production in the UK

The UK production base has grown significantly over the last 25 years. There has been a gradual increase in the number of UK feature films made, from an average each year of 40 in the 1980s to 80 in the 1990s and to 130 a year since 2000. In 2001, the UK was the tenth largest producer of feature films in the world in terms of the number of films made. By 2010, it was the ninth largest producer by volume and fourth largest by production spend (Screen Digest 2011).

Productions can involve either a single country of origin, or they may be co-productions involving more than one country and made under the terms of a bilateral co-production agreement or the European Co-production Convention. They may be significantly financed and controlled from outside the UK and attracted to the UK because of its infrastructure, locations or tax relief, in which case they are classified as 'inward investment features'. Otherwise they are considered to be a 'domestic feature', made by a UK production company and shot wholly or in part in the UK.

Using these categories, the pattern of UK feature film production between 2001 and 2010 is outlined in Figure 3. The decline in domestic features between 2001 and 2004 occurred alongside a substantial growth in co-production activity, suggesting that it was easier at that time to make films as official co-productions than as stand-alone UK productions. From 2005 to 2008 the trend was reversed, reflecting a tightening in co-production certification requirements followed by the introduction in 2007 of the new UK film

Film in the UK, 2001–10

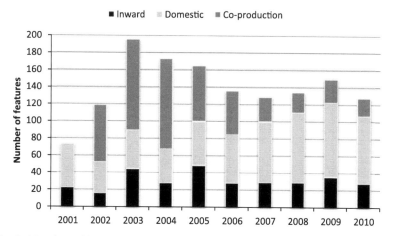

Fig. 3. Number of inward, domestic and co-production features, 2001–10. (Films with budgets under £500,000 are not included.) (Source: BFI 2011a)

production tax relief based on the amount spent in the UK rather than the whole production budget of the film. After a decline from the peak of 2003, the total number of films has levelled out at around 130 a year but domestic UK productions have grown as a proportion of the total. Production numbers continued at the highest level achieved after the introduction of tax relief and Lottery support for film in the mid-1990s. In 2010, 128 feature films (with budgets of £500,000 or more, which was the starting point for the UK Film Council's production tracking until 2010) were produced in whole or part in the UK (BFI 2011a).

The value of UK production in 2010 increased by 7% compared with 2009, making 2010 the highest value production year on record (Figure 4). The value of inward investment, at £935 million, was also the highest yet tracked. In 2010, inward investment accounted for 80% of UK spend demonstrating the importance of the link with the major US studios to the UK film economy. Since 2001, the fluctuation in production value has been driven principally by fluctuations in inward investment. In contrast, the combined UK spend of co-productions and UK domestic films declined from £386 million in 2003 to £230 million in 2010, reflecting tougher economic conditions and changing arrangements for film tax relief. The majority of this fall is due to the decline in co-productions, the UK spend of which fell from £169 million in 2004 to £35 million in 2009, although this recovered to £54 million in 2010. Spend on domestic UK production in 2010 declined by 22% compared with 2009 from £226 million to £176 million as the

315

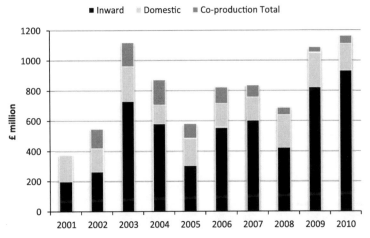

■ Inward   ▪ Domestic   ■ Co-production Total

Fig. 4. Value of UK spend of inward, domestic and co-production features, 2001–10. (Spending on films with budgets under £500,000 is not included.) (Source: BFI 2011a)

independent sector experienced the impact of the credit crunch on traditional sources of finance and revenues from DVD sales began to decline.

Until 2010, UK Film Council production tracking had focused on feature film production above a £500,000 budget level. However, a variety of sources, such as data on British film certification and the 2008 UK Film Council report *Low and Micro-Budget Film Production in the UK* (UK Film Council and Northern Alliance 2008), indicated an increase in the number of low-budget productions shooting in the UK. Figure 5 shows the number of low-budget films (with budgets under £500,000) produced in the UK between 2008 and 2010. The overwhelming majority of the 397 low- and micro-budget feature films made in that period were UK domestic productions (94%). In 2010, 147 low-budget films were made in the UK, up from 133 in 2009. UK spend associated with the 147 low-budget films shot in the UK in 2010 was £17.7 million and this spend represented 95% of the total budget of low budget films. The median budget over the three-year study period was £100,000 (BFI 2011a).

The UK box office

Cinema remains the crucial first step in the release of a feature film, providing the initial showcase and promotional platform for subsequent elements of the film value chain.

Film in the UK, 2001–10

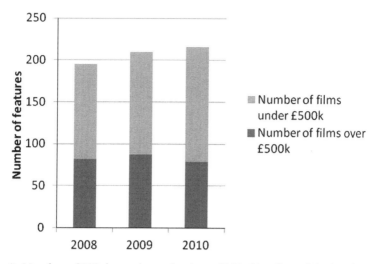

Fig. 5. Number of UK domestic productions, 2008–10, adjusted for low-budget films. (Source: BFI 2011a)

Cinema-going in the UK increased rapidly during the Second World War, with ticket sales reaching a peak of 1.64 billion in 1946. However, admissions plummeted through the 1950s and 1960s as television ownership became commonplace. The introduction of the VCR in the early 1980s had a further impact on admissions and the nadir was reached in 1984 with cinema-going levels down to 54 million, an average of one visit per person per year. However, the introduction of multiplex cinemas to the UK from 1985 onwards reversed the trend and ushered in a decade and a half of steady growth. By 2002, admissions had increased to a 30-year high of 176 million but since then ticket sales have reached a plateau with 2010's figure of 169 million slightly above the decade's average (166 million) (Figure 6). Box-office earnings increased 53% in the same period due to ticket price inflation and 3D premium ticket prices. By 2010, the UK represented the seventh largest theatrical market in the world based on admissions and the fourth largest by box-office revenue (Screen Digest 2011).

The UK theatrical market is dominated by US studio-produced titles, which together with UK/US studio collaborations such as the *Harry Potter* series typically earn 90% of the total gross box office (Figure 7). This has meant that the combined share of UK independent films and films from international territories other than the USA has rarely climbed above 10%. Earnings are also concentrated on a

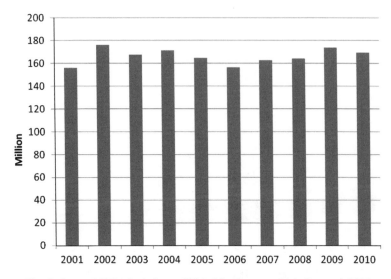

Fig. 6. Annual UK admissions, 2001–10. (Source: CAA, Rentrak EDI)

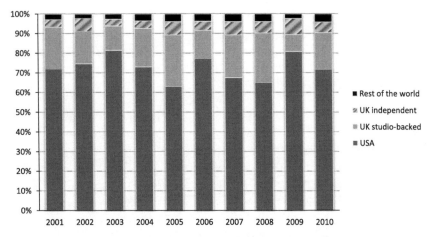

Fig. 7. Market share by country of origin, 2001–10. (Source: Rentrak EDI,
RSU analysis)

relatively small number of titles – in 2010, the top 20 films earned
almost half of UK box office revenue (48%), the top 50, 72% and
the top 100, 90%. The majority of releases – 457 (82%) – shared
just 10% of revenues, underlining the challenge for distributors of
independent UK titles and films from Europe, India and the rest of the
world.

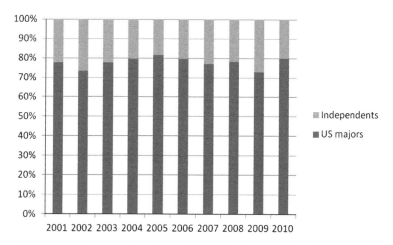

Fig. 8. Distributor market shares, 2001–10. (Source: Rentrak EDI, BFI RSU analysis)

Film distribution in the UK is dominated by a few very big companies, although a large number of smaller companies distribute almost as many titles. In 2010, the top ten distributors had a 94% share of the total gross box office from 237 titles, up from 92% in 2009 but down from 97% in 2001. As Figure 8 shows, the six major US studios – Paramount, Sony Pictures, Twentieth Century Fox, Universal Pictures, Walt Disney Studios and Warner Bros – accounted for 80% of market share from 151 titles, the same levels as at the beginning of the decade (BFI 2011a). The most successful independent UK distributor of the decade, Entertainment, averaged a market share of 9.5%, largely due to the success of the *Lord of the Rings* trilogy in the early part of the decade.

The best-performing films at the UK box office over the period 2001–10 again highlight the dominance of the US studios, although the list draws heavily on UK story material (Table 1). In the absence of admissions data on individual films, top films can be measured only in terms of earnings at the box office. *Avatar* (2009) is the highest grossing film of the last decade at the UK box office, with a final gross of just over £94 million, of which £84 million (89%) was earned from 3D screenings. The list is dominated by the major franchise films of the decade, *Harry Potter* and *The Lord of the Rings*, and sequels and franchise titles account for eight of the top ten films.

Table 2 highlights the top-earning independent (that is, made without US major studio involvement) UK titles. The highest grossing

Table 1. Top films at the UK box office, 2001–10

	Title	Country of origin	UK box-office total (£ million)	UK distributor	Year of release
1	Avatar	USA	94.0	20th Century Fox	2009
2	Toy Story 3	USA	73.8	Walt Disney	2010
3	Mamma Mia!	UK/USA	69.2	Universal	2008
4	Harry Potter and the Philosopher's Stone	UK/USA	66.1	Warner Bros	2001
5	Lord of the Rings: Fellowship of the Ring	USA/NZ	63.0	Entertainment	2001
6	Lord of the Rings: The Return of the King	USA/NZ	61.1	Entertainment	2003
7	Lord of the Rings: The Two Towers	USA/NZ	57.6	Entertainment	2002
8	Casino Royale	UK/USA/Czech	55.6	Sony Pictures	2006
9	Harry Potter and the Chamber of Secrets	UK/USA	54.8	Warner Bros	2002
10	Pirates of the Caribbean: Dead Man's Chest	USA	52.5	Walt Disney	2006

(Source: Rentrak EDI, RSU analysis.)

Table 2. Top independent UK films at the UK box office, 2001–10

	Title	Country of origin	UK box-office total (£ million)	UK distributor	Year of release
1	*Slumdog Millionaire*	UK	31.7	Pathé	2009
2	*St Trinian's*	UK	12.3	Entertainment	2007
3	*Gosford Park*	UK/USA*	12.3	Entertainment	2002
4	*StreetDance 3D*	UK	11.6	Vertigo Films	2010
5	*Kick-Ass*	UK/USA	11.6	Universal	2010
6	*Bend It Like Beckham*	UK/Ger	11.6	Lionsgate	2002
7	*Run, Fat Boy, Run*	UK/USA*	11.0	Entertainment	2007
8	*Kevin and Perry Go Large*	UK	10.5	Icon	2000
9	*The Queen*	UK/Fra/Ita	9.4	Pathé	2006
10	*Valiant*	UK/USA*	8.5	Entertainment	2005

* Made with independent (non-studio) US companies.
(Source: Rentrak EDI, RSU analysis.)

independent British film of the decade was *Slumdog Millionaire* (2009), £31.7 million, followed by *St Trinian's* (2007), £12.3 million, *Gosford Park* (2002), £12.3 million, and *StreetDance 3D* (2010), £11.6 million. *Slumdog Millionaire* was backed by Film4 while National Lottery funding through the UK Film Council supported the other three, highlighting the crucial role of public support in the production of independent UK films. Although outside the scope of the period in question, it is worth mentioning here two releases from 2011 which have surpassed *Slumdog Millionaire* as the highest grossing independent UK films at the UK box office – *The King's Speech* (2011), £45.7 million, and *The Inbetweeners Movie* (2011), £45 million.

The development of digital 3D exhibition is having an increasing impact on the UK box office (Table 3). In 2010, 28 3D films were released (double the number for 2009), generating £242 million from their 3D screenings (24% of the UK and Republic of Ireland box office). Of the top ten highest grossing 3D films of the decade, seven were animations (eight if *Avatar* is included, which is mostly computer-generated animation). Almost 90% of *Avatar*'s total gross was earned

Table 3. Highest grossing 3D releases in the UK, 2001–10

Title	3D gross (£ million)	3D gross as % of total gross	Distributor	Year
Avatar	84.0	89.9	20th Century Fox	2009
Toy Story 3	53.3	74.5	Walt Disney	2010
Alice in Wonderland	32.2	80.5	Walt Disney	2010
Shrek Forever After	21.5	68.6	Paramount	2010
Up	20.8	59.9	Walt Disney	2009
Ice Age III	18.2	51.9	20th Century Fox	2009
Clash of the Titans	15.6	77.7	Warner Bros	2010
A Christmas Carol	14.3	77.0	Walt Disney	2009
Despicable Me	14.2	70.8	Universal	2010
How to Train Your Dragon	12.4	76.1	Paramount	2010

(Source: Rentrak EDI, RSU analysis.)

from 3D showings compared with 52% for *Ice Age III* (2009) and 60% for *Up* (2009).

The UK theatrical market is highly competitive, with over ten new releases per week, on average, in 2010. Over six in every ten films released are specialised films, offering audiences an experience of cinema that is very different from mainstream commercial releases. These specialised films include foreign language releases, documentaries, re-releases from the archives or 'arthouse' titles offering an innovative cinematic style or engaging with difficult subject matter. An analysis of specialised film releases is shown in Figure 9. The proportion of specialised releases increased steadily from a low point of 51% in 2003 to 69% in 2009. During the same period, market share increased from 5% to over 15%, falling back to 6.3% in 2010. One particular feature of the last decade has been the rise in the number of documentaries securing a theatrical release, from just four in 2001 to 58 in 2010. The number of foreign language releases increased from a low point of 96 in 2001 to a peak of 193 in 2005 but has since fluctuated. While the overall market share for all specialised film categories remains low, interventions such as the National Lottery Prints and Advertising Fund have increased the

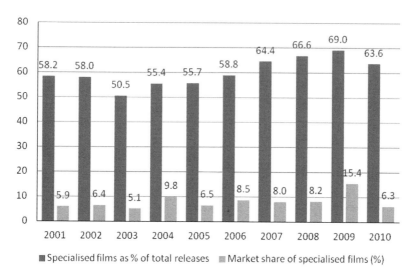

Fig. 9. Specialised films, 2001–10: percentage of releases and market share.
(Source: BFI 2011a)

release width of many specialised titles, enabling these titles to reach audiences outside London and the major cities.

The UK exhibition sector

In terms of commercial exhibition infrastructure, the UK had 3,671 screens in 716 cinemas in 2010, the equivalent of six screens per 100,000 people. This level of screen access falls short of the numbers in other major film territories such as the USA (12.8), Australia (9.2), Spain (9.0), France (8.7) and Italy (7.2) but slightly above Germany (5.8). The number of UK cinema screens grew by 16% between 2001 and 2010, compared with growth of 64% in the previous decade. The number of multiplex screens increased by 31% from 2001 to 2010 compared with a 14% decline in the number of traditional and mixed use screens. Although there has been a slowing down in the growth of the number of UK sites and screens, the key shift in the last decade has been the introduction of digital projection. The number of high-end digital screens in the UK increased from just four in 2002 to 1,415 by the end of 2010. Of these, 1,067 (75%) were 3D-capable digital screens.

In terms of the regional distribution of cinemas, London had the highest number of screens in 2010 (796) with a density of 6.5 screens per 100,000 people, lower than that of Northern Ireland (10.5) but the same as Central Scotland and Wales. The North East had the lowest screen density (4.1) in the UK. The North West and Yorkshire and the Humber had the highest proportion of multiplex screens (90% and 83% respectively) while the South West and London had the highest proportion of traditional and mixed use venues (40% and 35% respectively) (BFI 2011a). Eleven exhibitors owned or programmed twenty or more screens in the UK in 2010, with the five largest exhibitors accounting for 75% of all UK screens. Odeon was the largest exhibitor with 106 sites and 840 screens (23% of UK total) followed by Cineworld with 784 screens (21%), Vue with 642 (18%), National Amusements with 274 (7.5%) and Ward Anderson with 229 (6%). Screens showing mainly specialised films were concentrated in London and the South East, which accounted for 43% of the overall UK specialised film screen base. Scotland and the South West had 11% and 10% respectively but the North East (3.2%), Wales (2.8%) and Northern Ireland (0.8%) had the smallest number of dedicated specialised screens.

The screening of feature films in the UK is not limited to cinemas belonging to the major operators. In addition to commercial exhibitors there is a thriving non-theatrical sector of voluntary providers bringing a wide variety of programming, often specialised in nature, to local communities which would otherwise be under-served by the commercial operators. This sector is often referred to as community cinema with screenings taking place in venues as diverse as village halls, mixed arts venues and independent cinemas. The British Federation of Film Societies (BFFS) estimates a total membership of around 46,000 across all the film societies known to them, with a total number of admissions in 2009–10 of around 375,000 (2010).

The rapid introduction of digital technologies has also facilitated the screening of alternative content (AC) or non-feature film programming. The availability of a digital screen base has allowed a wider range of content onto the big screen, enabled interactivity between the screen and the audience, and potentially improved the use of auditorium capacity during typically quiet periods, for example special screenings of children's television programmes for parents with babies in the morning. Also, since AC events usually have only one or two screenings they tend to generate higher occupancy rates than feature films. In the past few years such events have ranged from live or recorded operas, ballets and pop music concerts to film screenings with live Q&A sessions and live sporting events. There were 54 such events in UK cinemas in 2010 (BFI, 2011). Notable alternative content events screened in 2010 included a live performance of *The Nutcracker* by the Bolshoi Ballet, the Six Nations Rugby Championships and the

Film in the UK, 2001–10

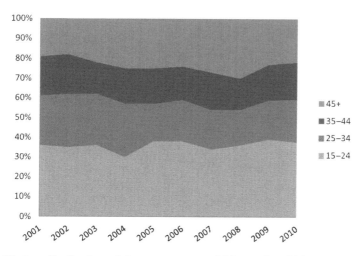

Fig. 10. Age distribution of cinema-goers aged fifteen-plus, 2001–10. (Source: BFI 2011a)

semi-finals and final of the FIFA World Cup. As in previous years, opera accounted for the largest number of events (24), followed by film with Q&A sessions (fifteen), theatre (five) and sport (two) (Screen Digest 2011).

Cinema audiences, 2001–10

According to the Cinema Advertising Association's *Film Monitor* survey (2011), more than six out of ten (62%) of the UK population went to the cinema at least once in 2010, while almost one person in five (19%) went to the cinema once a month or more. Teenagers and young adults were the most frequent cinema-goers in 2010 with 89% of 7–14-year-olds and 85% of 15–24-year-olds going to the cinema at least once per year whereas only 34% of the population aged over 55 had visited the cinema on at least once occasion. However, between 2001 and 2008 there was an increase in the proportion of over-45s going to the cinema, from 19% of the audience (aged fifteen-plus) to 30% in 2008, when the most successful film of the year, *Mamma Mia!* (2008), had an older audience profile (Figure 10). The last two years of the decade saw an increase in the number of 25–44-year-old cinema-goers at the expense of the over-45s which may reflect the number of animations and family films in the top twenties and the absence of a major hit with particular appeal to the over-45 audience. The most significant demographic in terms of audience share was the 15–24 category, which

325

declined from 36% to 30% of the fifteen-plus cinema audience between 2001 and 2004 before rising again to 38% of the audience in 2010 (BFI 2011a).

Two recent reports based on large-scale national surveys, *Opening Our Eyes: How Film Contributes to the Culture of the UK* (BFI 2011b) and *Portrayal vs. Betrayal?* (UK Film Council and Harris Interactive 2011) revealed wider film consumption patterns across a range of platforms. In terms of overall film viewing, over half (52%) of the population watched six or more films per quarter and one in ten watched more than 25. Just 12% of respondents had not seen a feature film on any platform over the three-month period prior to the survey (UK Film Council and Harris Interactive 2011). Respondents in the 45–54 age category were more likely to be heavy consumers of film, with 62% having watched six or more films in the three-month research period, compared with 55% of 16–24-year-olds, 56% of 25–34-year-olds and 42% of those aged over 55. Then respondents were asked to think about the last ten films they had watched and how they had watched them. The findings underlined the youthful nature of the cinema audience and the importance of television to older audiences, where 62% of viewings in the 55-plus age category were on broadcast television. In terms of home entertainment, DVD accounted for three in ten film viewings in the 15–24 age category and 27% in the 25–34 age group. Blu-ray viewing occasions were low, with a peak of 9% in the 25–34 age group. Peer-to-peer (P2P) piracy, film theft and infringement via cyberlockers or other Internet file hosting services accounted for 7% of film viewings in the 16–24 age category rising to 10% in the 25–34 age group while films downloaded via legal services represented 3% of viewings among 16–24 year-olds (the peak for this platform).

The changing home entertainment market

In addition to their theatrical release, films are distributed through physical video (DVD, Blu-ray and, historically, VHS) rental and sell-through, as well as, increasingly, via digital streaming and video-on-demand (VoD) platforms. The physical video retail market represented the most important revenue stream for the UK film industry over the last decade, with the increase in value fuelled by the growth in DVD ownership as household penetration of players increased from just 12.1% in 2001 to 92% in 2010.

However, the increase in DVD sales corresponded with a major decline in the physical video rental sector (Figure 11). Over 198 million

Film in the UK, 2001–10

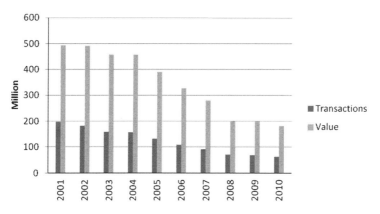

Fig. 11. Film-on-video rental market, 2001–10. (Source: BFI 2011a)

film-on-video rental transactions were made at the beginning of the decade but by 2010 the number of rentals had fallen to 63 million due to the rapid decline of the over-the-counter rental market in the wake of competition from multi-channel television, rental downloads (from providers such as iTunes), film theft and in particular the availability and lower cost of retail DVDs. Online video renting (with postal delivery) accounted for 56% of film-on-video rental transactions in the UK in 2010, but the emergence of this form of distribution has failed to offset the rapid decline in the over-the-counter rental video sector.

The number of films sold on video more than doubled between 2001 and 2008, from 96 million units to 196 million units, before falling in 2009 to 180 million units and then falling further to 160 million units in 2010 (Figure 12). In 2001, the VHS format accounted for 69% of the physical video market but in six years it had virtually disappeared – by 2006, 99% of volume sales were in the DVD format. Catalogue titles represented the bulk of DVD sales as consumers sought to build-up their home entertainment libraries. The top-selling video of the decade in all formats was *Mamma Mia!* with over six million copies sold and the decade's dominant franchise, *Harry Potter*, has sold over 27 million copies on DVD and Blu-ray in the UK alone.

Blu-ray, the high-definition video format, overcame the challenge of HD-DVD in an echo of the VHS/Betamax format wars of the 1980s. Although Blu-ray sales have increased markedly since the launch of the technology in 2007, it has yet to fully capture the public's imagination. Blu-ray players have been available in the UK since the end of 2006 but by 2010 household penetration was only 8%. However, it should be

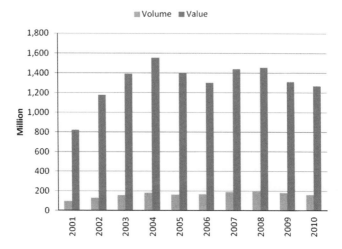

Fig. 12. Film-on-video retail sales, 2001–10. (Source: BFI 2011a)

noted in this respect that the PlayStation 3 (PS3) games console also functions as a Blu-ray player.

Film audiences are increasingly turning to online sources in order to access content. VoD brings films direct to TV screens, computers and to a range of portable devices. However, the nascent market remains a small part of the film value chain. The VoD market in the UK can be divided into television-based and online services and the total VoD and near-video on demand (nVoD) film market was estimated to be worth £159 million in 2010, up 22% on 2009. Over 15 million households were able to access television-based VoD and nVoD in 2010 and spent an estimated £118 million on films. Despite overall broadband penetration (fixed and mobile) of 71%, the online VoD market remained small in 2010. Online revenues increased by 86% to £41.2 million and Screen Digest (2011) estimated that 7.4 million films were downloaded to rent or own in 2010. Device-oriented services were the most successful, with iTunes being the dominant player in the online film market, followed by the Zune Marketplace with the Xbox 360 console.

Although there are signs of growth, the aggregate size of the UK VoD market remains small. According to Ofcom, average broadband speeds in the UK increased from 5.2 Mbit/s to 6.2 Mbit/s in 2010 but download speeds remain a factor in the slow growth of the market. Other issues to be addressed over the coming years include improving delivery to the television screen (although 2010 saw the launch of several services connected to Internet-enabled television sets such as LOVEFiLM's deal

Film in the UK, 2001–10

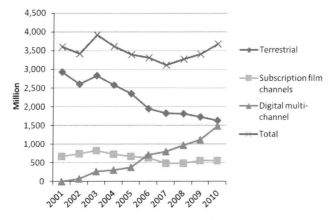

Fig. 13. Total audience for feature film on television (except nVoD), 2001–10. (Source: BFI 2011a)

with Sony and Samsung), enhancing the user interface via better menu options and recommendation engines, finding price points that work for both the industry and the consumer and increasing the size of VoD film catalogues so that a wider choice of material is available.

The emerging market also faces a challenge from illegal online sources. Based on a recent UK-wide survey, legal downloads represent just 1% of all film viewings, which is less than the reported volume of P2P file-sharing (2.5%) and file-sharing via cyberlockers or file-hosting services (1.1%). In all, 16% of respondents said they had watched films via P2P sharing and 11% via cyberlockers, although 17% said they had legally downloaded film content (UK Film Council and Harris Interactive 2011).

Film on television

In terms of viewer numbers, the single most important platform for film consumption is television. Almost eight out of ten film viewings in the UK are conducted via broadcast television and viewers had a choice of over 6,000 film titles across all channels in 2010. As in other sectors, the widespread adoption of digital technologies, via satellite, cable or digital terrestrial television, has led to major shifts in patterns of film viewing.

As Figure 13 shows, in 2010, there were 3.7 billion viewings of film on television, which is equivalent to approximately 64 film viewings per person per year. Film audiences have fallen on the traditional terrestrial channels over the last decade but this has been offset by the emergence of the free-to-air digital channels. Multi-channel television (freeview/satellite/cable) accounted for almost 44% of viewing in 2010, up from 17% in 2000. The digital switchover of UK television services was almost complete by the end of the decade with 96% of households having converted to digital TV by December 2010 (Ofcom 2011).

The number of feature films on the five main terrestrial channels fell from 2,394 in 2001 to 2,075 in 2010. However, the total number of films shown on UK television increased by 71% from 2001 to 2010 when factoring in digital multi-channel and pay-TV. A total of 42,682 feature films were shown on all types of television in 2001, increasing to 73,005 in 2010. The majority of film transmissions occur on the pay-TV film channels (50,756 or 70% in 2010), with BSkyB the dominant player in the sector with 9.9 million subscribers at the end of 2010.

The fragmented nature of multi-channel TV viewing has had a major impact on audience film viewing on the traditional terrestrial channels. Table 4 highlights the top feature films broadcast on terrestrial TV in the last decade. The highest audience total was recorded for *Billy Elliot* (2000) on New Year's Day 2003 with 12.7 million viewers. By 2010, audiences for the top film on terrestrial TV had fallen to 7.8 million for *Shrek the Third* (2007) (BFI 2011a). These shifts in television viewing look set to continue, as personal video recorders with large storage capacities and Internet-connected televisions have the potential fundamentally to alter the traditional schedule-driven broadcast model.

Conclusions

The period 2001–10 marked a major shift in the production and consumption of feature films in the UK, with the industry undergoing a period of transition from analogue to digital. It experienced fluctuating fortunes, with the level of cinema-going on a plateau, the rise and then maturing of the DVD market, the emergence of digital television and the lack of significant growth in new forms of digital distribution.

On the production side, the UK continues to be a regular partner in US studio-produced films, and the UK's infrastructure, locations, creative talent and expertise in areas such as visual effects attracted record levels of inward investment at the end of the decade. The most significant series of films of the last ten years was undoubtedly the *Harry Potter* saga and that series encapsulates many of the issues discussed in this article. Based on UK source material, shot in the

Table 4. Top ten film audiences on terrestrial TV, 2001–10

Title	Country of origin	Channel	Year	Audience (million)
Billy Elliot	UK/Fra	BBC1	2003	12.7
Deep Impact	USA	BBC1	2001	11.2
The Mummy	USA	BBC1	2002	11.1
Indiana Jones and the Last Crusade	USA	BBC1	2002	10.3
Indiana Jones and the Temple of Doom	USA	BBC1	2002	10.1
Mission: Impossible	USA	BBC1	2001	9.8
The World Is Not Enough	UK/USA	ITV1	2001	9.8
Chicken Run	UK/USA	BBC1	2002	9.6
Cast Away	USA	BBC1	2003	9.6
The Mask of Zorro	USA	BBC1	2001	9.6

(Source: BARB, Attentional, RSU analysis.)

UK with a British cast and crew, and produced by a UK company with finance from a major US studio (Warner Bros), the series has grossed £4.7 billion at the worldwide box office, sold 27 million copies on DVDs and Blu-ray in the UK alone, and has been watched 167 million times on UK television. The investment in films in the *Harry Potter* series has had positive effects beyond the franchise itself – Warner Bros has invested in Leavesden Studios as a permanent studio facility and UK visual effects companies have been able to invest in new CGI technologies. These developments underline the fact that the UK performs strongly in the global film market, both in terms of market size and film production, but it also underlines the UK's dependence on the USA for the scale of its industry.

While inward investment has thus flourished, there have also been major challenges for independent production and distribution in the UK. Traditional business models are under pressure, and although significant numbers of UK independent films are made, most find it hard both to raise finance and then to realise market revenues once they are made. Competition for available UK cinema screens is fierce and reaching audiences through other channels, such as pay-TV and online, is also problematic.

However, with broadband speeds increasing, smartphone and tablet ownership on the rise, and Internet-enabled televisions becoming more commonplace, the period of digital transition is by no means complete. Clearly, there will be significant new opportunities for UK film to reach audiences through these platforms in the years ahead.

References
BFI (2011a), *Statistical Yearbook*, London: BFI.
BFI (2011b), *Opening Our Eyes: How Film Contributes to the Culture of the UK. A Report for the BFI by Northern Alliance and Ipsos MediaCT*, London: BFI.
British Federation of Film Societies (2010), *Cinema for All: Annual Community Exhibitor Survey 2010/11*, Sheffield: British Federation of Film Societies.
British Video Association (2010), *BVA Yearbook and Directory 2010*, London: British Video Association.
Cinema Advertising Association (2011), *Film Monitor*, London: Cinema Advertising Association.
Ofcom (2011), *The Communications Market Report: 2011*, London: Ofcom.
Office for National Statistics (2009), *Annual Business Inquiry*, London: Office for National Statistics.
Office for National Statistics (2010), *Annual Business Survey*, London: Office for National Statistics.
Office for National Statistics (2011), *International Trade in Services, 2009*, London: Office for National Statistics.
Olsberg SPI and TBR (2010), *The UK Facilities Sector: A Key Contributor to the Film & Television Industries and to the UK's Creative Economy*, London: UK Screen Association.
Oxford Economics (2010), *The Economic Impact of the UK Film Industry*, Oxford: Oxford Economics.
PricewaterhouseCoopers (2011), *Global Entertainment and Media Outlook 2011–2015*, London: PricewaterhouseCoopers.
Screen Digest (2011), *Cinema Intelligence*, London: Screen Digest.
UK Film Council (2010) *Statistical Yearbook*, London: UK Film Council.
UK Film Council and Harris Interactive (2011), *Portrayal vs Betrayal: An Investigation of Diverse and Mainstream UK Film Audiences*, London: UK Film Council.
UK Film Council and Northern Alliance (2008), *Low and Micro-budget Film Production in the UK*, London: UK Film Council.

Sean Perkins is Head of the BFI's Research and Statistics Unit and is responsible for producing the *Statistical Yearbook*, official statistics releases and other research projects designed to contribute to evidence-based policy and to provide market intelligence to UK film stakeholders.

'This is for the *Batmans* as well as the *Vera Drakes*': Economics, Culture and UK Government Film Production Policy in the 2000s

John Hill

Following the UK general election of May 2010 and the formation of a Conservative-Liberal Democrat coalition government, a new team of Ministers was installed at the Department for Culture, Media and Sport (DCMS), the government department with partial responsibility for film policy. Barely two months later, on 26 July, the new Secretary of State for Culture, Olympics, Media and Sport, Jeremy Hunt, announced the decision to abolish the UK Film Council (UKFC), the publicly funded agency with responsibility for the support of film. Although the decision was met with a general sense of disbelief, it was not, perhaps, as unexpected as it might at first have appeared. Prior to the election, the Conservative Party, the major Coalition partner, had been decrying public-sector waste under Labour as a way of preparing for the cuts that were to follow. In a much commented upon speech, the future Prime Minister, David Cameron, had specifically called for reform of non-departmental government bodies, or quangos, which, he argued, had contributed to the growth of public sector expenditure. Although he was wary of announcing a forthcoming 'bonfire of the quangos', it was clear that many such bodies were destined for the axe. In the wake of the crisis over MPs expenses in 2009, the UKFC had also come under press scrutiny for both the high salaries and expenses of its chief executive and main officers and, therefore, looked set to be one of the quangos most at risk from any impending 'bonfire'.

Journal of British Cinema and Television 9.3 (2012): 333–356
DOI: 10.3366/jbctv.2012.0094
© Edinburgh University Press
www.eupjournals.com/jbctv

The decision to end the Film Council was also made easier by virtue of the fact that the DCMS, prior to the election, had been encouraging merger discussions between the UKFC and the British Film Institute, the body responsible for various aspects of cultural and educational policy (including the maintenance of the National Film and Television Archive). These negotiations had, however, made relatively little progress and it was reported that the new Minister for Culture, Communications and Creative Industries, Ed Vaizey, had called off the negotiations on the grounds that the remits of the two organisations were incompatible (Dawtrey 2010). The main surprise, therefore, was not so much that the new government should choose to review the arrangements for the delivery of government film policy but that the abolition of the UKFC should have occurred without any consultation or clear vision of how the responsibilities of the UKFC were to be discharged in the future. One of Cameron's arguments had been that ministerial responsibility for policy outcomes should not be devolved onto unelected bodies unless there was a demonstrable need for political independence. However, what rapidly became evident was that the abolition of the Film Council was less an attempt to alter – or reclaim – the direction of policy than a speedily contrived response to Treasury demands for savings. Even this, however, was not as clear-cut a matter as it was presented and the government was subsequently taken to task by the National Audit Office for having failed to undertake an adequate assessment of the 'financial implications' of its decision (National Audit Office 2011: 29).

Despite the inconclusive nature of its earlier merger talks with the UKFC, it turned out to be the British Film Institute that was called upon to assume the bulk of the UKFC's former functions (along with the newly established Creative England which took over from the UKFC-funded Regional Screen Agencies and Film London which, somewhat controversially, assumed responsibility for the British Film Commission). It was, however, only after these arrangements were agreed, and set in motion, that the government announced, in May 2011, that it was to establish a review of film policy. Given that key policy decisions had already been made, this appeared to be something of an afterthought designed to cover over the ad hoc nature of the policy-making process so far. This was further confirmed by the unexpected choice of Chris Smith as chair of the review panel. Smith had not only been the first Secretary of State for Culture, Media and Sport, following the renaming of the Department of National Heritage by the newly elected Labour government in 1997, but he had also been responsible for establishing the review group that had led to the formation of the Film Council in 2000. Given that it was politically inconceivable that this second review group should propose the reinstatement of the Film Council, Smith's appointment not only helped to legitimise, retrospectively, the destruction of his creation but also served as a reminder that, for all the *Sturm und Drang* accompanying the decision to close the Film Council, fundamental continuities in film policy remained. Indeed, while the review group was still in session, the government announced that, following an EC decision, it would be extending the tax breaks introduced by the previous government until at least the end of 2015 (HM Treasury 2011).

Continuities of policy

However, if Coalition film policy did not signal as dramatic a change in policy direction as the announcement of the UK Film Council's closure at first appeared to indicate, this might also be said of the policy decisions that took place under the new Labour government following its election to office in 1997. There is, for example, only one mention of film policy in Tony Blair's mammoth 718-page account of his premiership, *A Journey* (2010). It comes relatively early in the book when he boasts of how productive the first days of his government had been. Thus, along with the creation of a new Department for International Development, the awarding of independence to the Bank of England and introduction of bills for referendums on Scottish and Welsh devolution, he lists the announcement of 'a seven-point plan to revive the British film industry' (Blair 2010: 25). This refers to the plan, announced by Chris Smith at Cannes in May 1997, designed to help 'the film sector of small craft businesses into a properly integrated modern industry' (Smith 1998: 87). However, while Blair's account gives the impression of Labour rushing to the rescue of a beleaguered film industry, the most newsworthy aspect of Smith's appearance at Cannes was, in fact, the announcement of the Lottery-funded franchises that had already been decided upon under the outgoing Conservative administration.

It had, of course, been the case that for a long time the Conservative government had done little to help the UK film industry. Determined to remove all restrictions on 'free trade', the Conservatives under Margaret Thatcher abolished the quota (whereby British cinemas were required to show a certain proportion of British films), ended the Eady levy (whereby a small percentage of exhibitors' earnings was returned to film producers) and 'privatised' the National Film Finance Corporation which – as British Screen – had remained one of the few sources of public finance for film-making during the 1980s and early 1990s (Hill 1993). There was, however, a significant change in direction in 1994 when John Major's Conservative administration, partly in response to mounting criticism of the government's neglect of film, agreed to allocate a share of revenues from the newly established National Lottery to film funds to be administered by the Arts Councils of England, Wales, Scotland and Northern Ireland. Arriving at this point had involved a fair amount of manoeuvring on the part of the British film industry as, in order to qualify for Lottery funding, it had been necessary to argue that not only did British films constitute a 'good cause' but that, based on the precedent of tax law, they constituted capital expenditure as well. However, once the principle of Lottery funding for film had been established it quickly became a central plank of UK film policy as well as a source of considerable controversy. This was particularly so in the early years when the alleged poor quality and poor box-office performance of the films funded by the 'People's Lottery' became the focus of sustained press criticism (Petley 2000; Caterer 2011).

Although the attacks upon Lottery-funded films often appeared to misunderstand the guidelines that governed the allocation of Lottery funds, the strength of the press campaign against the films, nevertheless, helped to ensure that the original policy would be changed. In the case of English Lottery funding these changes were implemented by what was then referred to as a new 'super-body', the Film Council (subsequently renamed the UK Film Council), established in 2000. In order to advance his seven-point plan, Smith set up a working party to produce an agenda for action in support of British film. The Film Policy Review Group's report, *A Bigger Picture*, was published in 1998 and recommended, *inter alia*, the rationalisation of the various public bodies supporting film. Under this new arrangement, the Film Council replaced the Arts Council of England as the distributor of Lottery funds for film production as well as taking over British Screen and the British Film Commission (the body responsible for promoting Britain as a film location and attracting inward investment). At the time, it also seemed possible that the BFI, the oldest of the various film bodies, might be incorporated into the new organisation (and probably it would have been had it not been for its Royal Charter and charitable status). It is, therefore, something of a historical irony that it survived to subsume its short-lived parent organisation.

To this extent, the arrival of the Coalition and the 'New Labour' governments were marked by broadly similar initiatives (albeit that these occurred in a different order): the establishment of a policy review and the amalgamation of existing film organisations (indeed, it was Gordon Brown, when Shadow Chancellor, who had first promised a 'bonfire of the quangos' in 1995). Moreover, despite the sense of ushering in the new that these actions generated both governments nonetheless maintained a strong sense of continuity with the film policies of the preceding administration. To some extent, this might be said to derive from the peculiar status that film has occupied within policy discourses. As I have suggested elsewhere, government policy and legislation directed at film has been driven by a number of different imperatives (Hill 2004). Historically, government film policy has primarily been conceived as an *economic* policy concerned with the maintenance and support of commercial film production within the UK. However, in recognition of both the social effects and cultural importance that may be attributed to films, governments have also implemented film policies on both *social* and *cultural* grounds. Indeed, given the precarious economic position of the UK film industry since the 1920s, it is possible to argue that film policy has rarely been a matter of economics alone but has also depended upon cultural assumptions about the significance of film for the projection of 'national culture' at home and abroad (see, for example, Board of Trade 1936: 4). This interweaving of policy objectives became even more evident during the 2000s as a result of the way in which economic and cultural goals were increasingly linked together, as in the case of the Film Council which was discharged with the responsibility for not only developing 'a sustainable UK film industry' but also supporting 'film culture in the UK' through the encouragement of 'access to, and education about, the moving image' (a remit which it, in large part, fulfilled through its funding of the already existing BFI) (Film Council 2000: 6). Thus, while it has been common to comment upon the way in which cultural objectives were subordinated to economic ones during the 'New Labour' years, the actuality was rather more complicated. What might be said to have occurred is that the boundaries between the economic and cultural became increasingly blurred with the result that not only did 'cultural' policies increasingly come to rest upon economic justifications but also that 'economic' policies increasingly came to depend, both explicitly and implicitly, upon 'cultural' assumptions as well. Thus, while government film policy has sometimes been promoted as a hard-headed commercial industrial strategy it has rarely turned out to be so straightforwardly the case.

This may be seen in relation to policies in support of film production which have not only tended to dominate public debates but have also accounted for the lion's share of public spending. Thus, according to the *BFI Statistical Yearbook* (2011: 162), over 50 per cent of public spending on film is directed towards production (a percentage that is actually higher given that other listed activities – such as script development and training – are primarily forms of support for production). The two main ways in which funding for film production has been routed is through grants and loans and through fiscal incentives. Although not all of this expenditure has been governed by explicitly economic imperatives, much of it has been focused on 'commercial' production. By examining how this particular aspect of film funding has operated, this article will indicate how difficult it is to conceive of film policy as purely an economic matter even when it may have been presented, or intended, as such.

Production funding

Although direct government support for film production stretches back to 1948 when the then Labour government established the National Film Finance Corporation (subsequently British Screen) as a specialised bank to make loans in support of British film, the beginning of the modern era of funding was undoubtedly the decision to make Lottery funds available for film production. This was particularly so given that core grant-in-aid from the government did not increase significantly during the Film Council's existence. Thus, in 2009–10, the UKFC (2010: 11) reported that core grant-in-aid had increased for only the second time since 2003 (by £0.6 million to £25.3 million). As a substantial proportion of this grant-in-aid (£16 million) went straight to the British Film Institute, this meant that it was Lottery revenues accruing to the UKFC (£34.2 million in 2009–10), along with the funding provided by other national and regional agencies, that constituted the main source of grant-in-aid to film production. However, as previously noted, the administration of Lottery funds by the Arts Councils (especially the Arts Council of England) had quickly come under fire from the press and one of the first tasks undertaken by the newly established Film Council was the reconfiguration of Lottery funds. Although the Film Council was obliged to continue funding (to the tune of £17.2 million in 2000–1) the three ill-fated Lottery franchises announced in 1997, it also proceeded to launch two new production funds – the Premiere Production Fund (initially amounting to £10 million per year) and the New Cinema Fund (initially budgeted at £5 million) – as well as a Film Development Fund (worth £5 million) and a Training Fund (worth £1 million). The establishment of the Premiere Fund, in particular, appeared to signal the new direction in which the Film Council sought to take Lottery film funding insofar as it was designed to help fund bigger-budget productions that would prove 'profitable and attract significant audiences at home and abroad' (Film Council 2000: 15). Although the Film Council's launch document, *Towards a Sustainable UK Film Industry* (2000) indicated that that there would be an investment ceiling of £1 million per film, awards soon exceeded this figure. *Mike Bassett: England Manager* (2001), for example, received £1.2 million in 2000 while Gosford Park (2001) obtained £2 million in 2001. Other beneficiaries of large awards were subsequently to include *Valiant* (£2.5 million), *Five Children and It* (£2.1 million), *Stormbreaker* (£2 million), *The Constant Gardener* (£1.9 million), *Life'n'Lyrics* (£1.1 million), *Closing the Ring* (£2 million), *St Trinian's* (£1.4 million), *How to Lose Friends and Alienate People* (£1.4 million), *Harry Brown* (£1 million), *Nowhere Boy* (£1.2 million) and *The King's Speech* (£1 million).

Inevitably, the size of these awards and the apparent pursuit of 'mainstream' projects generated rather different questions from those that had previously accompanied the Lottery awards to film made by the Arts Council of England (and, to a lesser extent, by other Arts Councils in Scotland, Wales and Northern Ireland). If ACE had been criticised for supporting films that appeared to lack commercial potential (and which may have been rejected by commercial investors), the Film Council faced the opposite criticism for appearing to invest in films that commanded sufficient commercial appeal as not to require public funding (the animated feature *Valiant* (2005), for example, which was awarded over £2.5 million by the Council, received distribution from Disney in the US and was estimated to have cost $35 million overall). The notorious example of *Sex Lives of the Potato Men* (2003), which received over £1.6 million of Lottery funding, also illustrated how the funding of a film on an apparently 'commercial' basis could nonetheless attract considerable hostility from the very same newspapers that had previously lamented the lack of commercial success of Lottery-funded films. Even though a spokesman for the Film Council defended the film on the grounds that it would appeal to young working-class males rather than middle-aged, middle-class critics (and the film did, it seems, eventually turn a profit on the back of video and DVD sales), the general sense within the press remained that, whatever its commercial appeal, the film was nevertheless undeserving of public support on both aesthetic and moral grounds.

However, if the press response to the Film Council's funding of *Sex Lives* suggested that public investment in film could not really be regarded as solely an economic matter, the UKFC's own emphasis upon supporting 'popular' films did mean, nonetheless, that the economic performance of its films became subject to particular scrutiny. Unlike conventional arts funding (and other Lottery funds), awards to films were not conceived of as straightforward grants (or subsidy) but loans upon which a degree of return might be anticipated. Thus, in its launch document, the UKFC (Film Council 2000: 15) had indicated that the Premiere Fund's recoupment targets would be 'pegged to commercial norms'. Given the high-risk nature of film investment whereby many films fail at the box office, this was an ambiguously worded statement. Nevertheless, the Film Council did succeed in securing a good return on some of its early investments such as *Gosford Park* (which had fully recouped by the end of 2003) and *Mike Bassett* (which successfully recouped most of its award during the same period). The box-office success of later films such as *St Trinian's* and *The King's Speech* also meant that the Film Council saw its money fully returned. However, even though the Film Council could lay claim to a relatively high recoupment in comparison to film funding bodies across Europe, the majority of the films it supported did not, of course, recoup fully (and some films appear to have provided no return at all). According to the UKFC's Chief Executive, John Woodward, the Board had set a recoupment target of 50 per cent for investments supported by the Premiere Fund (House of Lords 2010b: 38). However, as of the end of 2008, the actual figure for the Premiere Fund was 34 per cent (ibid.: 31). While this would be regarded as a good rate of return for a conventional system of cultural subsidy (and comfortably exceeded the targets set for the more culturally oriented New Cinema Fund), it was less impressive for a fund designed to operate on a commercial basis. In the light of this, Woodward sought to downplay some of the Film Council's original ambitions, explaining to the House of Lords Communications Committee that the UKFC was not in 'the business of profit maximising on investment' but helping 'the film industry to get films made' (ibid.: 38). However, while it would be fair to say that the profile of the commercially successful films funded by the Premiere Fund helped to rescue Lottery-funded films from some of the opprobrium that had been a feature of press coverage in the 1990s, the 'commercial' rhetoric surrounding the Fund also rendered it, in part, a hostage to fortune, particularly if the would-be commercial films it supported turned out to be flops. Although partly motivated by a reduction in support for film production, this consideration may also have contributed to the decision to merge the Premiere and New Cinema Funds into a single production fund in 2010.

It is, of course, worth remembering that the New Cinema Fund did not operate with the same commercial expectations as the Premiere Fund and had, among its aims, the ambitions 'to encourage innovation in form and content' and to 'challenge audiences' (Film Council 2000: 16). Although there were complaints that the types of films supported by the two funds overlapped and that the New Cinema Fund was less adventurous than its predecessors, the BFI Production Board and British Screen, the New Cinema Fund did, nonetheless, provide financial backing for a fairly diverse group of films, ranging from *The Magdalene Sisters* (2002) and *The Wind that Shakes the Barley* (2006) to *Fish Tank* (2009), *Nightwatching* (2007) and *Yes* (2004). What some of these films backed by the New Cinema Fund demonstrated, moreover, was the multiplicity of factors involved in the emergence of a film as 'commercial'. This was partly revealed when the Coalition Culture Minister, Ed Vaizey, reported UKFC recoupment figures for the period 2006–11 which showed how a relatively 'uncommercial' project such as the documentary *Man on Wire* (2007), funded by the New Cinema Fund, had proved to be much more successful than a supposedly 'commercial' comedy such as *How to Lose Friends and Alienate People* (2008), backed by the Premiere Fund. Thus, whereas *How to Lose Friends...* had only returned £9,977 on an award of £1,471,145, *Man on Wire* had returned £390,081 on a UKFC award of £385,000.[1] Given these complexities, it was, perhaps, unwise of the new Coalition Prime Minister, David Cameron, to seek to intervene in the formulation of film policy ahead of the publication of the Film Policy Review Panel's report, *A Future for British Film*, by declaring that public money should be employed in support of 'commercially successful pictures' (Kemp 2012). This was not, as some media coverage implied, a recommendation of the report itself which proposed, in a more nuanced manner, that the objective of UK film policy should be 'to connect the widest possible range of audiences throughout the UK with the broadest range of British films and films from around the world' (Film Policy Review Panel 2012: 91). It was also, as some observers were quick to point out, a highly problematic – as well as historically ill-informed – remark given how difficult it was for both private investors and public agencies to identify in advance the components that make up 'commercially successful pictures'. As the history of the Premiere Fund demonstrated, even when a fund was devoted to funding potentially 'commercial' projects this did not guarantee that this would turn out to be the case.

John Hill

Creative industries

Despite the more proactive, pro-market features of the two UKFC production funds, they can, nonetheless, be seen to belong to a tradition of supporting film-making established by the National Film Finance Corporation, on the one hand, and the BFI Production Fund, on the other. The real discursive shift in policy rhetoric, therefore, might be said to have occurred in relation to the grounds upon which economic investment in film was identified and validated (transforming, in the process, how the 'profitability' of the film industry itself came to be conceived). In a revealing remark concerning his time as Minister for Culture, Media and Sport, Chris Smith (2003) comments as follows:

> Spare a thought, however, for the poor old Minister, faced with the daunting task of getting the increased funding out of the Treasury to start with... So I acknowledge unashamedly that when I was Secretary of State, going into what always seemed like a battle with the Treasury, I would try and touch the buttons that would work... I would refer to the economic value that can be generated from creative and cultural activity... If it helped to get more funds flowing into the arts, the argument was worth deploying.

Although the emphasis upon the economic importance of 'creative and cultural activity' had strategic benefits for the DCMS, it also chimed with more general socio-economic trends. In the period from 1979 to 1997, over three million UK manufacturing jobs had been 'lost' (Froud et al. 2011: 18–19). The 'New Labour' government, first elected in 1997, did little to reverse this trend, presiding over the loss of a further 1.3 million manufacturing jobs during the following ten years. In the face of manufacturing decline, the government sought to stimulate economic growth and global competitiveness through the promotion of a 'post-industrial' services-led 'knowledge economy' and, in 1998, the Department of Trade and Industry published a White Paper with a foreword by Tony Blair identifying 'knowledge, skills and creativity' as the country's 'most valuable assets' (Blair 1998). It was this 'modern knowledge-driven economy' with which Smith sought to align his department by establishing an inter-departmental Creative Industries Task Force discharged with assessing what steps government might take to increase the 'wealth-creating potential' of cultural activity and publishing a *Creative Industries Mapping Document* that identified the 'economic value' of the UK creative industries (DCMS 1998: 3). As various commentators have observed, the definition of 'the creative industries' was undoubtedly problematic, giving rise to a variety of questions regarding the principles governing the inclusion – and exclusion – of specific industries and the legitimacy of bracketing together relatively distinct economic sectors and cultural activities (Oakley 2004; Garnham 2005; O'Connor 2007). Nevertheless, the Creative Industries discourse has proved to be remarkably resilient and has clearly succeeded in giving credence to claims regarding the economic contribution of cultural activities. This was estimated to be £57 billion a year of revenues in the first *Mapping Document* of which film was held to account for some £900 million. Towards the end of the 2000s, the DCMS suggested the contribution of 'film, video and photography' to 'Gross Value Added' (the income generated by the sector minus consumption of goods and services) had become even greater, rising from £1.9 billion in 1997 to £3.8 billion in 2006 (though falling to £2.7 billion in 2008) (DCMS 2009, 2010).

This emphasis upon revenues (and 'value added') necessarily altered the way in which state support for film was conceived. The sole policy document of the Thatcher era, *Film Policy* (Department of Trade 1984), had also claimed to be encouraging 'the creative talents and business skills' of those involved in film production but had sought to do so by setting the industry 'free' from 'the paraphernalia of Government intervention', including state economic support (Department of Trade 1984: 18). Thus, while the report does refer to the economic turnover of the film industry (an estimated £300–400 million per annum), it does not consider the size, or economic contribution, of the industry to be salient to the formulation of government policy. However, subsequent to the DCMS initiative surrounding the creative industries, the measurement of economic value (however defined) became central to both the case for government 'investment' in – rather than 'subsidy' of – the film industry and the demonstration of the benefits that might be seen to accrue to the taxpayer (or Lottery-player). This was not, of course, an entirely new phenomenon. John Myerscough's well-known study, *The Economic Importance of the Arts in Great Britain* (1988), had paved the way for research into how the arts – including film – not only constituted economic activities in their own right but also contributed to the growth in ancillary industries, created additional employment, provided a catalyst for urban renewal, raised the profile and business attractiveness of a region and stimulated tourism. In the wake of the 1998 and 2001 *Creative Industries Mapping Documents*, however, studies of the economic impact of the arts and creative industries became increasingly common and, in the case of the UK film industry, a key component of policy debates (Cambridge Econometrics 2005; Oxford Economic Forecasting 2005; Oxford Economics 2007, 2010).

Much of this concern was in line with a broader government agenda to measure and audit the benefits of public investment of all kinds. However, in the case of the UK film industry, the new emphasis upon 'economic impact' also shifted the terms of the debate away from the profitability, or otherwise, of individual films (as occurred in relation to the use of Lottery monies) towards the economic benefits of film production in a country or region more generally. Thus, in the case of Northern Ireland, for example, it could make sense for the Northern Ireland Film Commission to argue that the Lottery funding of films had delivered a positive return to the local economy even when the majority of films that had received support had performed poorly at the box office (and thus provided relatively low levels of recoupment to the Northern Ireland Arts Council and NIFC) (Hill 2006: 185).[2] In this respect, what was decried in some circles as crude instrumentalism (the measurement of support for culture in terms of economic effects) became, in the case of film, quite an effective lobbying tool by virtue of the way in which it permitted a shift away from arguments about whether the industry was capable of 'standing on its own feet' towards arguments about the more general contribution that the film industry made to the economy, both directly and indirectly. This may be seen in the way in which tax incentives, previously regarded by the Thatcher government as an inappropriate interference in the market, came to be regarded as an acceptable form of government 'subsidy' that could be claimed not only to help remedy 'market failure' but also to constitute a net economic benefit to the Exchequer.

Tax incentives

The rise of tax incentives as a key plank of government film policy since the 1990s is not difficult to understand. From the Thatcher era onwards, both Conservative and 'New Labour' governments displayed a suspicion of what was regarded as state 'subsidy'; in such circumstances, fiscal incentives were seen to constitute a more market-friendly form of economic stimulus than grant-in-aid. By ruling that films could henceforth be regarded as 'plant', the Inland Revenue had ushered in capital allowances for film as far back as 1979. These had, however, been phased out by 1986 on the grounds that they constituted a part of the 'paraphernalia of Government intervention' that the 1984 White Paper had set out to eliminate. Partly due to the problems facing the industry by the end of the 1980s and effective lobbying for 'a level playing field' in the wake of the Downing Street seminar of 1990, tax write-offs for film were admitted under Section 42 of the 1992 Finance

(No. 2) Act by the then Conservative Chancellor, Norman Lamont. In a further example of the emerging political 'consensus' surrounding film policy, the new Labour Chancellor, Gordon Brown, extended these tax incentives in his 1997 budget by permitting (under Section 48 of the Finance Act) accelerated tax write-offs for films costing less than £15 million. Although debate within the press about film policy during this period characteristically focused on the use (and alleged misuse) of Lottery funds, the amounts provided through tax relief were by far the more substantial (though the more difficult to associate with specific films). Referring to the tax costs of Section 42 and 48 in the Commons in 2006, the Paymaster General reported a growth from £10 million in 1997–8 to £560 million in 2005–6 involving a total sum of £2 billion for the period from 1997 to 2006.[3] This constituted over four times the amount of direct funding that had gone into film over the same period as well as accounting for a significant proportion of overall production expenditure.

Although these tax incentives were associated with an increase in production spend and numbers of films made, they were also to prove controversial due to the opportunities they provided for tax avoidance of various kinds (HM Treasury 2005: 13). This led to the introduction of a number of changes aimed at eliminating tax loopholes and, ultimately, a decision to overhaul the whole framework of tax relief in 2004. As John Woodward, Chief Executive of UKFC, explained to a gathering of industry personnel at the time, the government was 'fed-up with the middlemen who were seen to be pillaging the tax system' and had little appetite for the renewal of Section 48. As he went on:

> These are days of tough Government spending rounds, tough choices, tough Treasury decisions. State pensions or private pensions? Cancer research or movies? More money for schools or bigger tax shelters for high net worth individuals? We need to understand how special the bubble we live in really is in the context of the big picture. (Woodward 2004)

Given such sentiments, it was, perhaps, something of a triumph for the film industry (and testimony to the government's continuing belief in the virtues of the 'creative industries') that it was able to emerge from the consultation process with a new revised tax relief in place (beginning in January 2007). This sought to minimise tax evasion by making a tax credit available to film production companies rather than to film financiers (and would-be tax dodgers) that was calculated on the basis of UK expenditure (which had to amount to at least 25 per cent of the total). This new set of arrangements also had the effect of reducing the cost to the Treasury though the sums involved still remained substantial. Thus, in August 2011, HM Revenue and Customs reported that claims amounting to £645 million had been received, of which £570 million had so far been paid.

The revised tax credit also succeeded in winning widespread political approval. Both the House of Lords Select Committee (2010a) and the Film Policy Review Panel (2012) expressed support for the continuation of the system. The Office of Tax Simplification, launched in 2010 by the incoming Coalition government, also recommended that the relief be retained despite the Coalition's adoption of a range of 'austerity' measures. To some extent, this was a tribute to the efforts that had gone into demonstrating the economic impact that the film industry could be shown to command. The Office of Film Tax Relief, for example, explicitly cites the research of Oxford Economics, a fairly open piece of 'lobbynomics' commissioned by the UK Film Council and Pinewood Shepperton, that not only argues that the film industry makes a substantial contribution to GDP (over £4.5 billion in 2009) and to the Exchequer (£1.2 billion in the same year) but that, in the absence of tax relief, these figures would have been significantly smaller (Oxford Economics 2010; Brown 2010). Thus, while Magor and Schlesinger (2009: 317) query the extent to which the post-2006 Film Tax Relief may be regarded as the product of 'creative industries policy' as opposed to a longer-standing tradition of Treasury interventionism, it does seem to be the case that the emphasis upon 'economic value' and 'economic impact' to be found in creative industries discourse–and research–did, nevertheless, come to exert a growing influence upon Treasury thinking (and help to make the case that tax relief should not necessarily be regarded as simply a drain on the exchequer).

This does not mean, however, that tax policy has been free of ambiguities and tensions in the way in which it has been conceived and implemented. For, while the use of tax incentives has been understood primarily as an 'economic' policy concerned with support for industrial activity, the Treasury, in establishing its review of tax reform, actually declared that the 'specific case' for government support of film production rested upon the 'important role that film plays in British cultural life' (HM Treasury 2005: 5). As a result, the review document goes on to propose that 'the core aim of tax reliefs' must be 'to promote the sustainable production of culturally British films' (ibid.: 8). This, however, is a more complex formulation than it at first appears and the precise ways in which the terms 'cultural Britishness' and economic 'sustainability' are to be understood has been a matter of some dispute.

While there is, as previously suggested, a long tradition of governments invoking the contribution of cinema to 'national life' in support of government measures on behalf of film, the specific impetus for the contemporary emphasis upon 'cultural' film may be linked to the UK's membership of the European Union. Under Article 87 of the EC Treaty, any use of state resources that 'distorts or threatens to distort competition by favouring certain undertakings or the production of certain goods' was deemed to be 'incompatible' with the common market. Although 'aid to promote culture and heritage conservation' was held to be an exception, this was only the case where such aid did 'not affect trading conditions and competition in the Community' (European Commission 1997). This, however, was insufficient to allay concerns that EU competition law might prevent member states 'from supporting their cinema sector in an international environment marked by tough competition with other continents' and led the European Commission to lay out new rules that permitted governments to assist film and television production provided they took steps, in line with the principle of subsidiarity, to ensure that 'the cultural content of the works supported' was established 'on the basis of verifiable national criteria' (European Commission 2001). Although tax reliefs do not constitute direct grant-in-aid, the EC nonetheless regards them as a form of 'state aid' that involves the deployment of state resources in a manner that is selective and liable to distort competition (European Commission 2006: 9). As a result, it became necessary for the UK government to demonstrate that the films benefiting from the proposed new tax reliefs exhibited the 'cultural content', based on 'verifiable national criteria', that exemption from EU competition law required.

This resulted in the adoption of a 'cultural test' for British films by the UK government; however, the basis upon which a 'culturally British' film might be defined provoked something of a political tussle insofar as the European Commission rejected the UK government's initial version of the test. To some extent, it could be said that this became the case due to a need to reconcile what had originally been conceived as an economic policy, designed to stimulate private investment in film production, with the EU's insistence that tax incentives constituted 'state aid' that had to be justified on 'cultural' grounds. The Chancellor's original extension of tax relief in 1997, for example, had been planned to 'promote growth, employment, investment and opportunities in the British film industry' rather than achieve specific cultural objectives (HM Treasury 1997). Tax incentives, under both Section 42 and Section 48, were, of course, only available to 'British qualifying' films but the definition of a 'British film' at this time rested upon purely industrial criteria (such as the use of a UK studio or the registration of a production company as British). This also meant that what counted as 'British' could vary considerably. Addressing the House of Commons in 1997, the Chancellor, Gordon Brown, declared that 'too many British films that could be made in Britain are being made abroad, or not at all'.[4] This is, however, an ambiguous formulation that suggests something of the 'Janus-faced' character of tax policy as it has evolved. On the one hand, it appears to be a policy concerned to address 'market failure' and encourage the production of British films that might not otherwise attract investment and get made. On the other hand, it is also a policy designed to encourage the production of films in Britain that would otherwise be made 'abroad' (and, thus, which might be said to be only potentially 'British').

Brown's measures were informed by the Middleton Report on Film Finance which had argued that, as tax incentives constituted 'a significant feature' of most film-making countries, similar incentives at a similar level were necessary in the UK if the film industry was 'to compete effectively in an open international market' (Advisory Committee on Film Finance 1996: 38). This recommendation had, of course, less to do with the encouragement of 'British films' as commonly understood than with the attraction of much bigger-budget international productions to Britain (and the economic benefits with which they are associated). Britain has, of course, a long history of inward investment, particularly on the part of the Hollywood majors which have made extensive use of UK studios (encouraged, in part, by quotas or favourable exchange rates). However, under pressure to reduce production costs (especially labour costs) and increase international box-office earnings, Hollywood production has become increasingly mobile in character, thereby encouraging increasing competition among countries (such as Ireland, the Czech Republic, Canada, New Zealand and Australia) to attract films to their territories through the use of tax incentives (Miller et al. 2001).[5] As a result, the view that the UK has to remain competitive by matching the tax incentives of other countries has become a key feature of arguments in support of fiscal incentives for UK film production. These incentives were, in turn, linked to the Film Council's ambition to promote the UK as a 'film hub' (and the Labour government's even grander aim of turning the UK into 'the world's creative hub') that would, in the words of the UKFC's first Chairman, Alan Parker, supply 'skills and services to the global film market' (Parker 2002:10; DCMS 2005).

This idea of a 'creative hub' may also be seen to be connected to the arguments over the 'cultural test'. Under the British government's original version of the UK cultural test, the 'use of cultural hubs' (including the use of UK studios and post-production facilities) constituted the most important component. The purpose of this was clear from the pronouncements of the Creative Industries Minister, James Purnell, when announcing the government's plans for tax reform in 2005. Indicating that 'the test would not dissuade Hollywood productions from taking productions to the UK', he argued that 'cultural goals go hand in hand with the industrial goals' and that the proposals were aimed at 'the Batmans as well as the Vera Drakes' (Milmo and Gibson 2005). However, as the European Commission noted, the title of 'cultural hub' was something of a misnomer insofar as it pertained to economic expenditure rather than what would commonly be regarded as the 'cultural content aspects of filmmaking' (European Commission 2006: 11). As a result, the UK government was obliged to reduce significantly the score it attached to the use of 'cultural hubs' and increase the number of points it awarded for 'cultural content' and 'cultural contribution'. However, although there were concerns that the revised version of the cultural test might deter Hollywood productions, it was crafted in such a way (awarding four points, for example, for the mere use of the English language) that, according to the US trade magazine *Variety*, it was 'a hard test' for Hollywood films involved in filming in the UK 'to fail' (Dawtrey 2008). Indeed, once the relatively low hurdle of the cultural test was jumped, the new tax credit was actually more generous to Hollywood productions in comparison to its predecessors insofar as it applied to all UK expenditure, including the salaries of American talent, and did not specify an overall ceiling on production spend.

Given these circumstances, it is hardly surprising that the co-Chairman of Working Title and subsequent Chair of the UK Film Council, Tim Bevan, felt able to tell the House of Lords Select Committee in 2010 that the tax credit scheme, introduced three years earlier, was 'working brilliantly for inward investment in terms of bringing the studios into this country to make big films here' (House of Lords 2010b: 309). This is borne out by the aggregate figures, released by HM Revenue and Customs, summarising the operation of the tax credit scheme in the years between 2007 and 2011. According to these, over 100 claims were made on behalf of 'large-budget films' (defined as costing over £20 million) for which the average tax-credit payment amounted to £3.7 million (though given that a 20 per cent tax relief can be claimed on 80 per cent of qualifying expenditure some of these payments will have been substantially higher). As the majority of these 'large-budget films', as well as some of the 'low-budget' ones, will have been US-backed, this means that a policy in support of 'the sustainable production of culturally British films' has entailed the provision of financially generous 'state aid' to numerous big Hollywood productions such as the *Harry Potter* films, *Mr Bean's Holiday*, *Prince of Persia*, *Hugo* and *Pirates of the Caribbean 4* (all of which passed the cultural test).

That this should be the case also sheds light on how the idea of 'sustainability' has tended to function within policy discourse. As previously noted, the Film Council was initially established with the brief to promote 'a sustainable UK film industry' while, for the Treasury, the primary aim of tax policy was 'the sustainable production of culturally British films'. The term 'sustainable', however, has rarely possessed a clearly defined meaning. At times, it has been taken to mean 'profitable', 'commercially successful' or 'self-sustaining'. However, the appeal of the term has also seemed to be, in part, that it is vaguer (and gentler) than many of these possible synonyms. As the former Head of Research and Statistics at the UK Film Council, Jim Barratt, has suggested, it is possible to draw a distinction between 'a hard concept of sustainability' that aspires to the creation of an industry that survives 'without outside support or influence', and a 'soft conception' that involves the idea of 'sustaining' the film industry within (or without the exhaustion of) 'available resources' (Barratt 2010). The Conservative administration, under Margaret Thatcher, might be said to have experimented with a 'hard concept' of sustainability by withdrawing various forms of state support and subjecting the film industry to the rigours of the 'free market'. However, faced with the slump in British film production to which this led, the succeeding Conservative government, under John Major, signalled a degree of retreat from earlier policies by introducing tax reliefs and providing film with Lottery support. Although 'New Labour' inherited the 'pro-market' sentiments of the preceding government, it also, in the case of film, maintained a 'soft concept' of sustainability by introducing additional forms of fiscal support and relaxing the ways in which Lottery funds could be employed to assist film. Thus, notwithstanding some of the rhetoric with which they have been associated, the policies for promoting 'a sustainable UK film industry' might be said to have involved the acceptance of two kinds of dependency. In the first case, it has involved an acceptance that the UK film industry is dependent upon Hollywood for investment in film production and the maintenance of a creative and technical infrastructure or 'film hub' (involving skilled technicians, studios and post-production facilities). However, given the mobility of Hollywood production and the vulnerability of investment to international competition (and fluctuations in the exchange rate), the maintenance of a 'sustainable' film industry has also come to be seen to depend upon the continuing availability (and, indeed, extension) of generous tax inducements (along with other kinds of state support).

As Goldsmith and O'Regan (2005: 59) suggest, it has been the assumption of governments that the presence of international productions and studios will benefit local film production (rather than simply provide employment on inward investment films). However, the development of 'convergent and productive relations' between the two is neither automatic nor guaranteed. Indeed, given the huge percentage of production spend accounted for by 'inward investment' films (over 80 per cent in 2010), the published figures on the state of 'the UK film industry' often disguise the diversity of production practices that constitute UK film production and the fragile economic basis upon which the bulk of UK 'independent' production is conducted. In its 1998 report, *A Bigger Picture*, the Film Policy Review Group accounted for the weakness of the British film industry in terms of a 'production-led and fragmented... 'cottage industry" in which distribution is 'dominated by big US companies' (1998: 14). At the end of the 'New Labour' era, the situation of the film industry in Britain remained much the same. In 2010, subsidiaries of the Hollywood majors still accounted for over 80 per cent of UK box office which was practically the same figure that it had been in the late 1990s (BFI 2011: 77). Production also continued to be fragmented with production activity spread across 232 production companies, of which 219 were involved in only one feature film (ibid.: 154). The majority of British films also continued to struggle to obtain adequate distribution and exhibition with only a handful each year achieving significant box-office returns (primarily those funded and/or distributed by the Hollywood majors). In line with the EU more generally (in which US distributors have typically accounted for over 70 per cent of market share), the continuing fragility of 'independent' UK production is indicative of the failure on the part of 'pro-market' policies to address the ways in which the imbalances of power associated with film distribution have themselves distorted the operations of the 'free market' and restricted the access that audiences have to see a full range of British (and European) films in cinemas. As such, the political strategy of 'New Labour' to go with the grain of globalisation may have served to sustain UK film production in some ways but also to have maintained its underlying weaknesses in others. In this regard, it is also worth recalling the emphasis that *A Bigger Picture* placed upon the role of television in supporting 'a sustainable British film industry' (Film Policy Review Group 1998: 24). Although Channel 4 and the BBC have continued to invest modest sums in British film production, the enhanced role envisaged for television in sustaining film-making has not materialised despite the continued popularity of television as a medium for film viewing. In this respect, it is another minor irony that one of the headline recommendations of the most recent film policy review in 2012 should have been a call for increased support for British film production (enforced by legislation if necessary) on the part of the major broadcasters (Film Policy Review Panel 2011: 55).

Conclusion

In its report on film finance in 1996 (which led to the extension of tax reliefs in 1997), the Middleton group noted that the Treasury appeared to have accepted that the film industry was a 'special case' by virtue of the way it had permitted benefits that were unavailable to other industries (Advisory Committee on Film Finance 1996: 38). If, at that time, the cultural underpinnings of fiscal policy were implicit rather than explicit, they have become much more overt since the introduction of the 'cultural test' for a 'British film' in 2007. In a slightly odd twist of the creative industries discourse, this has also led other industries to lay claim to 'state aid' on the grounds that they too may be seen to generate 'cultural', rather than simply 'economic', value. This has been so in the case of the video games sector, for example, which initially failed to win government support for tax relief on purely economic grounds but now seems set to obtain a tax subsidy provided the EC accept that it, like the UK film industry, may be held to be engaged in the production of 'culturally British' goods (TIGA 2011: 13).[6] However, if film has historically enjoyed a 'special' status as an industry it might also be said to have enjoyed a certain degree of favour as a 'cultural asset' as well. Thus, when the revised version of the 'cultural test' was debated in the House of Lords, the composer and owner of seven London theatres, Andrew Lloyd Webber, felt moved to ask why such reliefs were not also available to the theatre.[7]

In a sense the demands on behalf of both the theatre and video games for tax reliefs similar to those enjoyed by film indicate how blurred the lines between 'economics' and 'culture' have now become within policy discourse. In the case of film, this means that while the value of cultural activity has increasingly been measured in industrial and economic terms, it is also the case that economic policy (even for the most commercially successful of films) has itself been underpinned by cultural considerations. However, although 'economic' and cultural' goals are now routinely linked together within UK film policy discourse, this does not mean that the relationship between the two is clearly agreed and settled. Indeed, the use of state aid in support of film looks set to become a matter of political dispute once more in the wake of the publication of a draft EC Cinema Communication, planned to replace the Cinema Communication of 2001. Partly motivated by the fear of a 'subsidy race' among member states keen to attract inward investment films, the new Communication proposes a reduction in the proportion of a film budget that governments can require to be spent within a particular territory as well as a new definition of a 'European audiovisual work' that would potentially restrict the aid currently available to Hollywood films shooting within the EU (European Commission 2012). Given that these changes will almost certainly have a greater impact upon the UK than other EU states, the outcome of the current consultation may well be of considerable significance for the future implementation of UK policy in support of 'the sustainable production of film as a cultural product'.[8]

Notes

1. House of Commons, Written Answer, 20 July 2011, col. 1056W, http://www.publications.parliament.uk/pa/cm201011/cmhansrd/cm110720/text/110720w0003.htm.
2. Due to the devolution of Lottery funding to bodies in Scotland, Wales and Northern Ireland, it is, of course, difficult to identify a unitary UK film policy. However, although different 'national' film bodies have pursued distinct 'regional' policies, the influence of 'creative industries' discourse has, nonetheless, been evident across the UK.
3. House of Commons, Written Answer, 27 February 2006, vol. 433, col. 328w, http://www.publications.parliament.uk/pa/cm200506/cmhansrd/vo060227/text/60227w84.htm#60227w84.html_spnew7.
4. House of Commons, Debates, 2 July 1997, vol. 297, col. 308, http://www.publications.parliament.uk/pa/cm199798/cmhansrd/vo970702/debtext/70702-21.htm#70702-21_spmin1.
5. Different states within the US have also become involved in the global battle for Hollywood business, generating lively debates regarding the costs and benefits of these and how they are to be measured and assessed (see Wells and Posey 2011).
6. In his March 2012 budget, the Conservative Chancellor, George Osborne, announced his intention to introduce tax schemes, similar to the film tax credit, for the video games, animation and high-end television production industries subject to state-aid approval by the EC (Sabbagh 2012).
7. House of Lords, Debates, 7 December 2006, vol. 687, col. 1335, http://www.publications.parliament.uk/pa/ld200607/ldhansrd/text/61207-0014.htm.

8. This is the objective for state aid identified by the UK government in response to an EC 'Issues Paper' on 'Assessing state aid for films and other audio visual works' that preceded the publication of the draft Cinema Communication. See the letter from Gemma Cook, UK Representation to the EU Brussels, 5 October 2011, http://ec.europa.eu/competition/consultations/2011_state_aid.../uk_en.pdf.

References

Advisory Committee on Film Finance (1996), *Report to the Secretary of State for National Heritage*, Chair Sir Peter Middleton, London: Department of National Heritage.

Barratt, Jim (2010), 'On sustainability: UK film policy after the UK Film Council', *Bigger Picture Research*, 2 December, http://www.biggerpictureresearch.net/2010/12/on-sustainability-uk-film-policy-after-the-uk-film-council.html.

BFI (2011), *Statistical Yearbook 11*, London: BFI.

Blair, Tony (1998), 'Foreword by the Prime Minister', *Our Competitive Future: Building the Knowledge Driven Economy*, Cmnd 4176, London: HMSO.

Blair, Tony (2010), *A Journey*, London: Hutchinson.

Board of Trade (1936), *Cinematograph Films Act, 1927. Report of a Committee appointed by the Board of Trade*, Chair Lord Moyne, Cmnd 5320, London: HMSO.

Brown, Mark (2010), 'Economists defend UK film tax breaks', *Guardian*, 7 June, http://www.guardian.co.uk/uk/2010/jun/07/report-warning-uk-film-tax-cuts.

Cambridge Econometrics (2005), *Economic Impact of the UK Screen Industries*, Cambridge.

Cameron, David (2009), 'People Power – Reforming Quangos', http://www. conservatives . com / News / Speeches / 2009 / 07 / David_Cameron_People_Power_-_Reforming_Quangos.aspxSpeech.

Caterer, James (2011), *The People's Pictures: National Lottery Funding and British Cinema*, Newcastle: Cambridge Scholars Publishing.

Dawtrey, Adam (2008), 'Tax credits are U.K.'s secret weapon', *Variety*, 16 October, http://www.variety.com/article/VR1117994180.

Dawtrey, Adam (2010), 'How is the BFI suddenly able to take over from the UK Film Council?', 'Film Blog', *Guardian*, 29 November, http://www.guardian. co.uk/film/filmblog/2010/nov/29/uk-film-council-bfi-ed-vaizey.

Department for Culture, Media and Sport (1998), *Creative Industries Mapping Document*, London: DCMS.

Department for Culture, Media and Sport (2001), *Creative Industries Mapping Document*, London: DCMS.

Department for Culture, Media and Sport (2005), 'Making Britain the World's Creative Hub – Purnell', Press Release, 16 June, http://www.gov-news.org/gov/ uk/news/quotmaking_britain_world39s_creative_hubquot/18221.html.

Department for Culture, Media and Sport (2009), *Creative Industries Economic Estimates Statistical Bulletin*, January, London: DCMS.

Department for Culture, Media and Sport (2010), *Creative Industries Economic Estimates (Experimental Statistics) Full Statistical Release*, 9 December, London.

Department of Trade (1984), *Film Policy*, Cmnd 9319, London: HMSO.

European Commission (1997), *Article 87 of the EC Treaty (ex Article 92)*, http://ec.europa.eu/competition/legislation/treaties/ec/art87_en.html.

European Commission (2001), *Communication from the Commission to the Council, the European Parliament, the Economic and Social Committee and the Committee of the Regions on certain legal aspects relating to cinematographic and other audiovisual works*, COM (2001) 534 final, 26 September, Brussels.

European Commission (2006), *State Aid N 461/2005 – United Kingdom UK Film Tax Incentive*, C (2006) 3982 final, 22 November, Brussels.

European Commission (2012), *Draft: Communication from the Commission on State Aid for Films and Other Audiovisual Works*, Brussels.

Film Council (2000), *Towards a Sustainable UK Film Industry*, London: Film Council.

Film Policy Review Group (1998), *A Bigger Picture: The Report of the Film Policy Review Group*, London: DCMS.

Film Policy Review Panel (2012), *A Future for British Film: It Begins with the Audience . . .* , London: DCMS.

Froud, Julie, Johal, Sukhdev, Law, John, Leaver, Adam and Williams, Karel (2011), *Rebalancing the Economy (or Buyer's Remorse)*, CRESC Working Paper No. 87, Milton Keynes: Open University.

Garnham, Nicholas (2005), 'From cultural to creative industries: an analysis of the implications of the "creative industries" approach to arts and media policy making in the United Kingdom', *International Journal of Cultural Policy*, 11: 1, pp. 15–29.

Goldsmith, Ben and O'Regan, Tom (2005), 'The policy environment of the contemporary film studio,' in Greg Elmer and Mike Gasher (eds), *Contracting Out Hollywood: Runaway Productions and Foreign Location Shooting*, Lanham, Boulder: Rowman & Littlefield, pp. 41–66.

HM Revenue and Customs (2011), *Film Tax Relief Summary of Tax Credit Claims: 2006–07 to 2010–11*, August, http://www.hmrc.gov.uk/films/ftr-monitoring-summary.pdf.

HM Treasury (1997), 'Tax relief for film production expenditure', 2 July, http://archive.treasury.gov.uk/pub/html/budget97/ir11.html.

HM Treasury (2005), *Reform of Film Tax Incentives: Promoting the Production of Culturally British Films*, London: HMSO.

HM Treasury (2011), 'Government announces extension of film tax relief', 10 November, http://www.hm-treasury.gov.uk/press_124_11.htm.

Hill, John (1993), 'Government policy and the British film industry 1979–90', *European Journal of Communication*, 8: 2, pp. 203–24.

Hill, John (2004), 'UK film policy, cultural capital and social exclusion', *Cultural Trends*, 13: 2, pp. 29–39.

Hill, John (2006), *Cinema and Northern Ireland: Film, Culture and Politics*, London: British Film Institute.

House of Lords Select Committee on Communications (2010a), *The British Film and Television Industries – Decline of Opportunity?, Vol. I – Report*, HL Paper 37-I, London: Stationery Office.

House of Lords Select Committee on Communications (2010b), *The British Film and Television Industries – Decline of Opportunity?, Vol. II – Evidence*, HL Paper 37-II, London: Stationery Office.

Kemp, Stuart (2012), 'U.K. film industry gets commercial clarion call from Prime Minister David Cameron', *Hollywood Reporter*, 11 January 2012, http://www.hollywoodreporter.com/news/uk-film-industry-david-cameron-280462.

Magor, Maggie and Schlesinger, Philip (2009), ' "For this relief much thanks." Taxation, film policy and the UK government', *Screen*, 50: 3, pp. 299–317.

Miller, Toby, Govil, Nitin, McMurria, John and Maxwell, Richard (2010), *Global Hollywood*, London: BFI.

Milmo, Dan and Gibson, Owen (2005), 'Treasury's culture test aims to boost UK film-making', *Guardian*, 30 July, http://www.guardian.co.uk/politics/2005/jul/30/uk.filmnews.

Myerscough, John (1988), *The Economic Importance of the Arts in Britain*, London: Policy Studies Institute.

National Audit Office (2011), *Department for Media, Culture and Sport: Financial Management*, Report by the Comptroller and Auditor General, HC 821, Session 2010–11, London.

Oakley, Kate (2004), 'Not so cool Britannia: the role of the creative industries in economic development', *International Journal of Cultural Policy*, 7: 1, pp. 67–77.

O'Connor, Justin (2007), *The Cultural and Creative Industries: A Review of the Literature*, London: Creative Partnerships.

Office of Tax Simplification (2011), *Review of Tax Reliefs Final Report*, March, London.

Oxford Economic Forecasting (2005), *The Economic Contribution of the UK Film Industry*, Oxford.

Oxford Economics (2007), *The Economic Impact of the UK Film Industry*, Oxford.

Oxford Economics (2010), *The Economic Impact of the UK Film Industry*, Oxford.

Parker, Alan (2002), *Building a Sustainable UK Film Industry: A Presentation to the UK Film Industry*, London: Film Council.

Petley, Julian (2000), 'From Brit-flicks to shit-flicks: the cost of public subsidy', *Journal of Popular British Cinema*, 5, pp. 37–52.

Sabbagh, Dan (2012), 'Animation, drama and video games win tax break boost', 'Budget 2012', *Guardian*, 22 March, p. 14.

Smith, Chris (1998), *Creative Britain*, London: Faber & Faber.

Smith, Chris (2003), 'Valuing culture', *Valuing Culture: Event Speeches*, London: Demos, http://www.demos.co.uk/publications/valuingculturespeeches.

TIGA (2011), *Investing in the Future: A Tax Relief for the UK Video Games Development Sector*, second edition, London.

UK Film Council (2010), *UK Film Council Group and Lottery Annual Report and Financial Statements for the year ended 31 March 2010*, HC 276, London: Stationery Office.

Wells, Steve and Posey, Clyde (2011), 'Let's go to the movies – state tax incentives: heroes or villains', *Journal of State Taxation*, July–August, pp. 29–38.

Woodward, John (2004), *Keynote Address to Screen International Conference*, 21 October, London.

John Hill is Professor of Media at Royal Holloway, University of London. His most recent books are *Cinema and Northern Ireland* (2006) and *Ken Loach: The Politics of Film and Television* (2011). He was also a founding director of the UK Film Council and chair of the Specialised Distribution and Exhibition Committee that formulated a strategy in support of the distribution and exhibition of non-mainstream films through the establishment of a digital screen network and the Prints and Advertising (P&A) Fund.

Creative Industries and Skills: Film Education and Training in the Era of New Labour

Duncan Petrie

The first decade of the new millennium witnessed significant developments in the education and training of film and television practitioners. These developments were in turn informed by the broader policy agendas of Tony Blair's New Labour administration that had come to power in 1997. The government's policy for film was essentially part of a wider promotion of Britain's 'creative industries' as forms of high-profile cultural activity with great potential in terms of national branding – 'Creative Britain' being a kind of millennial update of 'swinging London' – and economic growth. Indeed, the advocacy of a primarily market-oriented imperative (rather than the concept of cultural value or social good) placed a priority on the creative industries to take full advantage of new global business opportunities. In the specific sphere of film, the Department for Culture, Media and Sport (DCMS) embarked on a major reorganisation of state support through the establishment in 2000 of a new all-purpose agency, the Film Council (subsequently the UK Film Council), the primary aim of which was the creation of an internationally competitive and sustainable British film industry. This involved the UKFC directly in various aspects of industry strategy and organisation, including the education and training of new entrants.

The relationship between the creative industries policy agenda and the formation of new media practitioners can be usefully located in the wider context of New Labour's approach to higher education and the needs of the post-industrial 'knowledge economy'. While seeking to increase substantially the numbers of young people going to university,

Journal of British Cinema and Television 9.3 (2012): 357–376
DOI: 10.3366/jbctv.2012.0095
© Edinburgh University Press
www.eupjournals.com/jbctv

Labour's education policy was less concerned with the social inclusion aspect than 'encouraging' higher education institutions to produce graduates with the appropriate and necessary skills to contribute to Britain's economic advancement. So just as the significance and value of the 'creative industries' had become increasingly subject to the language of business and enterprise, so too the HE sector has been gradually reframed by politicians and civil servants in relation to its economic relevance and utility.[1] Within the specific realm of film schools this policy initiative was to be driven primarily by Skillset – an organisation founded in 1992 in the wake of the boom in independent production in television to initiate and coordinate training across an increasingly fragmented sector – working in close collaboration with the UKFC. Skillset was subsequently well placed to take advantage of the new opportunities provided by the creative industries agenda, becoming the National Training Organisation for Broadcast, Film, Video and Interactive Media in 1997 and then, five years later, the Sector Skills Council for the Creative Industries, a significant expansion of its remit to include radio, computer games, advertising, publishing, photo-imaging and fashion and textiles. Skillset and the UKFC subsequently set about devising and implementing a new training strategy for film and television, a major consequence of which was the creation of a new relationship between the film and television industries and the higher education sector. In line with the macro-policy shifts indicated above, this placed universities and colleges much more clearly and firmly at the service of industry through the promotion of an overtly industrial and vocational model of education.

This article will critically examine film education and training in the UK during the 2000s, charting the development and implementation of major policy initiatives, considering the ideological underpinning and influence of the creative industries agenda on these initiatives, and assessing the impact on individual film schools and the HE sector more broadly. Such an examination is lent added importance by the fact that we are once again at a moment of transition following the 2010 general election and the formation of a new Conservative/Liberal Democratic coalition government – which immediately set about undoing the legacy of New Labour through the abolition of the UKFC and the initiation of a major review of film policy.

While many university programmes in film and media studies include some practical element within their curricula, my primary interest here is in 'film schools': institutions and departments where the teaching of production is the distinguishing or predominant feature. As this field of education developed in the UK, different types of institution started to lay claim to the designation 'film school'. The most high-profile example is the single-discipline conservatoire, of which only two examples exist in the UK: the National Film and Television School (NFTS) and the London Film School (LFS). The former was established by the government in 1970 following the report of the Lloyd Committee and has been supported since by a combination of public and industry funding. On the other hand, the latter, set up in 1957 and thus Britain's oldest film school, is a smaller, private institution financially dependent on student fees. Both schools have always had a close relationship with the mainstream industry and have primarily been oriented towards training students in orthodox production techniques and methods. A more overtly technical or scientific approach to teaching film production emerged within the Regent Street Polytechnic (subsequently the Polytechnic of Central London and now part of the University of Westminster), the site of the first public demonstration of the Lumière cinematograph in the UK in 1896, which had started running courses in still photography in the 1930s before subsequently moving into the realm of cinematography. Practice-based film education also began to develop in the 1960s within art schools informed more by a fine arts perspective that privileged aesthetic innovation and creative expression. Pioneering institutions here include the Royal College of Art, which established a department of film design back in 1961, Hornsey School of Art and Ravensbourne School of Art, followed later by Goldsmiths, Central St Martins and Bournemouth. The art school model also provided the impetus for the development of film education within several polytechnics including Sunderland, Sheffield, Leeds, Glamorgan and Birmingham. Within the universities, the only significant pioneer was the Department of Drama at the University of Bristol which introducing a postgraduate course in radio, film and television in the late 1960s which included a major practice-based component.

Subsequent developments within higher education led to the incorporation of art schools into the polytechnic and university sectors, followed by the wholesale upgrading of polytechnics to 'New Universities' after 1992. The 1990s also witnessed massive growth in film and media courses across the sector, driven by increasing student demand for courses that apparently provided access to much sought-after careers in the media. This trend was subsequently exacerbated by the advent of the new vocationalism in education and the promotion of the Creative Industries, further encouraging institutions – particularly post-1992 universities seeking to attract new students into the system – to invest in new production-based programmes, facilities and equipment.

At the same time, the UK's two single-discipline film schools were also keen to take advantage of the expansion in higher education and so secure much-needed new sources of income. In the case of the NFTS, the abolition of the Eady levy in 1985 had made the school more dependent on a disparate range of industry sources, a highly unsatisfactory state of affairs which was characterised by financial insecurity and the inability to plan for the future. Meanwhile, the London Film School – which had been forced into receivership in 1974 and reconstituted the following year as a staff/student cooperative – continued to eke out its own rather precarious hand-to-mouth existence, becoming increasingly dependent upon international students who by the late 1980s comprised 80 per cent of the school's intake. In order to access funding from the Higher Education Funding Council of England (HEFCE), both schools decided to replace their respective long-established diplomas in favour of university-validated degrees. Thus in 2000 the NFTS established a suite of MA degrees in various craft disciplines validated by the Royal College of Art, which had been forced to close down its own film production department in 1994. The director of the NFTS who negotiated the agreement with the RCA's rector Christopher Frayling was Stephen Bayly. As he suggests, offering degrees rather than diplomas had become essential for the School:

> In the world in which we found ourselves that was imperative. For example, none of the European students could get any support from their countries because it wasn't a degree course. Moreover, there were other degree courses growing up around us which, because they were degree courses, were attractive to some of the students we might like to attract ourselves... I chose to go with the Royal College of Art to validate the degree because the RCA had a special charter but unlike us they had a special standing and qualified for HEFCE funding based on practice... So they seemed the perfect partners for us... I think it was the perfect fit and it made the academic side of it palatable to our practitioner staff. (Bayly 2010)

Securing an institutional link with the Royal College of Art also meshed with Bayly's desire to move the NFTS from its home at Beaconsfield Studios in Berkshire into the centre of London, an ambition that would remain unrealised. One major impact that the introduction of the MA degree did have was the reduction in the NFTS's programmes from three to two years, arguably the most significant change since the school's original open curriculum devised by Colin Young in 1971 had been replaced by a structured curriculum with clear craft specialisations in the early 1980s following pressure from the industry. Bayly suggests that while the reduction had no serious implications for certain specialised areas such as documentary or animation production, it did have a detrimental effect on the fiction programme where students effectively no longer had the opportunity to develop and work on a longer piece of dramatic work and so various ill-fated attempts were subsequently made to introduce an additional third year to allow graduates to return to the school to complete a longer piece of work.

The LFS established a similar relationship with London Metropolitan University in 2001, transforming their two-year diploma course into an MA in Film-Making. This was followed four years later by the introduction of a one-year MA in Screenwriting and then in 2010 by an MA in Film Curating, taught in collaboration with the London Consortium postgraduate school. While similarly influenced by issues of international recognition, the impetus at the LFS was also driven by the desire to encourage more home students to apply to the school, something that had become increasingly difficult since the abolition of sources of local authority support, such as that previously provided by the Greater London Council which contributed ten student grants a year (Bernstein 2011). For Ben Gibson (2009), who became director of the LFS in 2000, the confirmation of this programme as a postgraduate qualification also ensured that applicants had a certain level of maturity and experience, something he considered important. On one level the introduction of the MA made remarkably little difference to the fundamental structure of the school's two-year programme in film-making, which had been introduced in the early 1960s and involved the students progressing through a highly structured programme of six production exercises over the course of two years. It did, however, create certain new pedagogical challenges, as Alan Bernstein, deputy director of the school, explains:

Two things have changed. One is that we now have an assessment system – and something in that past which I valued, and most of the more or less anarchic people in the school valued, was that there was no aesthetic assessment. So students were really free and there was no pressure for them to conform to an institutional aesthetic requirement... The other thing is that when we were validated the University had no knowledge of or interest in practical courses whatsoever... but they were very concerned about the academic content, they thought there should be a serious academic component in an MA. Every other course I looked at came up with the same solution in that they allowed a large chunk of the students' time to be farmed off, so there were two parts to the course – the practical and the academic side – students had to have academic class, write academic exams and dissertations and I was very opposed to that... (2009)

The compromise reached to resolve the problem was the new requirement for students to compile a critical journal. This provided an opportunity for critical reflection on their work and creative process and for discussing this in a sophisticated way, finding their own relevance in relation to other films and to theoretical and critical debates in the process. For Bernstein this represented a major development that 'encourage(s) students to be critical and thoughtful about what they do which I think is central to what a film school does' (ibid.).

Over at the National Film and Television School the introduction of a Masters degree also made it necessary for the first time in the institution's history for students to research and write a dissertation as a core assessed part of their degree. While the contextual study of film history and aesthetics had been available at the school from the early 1970s (when it was designated as 'general studies'), this had always been regarded as something of an adjunct to the real business of practice. But for Roger Crittenden, one of the longest-serving teachers at the school, the introduction of the dissertation has been beneficial in terms of counteracting a creeping anti-intellectualism within the student body:

> There is an opinion from some practitioners that theory... will pollute their focus on what they do as film-makers. But on the whole students doing dissertations has been a good influence, obviously we make them think of it as part of developing their practice. They have to choose their subject before the end of the first year and present 1,000 words, so they are already thinking of what interests them in relation to their practice. So they might write on Wong Kar Wai's use of colour if they are a cinematographer, and I think we should publish some of them, some are really good, and by and large they end up having done it and thinking 'actually it was a good thing to do'. (2009)

Let us now consider in more detail the key policy agendas that impacted upon the development of film education and training during the 2000s. The expansion in HE provision coupled with a renewed emphasis on addressing the needs of the economy and business can be seen as indicative of the general direction in which things were moving. But the ways in which the Creative Industries agenda was also elaborated is also significant as this provides useful insight into the kinds of thinking behind the realignment between the education sector and the film and television industries during the decade. The concept of the Creative Industries has its roots in the 1980s when policy-makers and academics on the left, such as Nick Garnham (1987) and Geoff Mulgan and Ken Worpole (1986), began to advocate a radical alternative to traditional arts funding, which they regarded as elitist and rooted in outmoded bourgeois views of both the individual artist and the privileged status of certain forms. By contrast the promotion of the 'Cultural Industries' placed a new, politically progressive emphasis on public support for popular forms of culture and mass media which provided the basis for greater social inclusiveness and pluralism. In breaking down barriers to access, the state needed also to become less a provider of art and culture and more an enabler and catalyst (Mulgan and Worpole 1986: 111). This also meant the cultural policy needed to work much more with the grain of the market rather than preserving the traditional bastions of high culture. But it still provided an important alternative to establishment thinking and, as such, helped to inform the cultural policies of the Labour-led Greater London Council (GLC) prior to its abolition by Margaret Thatcher's Conservative government in 1986.

Despite certain continuities, the subsequent progression from Cultural Industries to Creative Industries signifies more than a mere semantic shift. For Garnham (2005), this is bound up with the advent of the concept of the 'information society' and the bundling together of ICT with what were formerly called the cultural industries to form a new sector of activity that would increasingly provide a key source of economic growth and prosperity. Initially formulated in the early 1990s by a group of academics based at Queensland University of Technology in Brisbane Australia, the concept of the Creative Industries was picked up and enthusiastically embraced by New Labour, whose core team of policy advisors also included Geoff Mulgan.[2] Setting out his guiding philosophy in an essay entitled 'Culture and our sense of national identity', Chris Smith, the first Secretary of State at the newly created Department for Culture, Media and Sport (which replaced the former Department of National Heritage), identified the Creative Industries as 'where the jobs of the future and the wealth creation of the future are going to come from' (1997: 7). These were subsequently defined by Smith's department as

... those industries which have their origin in individual creativity, skill and talent and which have a potential for wealth and job creation through the generation and exploitation of intellectual property. This includes advertising, architecture, the art and antiques market, crafts, design, designer fashion, film and video, interactive leisure software, music, the performing arts, publishing, software and computer games, television and radio. (DCMS website)

In 2001 the DCMS estimated that these industries were generating £112.5 billion or 5 per cent of GDP and accounted for £10.3 billion of British export earnings; by 2008 this had increased to 5.6 per cent of Gross Value Added and £17.3 billion in exports (4.1 per cent of all goods and service exported).[3] Hence the clear attractiveness of this sector for a government that was particularly keen to appear trendy and youthful while at the same time demonstrating a sound management of the economy and enthusiastic support for business and enterprise.

The adoption of the new agenda meant that what had previously been considered 'the arts' had now been subtly transformed into the 'creative industries', signalling a new and apparently seamless integration of culture and the market in the process. For advocates of the new order, this continued the emphasis of cultural industries policy with the dissolving of old and outmoded distinctions between high and low culture, art and entertainment, sponsored and commercial activities. But now this was motivated more by the advent of a new phase in advanced capitalism in which the increased circulation of cultural products placed a new emphasis on the symbolic content of commodities and on the experiential desires of consumers rather than their use-value. Moreover, such transformations also had major implications for the future role of public support for cultural activities, as John Hartley, one of the formative Australian thinkers associated with the 'creative industries' debate, has noted:

> The 'creative industries' idea brought creativity from the back door of government, where it had sat for decades holding out a tin cup for subsidy – miserable, self loathing and critical (especially of the hand that fed it), but unwilling to change – around to the front door, where it was introduced to the wealth-creating portfolios, the emergent industry departments, and the enterprise support programmes. (2005: 19)

Hartley's language begins to reveal another dimension to the new philosophy: the wholesale (bordering on contemptuous) rejection of previous arrangements and justifications within a particular realm of public spending. It also marks a crucial distinction away from the original cultural industries concept as the new rhetoric placed a much stronger emphasis on entrepreneurial activity and on the market as a source of wealth and prosperity rather than a guarantor of choice and pluralism. Again this had great appeal to the architects of Blairism, whose very political project and identity was bound up in a deliberate erasure of the past and the enthusiastic embrace of all things 'new'. Moreover, as Philip Schlesinger has indicated, it also indicates the way in which Britain rebranded itself at the creative cutting edge within a competitive global arena in which 'education and training... become key policy areas' (2007: 379).

Within the specific realm of film, the impact of the Creative Industries agenda was a wholesale institutional reorganisation of public support spearheaded by the 2000 creation of the Film Council (subsequently rebranded the UK Film Council to counter perceptions that it was de facto the English Film Council in the light of the establishment of new national Screen Agencies in Scotland, Wales and Northern Ireland) to take over, integrate and expand a range of activities previously carried out by a number of public bodies which were subsequently disbanded. These included the British Film Institute's production department, British Screen Finance, the Film Department of the Arts Council of England – all of which had provided funding for development and production activities – and the British Film Commission – which had promoted British facilities and locations at home and abroad. The UKFC also assumed responsibility for the English regions, previously the remit of the English Regional Arts Boards, and this paved the way for the creation of a new network of Regional Screen Agencies (RSAs), which were subsequently able to access substantial levels of investment from the newly created Regional Development Agencies. The cumulative result of this institutional reorganisation was a simplified administrative structure of institutional support and a considerable increase in public funding for the sector. But, following the Creative Industries logic, it also ushered in a new focus on developing a sustainable British film industry through the investment in businesses and talent and the promotion of greater market responsiveness and competitiveness. As Margaret Dickinson and Sylvia Harvey have noted, the creation of the UKFC and the RSAs effectively 'moved public policy away from cultural criteria and concerns and towards almost exclusively market-based forms of judgement and evaluation' (2005: 424).

Inevitably, film education and training were to be guided by a similar industrial/market imperative and in September 2003, after a twelve-month period of research and consultation, Skillset and the UK Film Council published a national film skills training strategy. The clearly stated objective of the strategy, entitled *A Bigger Future* (the title of which deliberately invoked *A Bigger Picture*, the report that led to the establishment of the Film Council), was 'to ensure that the UK industry is able to compete successfully in the European and global marketplace on the basis of world beating skills' (Skillset/UK Film Council 2003: 9). Four key areas were identified for concerted action: the provision of careers information, advice and guidance; the role of further, higher and postgraduate education; support for new entrants to the industry and for professional and company development; and the need for an appropriate mechanism for collecting and analysing information. In addition, three overarching themes or 'golden threads' running across all four areas were flagged up, including the need for a more socially and culturally diverse workforce, a recognition of the crucial role to be played by the various national and regional screen agencies in delivering the strategy, and the importance of fully understanding and addressing the potential of new digital technology.

The part of the strategy of most interest here is the role to be played by the formal education sector in advancing the new skills agenda. As with the other key areas, this was posed in terms of a problem to which a solution was subsequently identified and elaborated. In this instance the problem was that while the expansion of post-school education had led to a wide array of film and media courses in universities and colleges, 'only a few of these courses deliver the right mix of vocational skills which equip students to enter the industry' (ibid.: 17). The solution to this lack of vocational relevance was simple: what was required was a greater responsiveness on the part of higher and further education to the needs and demands of the film and television industries. This would be achieved via a comprehensive system of industry accreditation comprising two major dimensions: firstly, a course approvals system to 'identify a select number of practice-based higher education film courses throughout the UK that provide the skills, knowledge and experience needed for individuals to confidently enter the industry direct from education' (ibid.: 18); and, secondly, the creation of a limited number of recognised centres of excellence to provide appropriate, high-quality and relevant training. In order to become a Skillset 'Academy', individual academic institutions would have to 'demonstrate the right mix of creative encouragement and vocational education that is needed to prepare students to succeed in the film industry' (ibid.: 10). The implementation of the five-year strategy, to commence in April 2004, anticipated investment of £10 million a year (including £6.5 million from the Lottery) of which £3.9 million would be directed towards the funding of the Screen and Media Academies and £600,000 for the course approvals initiative. This would all be overseen by a Film Skills Strategy Committee chaired by Stewart Till, a powerful and influential figure from the distribution sector of the film industry and at the time deputy chairman of both Skillset and the UKFC.

By July 2005 a network of seven screen academies had been created. This included the National Film and Television School (the only existing institution explicitly identified for inclusion in the strategy document), the London Film School and five new inter-institutional entities: the Bournemouth Screen and Media Academy (a collaboration between Bournemouth University and the Bournemouth Institute of Art); the Screen Academy at the London College of Communication and the Ealing Institute of Media; the Screen Academy Scotland (involving Napier University and the Edinburgh School of Art); the Screen Academy Wales (bringing together the University of Wales in Newport and the University of Glamorgan); and a specially created Film Business Academy at the Cass Business School, City University, London (such an entity had also been flagged up in the strategy as a necessary new development). A second network of nineteen Media Academies was also created to address the specific needs of the television and interactive media industries and featured a similar pattern of collaboration between exiting institutions – including a high representation from the new post-1992 universities and further education colleges. Skillset accreditation for individual courses and programmes (including many of those provided by academies) was targeted towards three designated areas – screenwriting, computer games and animation – considered priorities in terms of skills shortage. In addition to becoming part of the Skillset brand, valuable from the point of view of attracting students, academies and other accredited institutions have been supported via the provision of direct investment and student bursaries, the latter designed to boost the numbers of students participating in approved programmes and courses, while encouraging greater diversity and social inclusion.

During the first four years of the strategy, just over £29 million was invested (£26 million of which was Lottery funding), with more than £12 million channelled to the Screen Academies. The NFTS alone received just over £5.5 million during the period, underlining its strategic importance within the sector. The director of the School, Nik Powell, notes that Skillset support has underpinned the expansion of the digital post-production and VFX SFX programmes at Beaconsfield (2009). On the other hand, for the London Film School (awarded £1.04 million between 2004 and 2008) the main value of being an academy has been the provision of around twelve scholarships a year to enable the recruitment of more home students. This has facilitated an important new cultural perspective, as well as creating the opportunity for training more future film-makers for the British industry. As Alan Bernstein argues:

> What we have now, which we just didn't before, are students being challenged by English students off the streets who know a great deal about the other side of life in London. In the past they tended to be better off and while they may still have liked to make films about the seedy side they tended to be like Guy Ritchie films. Whereas we have a lot of students now who know something about it and they challenge and that is important to us. (2009)

The targeting of support to particular areas of industry training can also be seen in the various initiatives supported by the pan-European MEDIA programme, the existence of which also underlines another key priority, that of developing international networks and promoting international collaboration as a way of taking advantage of new opportunities within an increasingly global industry. Over the past decade the MEDIA programme has targeted training support to three key areas: screenwriting (including the funding of well-established schemes such as Arista and Moonstone), management (notably through producer-training programmes like EAVE (European Audiovisual Entrepreneurs) and ACE (Ateliers du Cinéma Européen) and the Film Business School) and new technologies (including workshops in animation and writing interactive fiction). MEDIA also contributes sponsorship to the Script Factory, initially established in the UK in 1996 to provide opportunities for developing writing talent and which continues to offer a range of training initiatives (including a diploma course run in collaboration with the NFTS), one-off events and performed readings of scripts in development. This focus on training writers and producers is significant as it represents a major shift from an earlier concentration on the formation of film-makers which in most cases translated into a particularly auteurist vision.

As we have seen, the vision guiding *A Bigger Future* is fundamentally a skills training agenda consistent with the UKFC's primary objective of creating a competitive and sustainable British film industry. The kind of industry being promoted was articulated in 2002 by the UKFCs first chairman, the film-maker Alan Parker, in terms of the need to 'abandon forever the "little England" vision of a UK industry comprised of small British film companies delivering parochial British films' in favour of a strategy that 'embraces the international market' built on the reinvention of the British film industry as a creative hub or core that would be 'a natural destination for international investment . . . a natural supplier of skills and services to the global film market' (2002: 8–9).

For Parker, the necessary components to deliver this vision were a new focus on distribution rather than production as the leading element, a state-of-the-art infrastructure (essentially to service the production of 'international' – i.e. Hollywood – films) and skills – to create a highly skilled and flexible workforce. Now while this may be a clear and coherent vision in which the Skillset training strategy is designed to play a key role, it also depends on a very singular, highly contestable and ultimately reductive vision of film and its wider purpose and role in society – a perfect illustration of the creative industries logic where cultural pluralism loses out to the powerful monopoly interests. And just as Parker rhetorically consigns to his dustbin of 'parochial British films' anything that doesn't fit his industrial/Hollywood model, so too *A Bigger Future* completely ignores the need to nurture those qualities of social engagement, of intellectual curiosity, of artistic expression that have underpinned film as a formally innovative and culturally relevant popular art form. This training strategy is only concerned with producing skilled technicians – noting bluntly that 'there is a clear distinction to be made between academic study and vocational provision' (Skillset/UK Film Council 2003: 17). Conspicuously absent is an acknowledgement, let alone discussion, of the importance of critical thinking to the propagation of creative, innovative, vibrant and socially relevant film and television production. Thus what was posited was a new and unambiguously one-way relationship between 'the industry' – consistently presented as an undifferentiated and unified entity – and its 'training providers', clearly differentiated between a new 'premier league' of officially approved institutions and courses and 'the rest'.

It is instructive to compare the paucity of this vision with that elaborated in the Lloyd Report of 1967 which had led to the establishment of a national film school in the UK. In considering and preparing their report, the Lloyd Committee visited a number of institutions in the UK but also beyond, including the national film schools of France, Italy, Sweden and Poland, to investigate various existing pedagogical models, philosophies and practices. This research was subsequently used to identify the type of institution that would prove most suitable for a putative British school and in this it is particularly notable that the Committee strove to find the most efficacious blend of theory and practice. While an approach based primarily on the academic study of film was deemed inappropriate, so an overtly technical approach was also rejected:

> ... a National Film School which was directed primarily or solely to technical training and accomplishment would almost inevitably fail to provide, and indeed by its very nature would be virtually incapable of providing, a centre where creative talent of the highest order could be fostered ... (Lloyd et al. 1967: 4)

This statement sums up perfectly the central limitations of *A Bigger Future*. Yet the group of people that produced the Lloyd Report included some very mainstream industry figures whose conservative views were well known. But unlike the Film Skills Action Group that oversaw the writing of the Skillset/UKFC strategy (and indeed the respective boards of the UK Film Council and Skillset), the Lloyd Committee represented a far greater range of interests and expertise, a fact reflected in the choice of the lawyer and scholar, Lord (Dennis) Lloyd of Hampstead, as chair. His Committee defined film as a medium of communication, a popular entertainment and an innovative art form (ibid.: 3), and this was subsequently used in profound ways to inform and direct their approach. In his introduction to *A Bigger Future*, Stewart Till asserts that film

> ... is not only a mature but growing industry, it also has profound abilities as an entertainment medium to impact upon people and their attitudes and views. Film is able to communicate the culture of a whole country's as well as an individual's point of view. (Skillset/UK Film Council 2003: 5)

Yet this has no ramifications whatsoever for the substance of the strategy – this statement has simply to be taken as read and that the best (the only?) way to preserve these virtues is to promote economic competitiveness. But the more a British industry fulfils Parker and Till's vision of becoming a 'creative hub', the less it is able to communicate any meaningful sense of the national culture. Thus, rather than dissolving old boundaries, the 'creative industries' vision of British film has ultimately reinscribed the polarisation between conceptions of 'commercial' and 'cultural' film-making. The main difference now, however, was that public support for film was being increasingly channelled into commercial productions (the primary objective of the UKFC's Premiere Film Fund) which often also had Hollywood studio involvement, a new emphasis justified via the rhetoric of investment in sustainable production and in building audiences for 'British' film.

The lack of direct involvement of academics and educationalists within the formulation and implementation of film policy during the 2000s is another major cause for concern, Dickinson and Harvey noting that of the fifteen-strong board of the UKFC, thirteen places were filled by members of the 'higher ranks of the mainstream industry' (2005: 426) and one by the chair of the BFI, leaving only one for someone from the education sector. Academic involvement in the development of Skillset's new training initiative was even worse, with not one member of the three key bodies – the Film Skills Action Group, the Communications Advisory Group and the Developing UK Film Talent Steering Group – being drawn from the formal HE sector, despite the key partnership role to be played by universities and colleges in delivering the strategy. Yet the dangers posed by a new vocationalism and the need to resist this in favour of developing a more productive relationship between education and the industry were being articulated long before *A Bigger Future* saw the light of day. For example, in 2001 Jan Worth drew attention to the ways in which HE institutions appeared to be responding to the new skills criteria laid down by Skillset by excluding critical or reflective components in favour of conformity to a narrow conception of industrial demand. This was something to be concerned about as '... vocational training without educational content, challenge and diversity does not provide the calibre of graduates to work in a profession that involves taking ethical, political and creative responsibility for the representation of the society that we inhabit' (Worth 2001:116). Elsewhere, the Education and Training Committee of the UK Film Parliament convened in 2003 by a range of interested parties supported by the magazine *Vertigo* and galvanised by a shared concern over the general direction of the UKFC agenda included in its recommendations that the Education sector be given the opportunity to become a more active stakeholder in the industry and that any moves to create a system of accreditation within educational provision give 'high priority ... to the recognition of innovation, risk and challenge' (Myer 2003: 15). Yet much of this concern fell on deaf ears as the UKFC and Skillset, acting on behalf of the industry and with the full support of government, pressed on with their reforms.

In February 2008 Skillset reported on the first four years of *A Bigger Future*, providing a welter of information and figures that suggested the strategy was succeeding on all fronts. But tucked in at the back of the document was a statement by Iain Smith, the new chair of the Film Skills Strategy Committee, that included an indication that tougher times lay ahead – notably the fact that current Lottery funding was due to run out in 2009 and the subsequent inevitable reduction in resources in light of the DCMS prioritising the 2012 Olympics. Moreover, the publication in October of the same year of an official UKFC review of the strategy sounded an even greater note of caution. Preparation for this report had taken on board the views of a range of stakeholders within the industry and the various organisations involved in the delivery of the strategy. While broadly positive, the report did raise some significant concerns, particularly in the light of a predicted reduction in available resources. In addition to the suggestion that the Screen Academies had become too dependent on direct Skillset funding and thus needed to find ways of becoming more self-sustaining in future, more serious problems were identified in relation to the performance of the Film Business Academy which had been slow to establish itself and had already received adverse feedback from the first cohorts of students. Consequently, a serious question mark was being raised concerning the future of the partnership with the Cass Business School (UK Film Council 2008: 21). This was a particular blow given the level of investment in the Film Business Academy – £1,480,000 over the first four years (ibid.: 14) – and Iain Smith's lauding of its MBA and MSc courses as 'an outstanding achievement' (Skillset 2008: 24). The UKFC report also pointed to wider structural changes that suggested the overall programme should be scaled back in line with a concern from the industry that it was 'over-delivering' during a period in which the workforce was actually declining.

Both reports appeared before the banking crisis of 2008, which ushered in a new era of economic austerity and substantial reductions in public expenditure. From 2010/11 the annual allocation of lottery funding from the UKFC to Skillset that underpinned the training strategy was reduced by 50 per cent to £3.25 million (Skillset 2010). Consequently, when Skillset launched 'A Bigger Future 2' in June 2010, the Screen Academy Network had been rebranded as 'Film Academies' with a drastically reduced membership from seven to just three: the National Film and Television School, the London Film School and the Scottish Film Academy in Edinburgh. There had also been implications for the level of support institutions now receive, for example the LFS's annual allocation of Skillset student bursaries was cut from ten to five. Meanwhile the network of media academies had increased slightly to 23 (five in London, six in the south of England, two in the Midlands, four in the north of England, and six in Scotland, Northern Ireland and Wales), but this included a rebranded Bournemouth and the former Welsh Screen Academy, and the inclusion of the NFTS and the Scottish Academy in Edinburgh–which were now branded as 'Film and Media Academies'. Skillset provided no information as to the motivation for these developments, and in contrast to the hubristic rhetoric and detail of *A Bigger Future*, this time information was minimal, the official strategy brochure (downloadable from the Skillset website and consisting of a mere two pages of text) outlining five new funding priorities: retraining in new technologies; supporting trainees, apprentices and new entrants; developing creative talent (including the Film Academies and accredited courses); enhancing business skills; and improving health and safety awareness and expertise.

It seems that just as after ten years and considerable levels of public investment the UK Film Council failed to create a sustainable British film industry, so too the future had ultimately proven less 'big' than Skillset and the UKFC had originally predicted. While clearly beneficial to those institutions who gained and have retained academy status, the closure of the Film Business School at Cass now reduced to a small research centre,[4] the scaling back of the number of academies oriented towards the film industry from seven to three and the dramatic reduction in overall funding available in 'A Bigger Future 2', all provide ample evidence of this major retrenchment. While the primary reason for this has undoubtedly been the economic crisis, this has arguably been exacerbated by certain flaws of the strategy as discussed above. But it also appears that Skillset seriously overestimated the potential for leveraging more funding from the HE sector to subsidise the training needs of the UK film and television industries, while at the same time imposing onerous compliance procedures on accredited institutions that cut across the already burdensome quality assurance procedures demanded by HEFCE. However, the massive cuts in public funding for universities and the introduction of a harsh new fees regime of up to £9,000 a year may actually prove beneficial to Skillset. With an even greater emphasis being placed on employability, forms of official industry approval will take on a new significance as universities compete for students. And at the time of writing, Skillset have embarked on a new phase of accreditation, but this time charging successful universities a fee for the privilege.

It is also important to note that while the new skills agenda by Skillset and the UKFC was the dominant feature on the film education and training landscape during the 2000s, the formation of future professionals has remained a more complex and multi-faceted terrain. As I have explored in detail elsewhere (Petrie, 2011), some of the institutions at the very heart of the Skillset initiative have attempted to preserve and even enhance a more integrated approach in which industrial and cultural imperatives can continue to be mutually reinforcing. For example, under the leadership of Ben Gibson, the London Film School has sought to maintain a significantly more pluralistic vision of film education and orientation of graduates towards developing careers as film-makers than the world invoked by Skillset and the UKFC. The LFS has also demonstrated a different kind of impact brought about by globalisation, one in which, rather than creating greater hegemony for the powerful industry players and their interests, the values of cultural pluralism and dialogue are promoted. This is rooted in the cosmopolitanism of a student body in which 75 per cent continue to come from overseas. Interestingly, while immersing themselves for two years in this resolutely transnational community located in the heart of London's West End, most of the students subsequently elect to make their graduation film back in their country of origin, using the experience to refocus a sense of identity and cultural distinctiveness.

Thus the Skillset Film Academy at the London Film School is helping to sustain the creative and cultural strength of British film, being both an alternative kind of production hub to that envisaged by Alan Parker and a vibrant and dynamic cultural space in which emerging film-makers can find new ways of communicating experience, cultural specificity and difference and forge new understandings, partnerships and alliances in the interests of something more than mass entertainment or corporate profit. For this reason, the continued survival of a Scottish Film Academy in Edinburgh also keeps alive the potential for a different kind of geographical and cultural centre within the (albeit dramatically reduced) Skillset network. And while the National Film and Television School may be more directly bound up with the industrial mainstream, introducing new MA programmes in VFX/SFX, digital post-production, producing and directing television entertainment and games design and development, under Nik Powell it has also sought to maintain the kind of pluralism that in the past produced graduates such as Nick Broomfield, Terence Davies and Lynne Ramsay. The increasing internationalisation of higher education has also led to a situation where 45 per cent of students at the NFTS now come from overseas (Powell 2009), creating a less overtly 'national' cultural environment.

Finally, we are once again at a moment of uncertainty. In 2011 the Conservative-Liberal Democrat coalition government launched a major review of film policy, including education and training. While the end of the New Labour era of film policy had apparently been signified by the abolition of the UKFC, the announcement that the new review was to be chaired by Chris Smith (who had been given a peerage and elevated to the House of Lords in 2005) and would comprise a panel of eight mainstream industry insiders suggested a certain continuity in both priorities and vision. But there are other facts that are even more important. Firstly, the new era of financial austerity and spending cuts will ensure that any new policy will almost certainly be considerably more modest in terms of public investment than was experienced during the previous decade. Secondly, the introduction of student fees and with it the extension of the market in higher education is likely to intensify the importance of employability and economic relevance and within a traditionally risky sector like film and media in which stable careers are notoriously difficult to establish, this may have a profoundly negative impact on recruitment should students become more conservative or risk-averse in their choice of programmes. At the same time apparent guarantors of vocational or industry relevance such as Skillset may find their significance enhanced within the new environment. Only time will tell.

Notes

1. Stefan Collini (2011) charts how this thinking has been reflected in the way that departmental responsibility for higher education has developed under New Labour. In 2001 the ministry responsible for universities, the Department for Education and Employment, was renamed the Department for Education and Skills; by 2007 this had been broken up and replaced by the Department for Innovation, Universities and Skills; and just two years later HE was incorporated into the new Department of Business, Innovation and Skills.
2. Between 1997 and 2004, Mulgan occupied various roles in the Blair government, including director of the government's Strategy Unit and Head of Policy in the Prime Minister's Office.
3. http://www.culture.gov.uk/what_we_do/creative_industries/default.aspx#Creative (accessed 5 August 2011).
4. The Film, Media and Entertainment Research Centre, http://www.cass.city.ac.uk/research-and-faculty/centres/fmerc.

References

Bayly, S. (2010), Interview with author, London, 24 June.
Bernstein, A. (2009), Interview with author, London, 6 July.
Bernstein, A. (2011), Interview with the author, London, 28 September.
Collini, S. (2011), 'From Robins to Mackinsey', *London Review of Books*, 33: 16, pp. 9–14.
Crittenden, R. (2009), Interview with author, Beaconsfield, 7 July.
Department of Media, Culture and Sport, http://www.culture.gov.uk/creative_industries/default.htm.

Dickinson, M. and Harvey, S. (2005) 'Film policy in the United Kingdom: New Labour at the movies', *Political Quarterly*, 76: 3, pp. 420–9.

Frayling, C. (2011), Interview with author and Rod Stoneman, London, 31 May.

Garnham, N. (1987) 'Concepts of culture: public policy and the cultural industries', *Cultural Studies*, 1: 1, pp. 23–37.

Garnham, N. (2005) 'From cultural to creative industries: an analysis of the implications of the "creative industries" approach to arts and media policy making in the United Kingdom', *International Journal of Cultural Policy*, 11: 1, pp. 15–29.

Gibson, B. (2009), Interview with author, London, 6 July.

Hartley, J. (2005), 'Creative industries', in J. Hartley (ed.), *Creative Industries*, Oxford: Blackwell, pp. 1–40.

Lloyd, Lord et al. (1967), *National Film School: Report of a Committee to Consider the Need for a National Film School*, London: Department of Education and Science.

Mulgan, G. and Worpole, K. (1986), *Saturday Night or Sunday Morning? From Arts to Industry – New Forms of Cultural Policy*, London: Comedia.

Myer, C. (2003), 'Recommendations from the Education and Training Committee', *Vertigo*, 2: 5, p. 15.

Parker, A. (2002), *Building a Sustainable UK Film Industry: A Presentation to the UK Film Industry*, London: UKFC.

Petrie, D. (2011), 'Theory, practice and the British film conservatoire', *Journal of Media Practice*, 12: 2, pp. 125–38.

Powell, N. (2009), Interview with author, Beaconsfield, 7 July.

Schlesinger, P. (2007), 'Creativity: from discourse to doctrine', *Screen*, 48: 3, pp. 377–87.

Skillset (2008), '*A Bigger Future*: four years on', *Skillset Film*, 1, February.

Skillset (2010), *Annual Report 2009/10*, London: Skillset.

Skillset/UK Film Council (2003), *A Bigger Future: The UK Film Skills Strategy*, London: Skillset.

Smith, C. (1997), 'Culture and our sense of national identity', in M. Jacobs (ed.), *Modernising Britain: Creative Futures*, London: Fabian Society.

UK Film Council (2008), *Review of a Bigger Future – The UK Film Skills Strategy*, London: UKFC/BOP Consulting.

Worth, J. (2001), 'Interrogation or conformity: journeys in film production education', *Journal of Media Practice*, 2: 2, pp. 114–25.

Duncan Petrie is Professor of Film and Television at the University of York. He is the author of *Creativity and Constraint in the British Film Industry*, *The British Cinematographer*, *Screening Scotland* and *Contemporary Scottish Fictions: Film, Television and the Novel*, and is currently researching the history and significance of film schools in collaboration with Rod Stoneman.

Digital Britain and the Spectre/Spectacle of New Technologies

Sarah Street

During the last ten years the most frequently cited aesthetic and economic shifts influencing the British film industry are the impacts of digital technologies. The words 'digital' and 'innovation' are frequently coupled, as in the UK Film Council's policy and funding priorities manifesto for April 2010–March 2013 entitled *UK Film: Digital Innovation and Creative Excellence*. This contributes to the idea that major transformations are being facilitated by new technologies as demonstrated by the all-pervasive trends towards high-definition television, high-resolution cinematography and digital colour grading in post-production, as well as profound changes in the ways films are distributed, exhibited, preserved and restored. This article examines some of the issues around the introduction of new technologies in relation to these areas. New technologies are often greeted with messianic enthusiasm by some and feared by others, resulting in the uptake of formats and systems which might be technically less advanced than others yet able to maintain a dominant position in the market for economic, political, aesthetic and cultural reasons. Negotiating innovation is a historic paradigm through which it is useful to reflect on our contemporary experience of the digital debate.

William Uricchio has noted the importance of historical precedent, looking at struggles in the past over new technologies which resonate with current trends, noting how

> new technological capacities achieve (new) media status through a series of struggles over identity, representational capacity, business model, mode of production, regulatory frameworks, and so on. Historically,

Journal of British Cinema and Television 9.3 (2012): 377–399
DOI: 10.3366/jbctv.2012.0096
© Edinburgh University Press
www.eupjournals.com/jbctv

such struggles have been profoundly social, resulting in cultural and institutional consensus around a particular set of constructions, the new medium of the moment, effectively marginalizing many viable alternatives. (2002: 220)

This raises the question as to whether digital can be described as the 'new medium of the moment' or whether its dominance is compromised by the continuing co-presence of analogue. In *The Virtual Life of Film*, David Rodowick is concerned to stress the simultaneous existence of media as processes of technological change occur:

> As film disappears into digital movies... a new medium may be created, not in substitution of one form or substance for another, but rather through a staggered displacement of elements. The electronic image has not come into being *ex nihilo* from the invention of digital information processing, but through a series of displacements in the relationship between the formative and constitutive of moving-image media: how an image is formed, preserved, placed into movement, expresses time, and is presented on detached displays. We may be confident in our ordinary sense that film, analogical video and digital video are relatively distinct media, without assuming that a medium is defined essentially by substantial self-similarity. Every medium consists of a variable combination of elements. (2007: 86)

This was the case with the development of television, for example, which was produced in technical terms to mimic film. Analogical video experimented with transitional forms such as Hi8, which in turn developed into Digital Video as represented by Digital8 and DV formats.

Writing from the perspective of film restoration and preservation, archivist Giovanna Fossatti similarly notes that it is not a case of digital simply replacing film but that a more transformative process is involved for both. She suggests that we must think of the 'middle ground' since it is here that 'things acquire their real dimension, namely in the very place of transition' (2009: 19). Following this line of thought analogue media will probably not disappear altogether even though 'digital technology is here to stay', and will become 'more and more intertwined with our daily life. What is open for discussion is what media will look like at the end of this transition and, again, if [this] transition will ever know an end' (ibid.: 19–20). So, we're living in a digital age, but this coexists with analogue even though this may become a residual technology in the future. This conclusion complicates any attempt to look for media specificity around digital technology since it is not always obvious what role digital has played and reports are seldom clear about technical details. The ghostly/spectral analogy is often invoked about digital for these reasons since, although increasingly all-pervasive, the nature of its materiality is not visible in the same way as with film; it is everywhere but nowhere to be seen. But this is not to argue that digital does not engage with many of the issues surrounding notions of materiality (Willis 2005: 95). The digital realm is full of such paradoxes: claims, for example, that it constitutes a lifeline in the restoration of decomposing nitrate films are countered with revelations about the vulnerability of digital technology to magnetic storage tape deterioration. While digital cameras may be of excellent quality (however you want to define that – the current assumption is that high resolution is the most desirable look) the resulting image for audiences is only as good as the quality of projection; the latter is improving all the time, with current specifications up to 4K in multiplex cinemas.[1] Yet digital cameras can record in higher definitions than it is possible for computers to process and for some projectors to project. Digital cameras are ubiquitous but as long as dominant notions of 'quality' prevail the images shot with them remain best projected after having been transferred to film. As Brian Winston (1996: 39–57) argues, technologies are made to 'fit' society, and while there is optimism that digital will produce radical new innovations in screen media it is likely that these too will be constrained by prevailing cultural and economic strictures.

In keeping with the capitalist logic around the development of consumer products, continued economic growth can only occur once the stages of introduction, development and mass saturation of the market have passed, when new features and refinements are delivered. Today this explains Blu-ray, the continuing pursuit of high definition and ambitions for 3D television. Digital encourages a fascination with seeing better, deeper, sharper, to attain 'perfect' vision and a greater colour range and depth which is manipulated during post-production. The premise is that the technology is delivering a visual experience that exceeds human perception. The cyborg self is realised through the visual sensations provided by digital technology; it is indeed the ghost in the machine. William Brown has classified digital cinema as 'post-humanist, or, at the very least, as anti-humanist' since its infinite capacity to manipulate 'the real', even on the level of altering colour and creating images without a camera, 'suggests a cinema that is no longer an indexical representation of a reality that existed before the camera (even if that 'reality' was part of a 'fictional' world)' (2009: 70).

The prevalent cultural assumptions around the desirability of high-definition television and high-resolution cinema are not dissimilar to preferences for line over diffusion in art theory or to past developments in the fields of advertising and animation. The first commercially successful Technicolor films were Disney's *Silly Symphonies* and colour in animation was praised by theorists such as Eisenstein for being clearly defined, subject to compositional control and as an integral, organic part of the whole film. It is no coincidence that when demonstrated for purchase new televisions most often play back animated features which show up high-definition lines most clearly. Line is good; diffusion is not. Grain is material and subject to change; pixels indicate numerical cipher. Paradoxically, a criticism often made of films projected digitally is that pixels are visible, even appearing similar to grains visible through an enlarger during photo-chemical processing. There is even discussion among cinematographers that it is desirable to mess up an image a little to give it 'soul'. The constant pressure towards re-mediation means that digital has acquired a tendency towards mimicry. To be mistaken for film is one of the highest compliments it can be paid. In this way any specificity around digital imaging is frustrated by its transitional positioning. As Branigan has perceptively noted: 'One should be cautious about focusing too quickly on physical characteristics, technology, and typical operations of a medium at the expense of radial sorts of connections to "older" media. The reality status of a new medium is relative' (2006: 118).

Another continuity between the history of colour and digital is the desire for control. Debates about how best to control colour date from the silent period and into the arrival of Technicolor. The ideological continuum with digital posits that the best technology enables hyper-control over results. In terms of current practice, this has resulted in shifts in the organisation of production whereby post-production is the place where a great degree of control can be exercised, particularly over colour. At first, and in common with the early presentation of many technologies, Technicolor was demonstrated so that colour became a unique and obtrusive feature. In time the cultural preference to tone-down colour in the name of 'restraint' became more prevalent. The application of digital colour has followed a similar path and it remains to be seen whether the full range of what is possible will ever reach the screen. The rest of this article will focus on three related aspects of contemporary development which raise different issues concerning the impact of the digital age. The first is the impact of high resolution on cinematographers and in post-production; second, the impact and implications of digital screen exhibition delivery; and, finally, the use of digital technologies in preserving and reviving 'classics' of British cinema such as *This Happy Breed* (1944), *Blithe Spirit* (1945) and *The Red Shoes* (1948) for current theatrical release as well as non-fiction titles considered to have historic value.

Production and post-production

The availability of lightweight, digital cameras has most certainly encouraged lower-budget production and to some extent influenced the aesthetics of contemporary cinema. When Duncan Petrie examined the first wave of British digital films in 2002 he found that the technology enabled new directors including Nichola Bruce to make low-budget films supported by bodies such as the UK Film Council's New Cinema Fund. He cited examples where the technology encouraged aesthetic strategies such as a stylised emphasis on subjective imagery facilitated by the ease of 'tricks' made possible with the new cameras. Such experimentation can be linked with the work of Derek Jarman who similarly embraced cheap, video formats to create innovative work. Digital facilitates effective night-time shooting and on locations that would be much more difficult for 35mm set-ups. In theory the practical conveniences of digital create possibilities for filming in previously off-limit locations and in innovative styles. Yet Petrie concluded that sustained experimentation was rare: 'Whatever the high level of personal control afforded by digital technology ... it is worth reiterating that, in aesthetic terms, the first wave of British digital features has relied heavily on existing cinematic traditions, rather than pioneering new approaches to visual language and representation' (2002: 72). It is not difficult to understand why apparently residual aesthetic forms persist since in most phases of technological change the old and the new are intertwined in aesthetic, cultural and economic terms. Film's longevity as the primary visual medium means that a digital film's success is often judged on how closely it resembles film. The persistence of the linearity of classic narrative modes is also evident outside artists' film and video and gallery installation work.

The debate around digital cameras and their aesthetic possibilities is polarised around two apparently contradictory positions: on the one hand enabling low-budget 'lifelike', realist image production available to all, suitable for showing on YouTube in the tradition of classic amateur film-making, while on the other hand enabling the professionalism associated with high resolution as a hyper-real aesthetic for high-end, bigger-budget film-making. To consider the first aesthetic imperative, for documentary specialists digital technology facilitates a greater sense of intimacy with the subject, since the camera is not obtrusive or noisy, enabling an enhanced level of natural interaction during shooting. From this perspective, capturing a sense of 'the real' is within the capability of digital cameras as a way of enhancing established conventions and regimes of documentary verisimilitude. Logistical problems can also be overcome when shooting in difficult locations with lightweight digital equipment, capable of working in very low light levels. Some sequences in *Touching the Void* (2003) were shot on digital for this reason. But digital's capacity to mimic other forms can sometimes lead to problems of perceived 'authenticity'. Cinematographer Steve Gladstone was asked, for example, to shoot footage for YouTube which was supposed to replicate an amateur's work. He was told it looked too good (Flaxton 2009). From this perspective digital can be seen as challenging professional codes as well as generic expectations; the footage needs to look 'real' rather than 'good'. Cinematographers speak about the changed relationship to their craft brought about by digital. While a great degree of control and latitude is possible it is easy to lose a sense of creativity, or to rely rather too much on technology. An example of this is paying excessive attention to the camera's monitor which enables shots to be erased. The possibility of instant playback suggests a different relationship to what has been shot and can be a lazy and less creative way of planning images (ibid.). As cinematographers such as Roger Deakins (2009: 24) have observed, the apparently limitless time available to shoot with digital encourages an approach which favours postponing key decisions until post-production.

In 2005 the UK Film Council's New Cinema Fund and Film4 established a digital film studio based in Sheffield called Warp X to revitalise low-budget British film-making. The first slate of films was funded until the end of 2010 by the New Cinema Fund, Film4, Screen Yorkshire and Optimum Releasing. A key feature was that 'creative talent should share in the gross revenue of any film once the commission and expenses of distributors and sales agents have been deducted'.[2] Films funded include *Hush* (2008), a horror/road movie shot on location in Sheffield and the East Midlands, *This Is England* (2006), *Donkey Punch* (2008), a thriller/horror about three young women on a hedonistic weekend in Spain, and a comic documentary *A Complete History of My Sexual Failures* (2008). The films aimed to combine low-budget digital production with commercial appeal. *This Is England* had the most significant box-office career, although *Hush* is associated with the 'new wave' of British horror films started by *28 Days Later* (2008) and *Shaun of the Dead* (2004). Statistics produced by the British Film Institute for 2007–10 show that low-budget production increased markedly, particularly films shot in Britain for under £500,000, which reflects the impact of low-cost digital equipment, even though the majority of registered British films are not in this category (British Film Institute 2011: 155). Lower-budget films are on average cheaper than works shot on film, particularly if specialist post-production facilities are not required. The British Film Institute attributes the burgeoning of low-budget film-making to pressures on budgets but also to the impact of digital (ibid.: 6). On the other hand, it should be noted that the costs of 35mm film have come down, so it is debatable in some cases whether there is a clear case for digital film-making being necessarily more cost-effective. That being said, it is clear that the affordability and apparent lighter touch of digital has been influential in the interest taken by bodies such as the UK Film Council in facilitating this kind of production.

At the bigger-budget, co-production high end of film-making, British-based companies provide expertise in skills such as digital visual effects. Cinesite, a London-based post-production house owned by Kodak, is one of the largest digital effects companies in Europe. Films worked on include *Harry Potter and the Deathly Hallows* (2010 and 2011). In this way British-based units contribute to an international structure of co-production and to advancing Hollywood's global saturation market strategy. Another leading London-based post-production house, The Mill, was founded in partnership with British directors Ridley and Tony Scott; the company also has offices in New York and Los Angeles. Visual effects expertise is not confined to film but encompasses television, games and music. Ascertaining exactly where digital input is most decisive or apparent is often difficult in this context because of the multiple, cascading outputs arising from high-budget blockbusters. A film as a product does not end with theatrical release; the forms of ancillary dissemination such as games also involve digital expertise.

The RED camera, first launched in 2007 by Jim Jannard's American company with the intention of taking digital cinematography into a new realm of technical development and affordability, has reduced the costs of higher-end digital production, facilitating increased flexibility around equipment and production scheduling. The RED company's website lists the mainly US films including *The Social Network* (2010) shot on RED.[3] It has also been used in a few co-productions with British involvement, such as Peter Jackson's *The Lovely Bones* (2009) and *Green*

Zone (2010), as well as in *Mrs Peppercorn's Magical Reading Room* (2011), a British film directed by Mike Le Han and set in Cornwall. The RED camera has also been used in television productions including *Red Dwarf: Back to Earth* (2009), *The Shadow Line* (2011) and *Shameless* (2011). New cameras are constantly being developed by the company, especially in its EPIC range, to offer higher resolutions. Using RED cameras on big-budget films such as *Pirates of the Caribbean: On Stranger Tides* (2011) and Peter Jackson's *The Hobbit: There and Back Again* (release due 2013) confirms their place within the technology choices for blockbusters.

Many cinematographers trained in film have found the transition to digital difficult, seeing it as threatening their expertise and established methods of controlling a film's 'look'. This is because many changes can be made in post-production. Craft levels are still high on a high-end digital shoot but expertise is spread with roles such as Digital Imaging Technicians becoming essential. Post-production is where control over the look of an image is primarily located, and this has implications for power relations within the crew and raises new questions around authorship. Colour graders – 'colourists' – have a great deal of expertise and can be the most highly paid members of a post-production team. Most cinematographers want to be involved in grading sessions but since they rarely get paid for this work it is possible that the images they shot end up looking very different after manipulations during post-production have taken place.

The impact on colour through digital technologies has been groundbreaking with systems such as Digital Intermediate, pioneered by Technicolor, revolutionising post-production. As Misek has commented, 'Since the spread of DI in the early to mid-2000s, screen colour has owed at least as much to computer-based postproduction processes as it has to camera-based production processes' (2010: 404). The range of shades, hues and saturation is immense, even though the quality of three-strip Technicolor has not quite been achieved. Many films are shot on film and then digitised for post-production effects/editing. Charlotte Crofts described the DI process: 'If originated on film, each individual frame is digitally scanned as a high-resolution (2–4K) digital data file. The film is edited and colour graded digitally and then either burnt back to film for traditional release prints, or formatted for digital distribution' (2008: 10). While many digital cameras are sold on the premise that practically anyone can use them, it is seldom pointed out that expertise is needed for post-production colour grading to ensure that the best-quality images are produced.

Misek notes the consequences of these changes: 'A film's "look" is now no longer set during production. Primary colour grading is now carried out digitally, and as a result can be used to adjust colour balance without the restrictions inherent in photochemical colour timing' (2010: 405). He explains that there are two types of grading: primary grading 'alters the colour balance of an entire shot; secondary grading allows specific colour values and areas of the frame to be altered in isolation' (blue sky, for instance, can be made pink without changing the hue of the sea). Cinematographers, and the American Society of Cinematographers (ASC) in particular, tried to exert an influence on the newly enhanced power of post-production over the 'look' of an image. The ASC's Technology Committee tried various strategies to control colour throughout post-production. A 'Colour Decision List' (CDL), for example, was developed as part of the general standardisation of capture to post workflow. The CDL lists the metadata attached to video files, detailing the original colour and exposure properties of each shot. As Misek explains: 'The metadata allows operators using any postproduction platform to adjust the colour values of video files so that they will look exactly the same as they looked on the cinematographer's monitor' (ibid.: 405). The principle is keeping control of colour from production into post-production. But tellingly, the CDL is only useful for primary colour correction; secondary colour changes are under the control of the colourist. So, what emerges is that 'cinematographers control the overall colour scheme of a film; colourists have control over more precise shot-by-shot colour effects' (ibid.: 405). But this applies to 'filmed' images and increasingly there are examples of moving images created without cameras: these are beyond the control of the ASC. As a subset of the ASC, members of the British Society of Cinematographers (BSC) generally subscribe to the same standardisation of capture to post workflow since they share similar concerns about developing trends about maintaining a close relationship between shooting and post-production. This is an attempt to put the Director of Photography back in their 'chief quality control clerk' position. As Flaxton (2011) explains: 'The system ensures that whatever you generate on and whatever you output in, the workflow will take account of the photo-chemical nature of ins and outs or the data values of ins and outs, combining all with meta-data values.'

Sally Potter's *Rage* (2009) was filmed using digital and as a comparatively low-budget film the main costs were for post-production ($325,000 to shoot and $450,000 to edit, grade, sound mix and 'deliver' the film in multiple sales formats, plus $225,000 in – 100 per cent deferred – producer, director and production company fees). A 35mm print was made, as well as a commercially projectable print in digital format. The actors were filmed against a green screen background. The decision not to include background images but instead add different colours in post-production was determined by practical and aesthetic reasons. When asked about the colours Potter explained:

> I had filmed on backgrounds of green screen. I had thought that I was going to put a whole bunch of other backgrounds in and then when I looked at them in the cutting room, it was distracting. It was too complex. And I realized I needed to really take this notion of an austere but rich aesthetic all the way, as far as I could take it. And that meant actually using simple color backgrounds. And so finding a logic for that was initially intuitive, and then I started to discover a system which was to take a color from somewhere in that person's face, body, clothes or whatever and to tie it to the background so that it began to have this kind of organic, integrated feeling. But funnily enough, that often then became the emotional tone of the character as well or was reflective of or was a counterpoint to the emotional tone. I always knew when it was right. When you have got the wrong color, it is just wrong! And that itself is fascinating. (2009)

As a film about a person shooting a series of interviews on his mobile phone with the intention of putting them on the web (which is the film we see), *Rage* is an experiment in negotiating with new technology on many levels. It typifies many of the contradictory aspects of digital recording. The images are large, brightly lit and extremely clear. The actors in close-up stand out almost as animated characters from the various deeply saturated backgrounds against which they are sharply defined. These images are almost too much on a large screen – their brightness and clarity almost hurt the eyes. Their size seems to favour a smaller screen; if seen on a phone they would be very impressive. The aesthetic result belies the method by which the images we see were supposed to have been filmed by the boy Michaelangelo on his mobile phone. The arresting colours were produced in post-production as a sleight of hand typical of digital imagery which is advertised as available to everyone yet the distinguishing features which constitute its claims to quality and artistic aspiration can be expensive. An auteur director posing as an amateur has produced images which are in themselves worthy of gallery installation work. The arresting visual style is thus a combination of factors which highlight the transitional positioning of digital between various aesthetic modes and economic realities.

Creativity has been enabled on many levels and, as many of the following examples demonstrate, the record of British digital film-making is more impressive than when Petrie conducted his initial assessment in 2002. While it may be hard to discern major patterns, some British directors have nevertheless found digital technologies liberating with major contributions to British cinema. Sally Potter is a good example, as well as Shane Meadows who used digital for films such as *This Is England*. Meadows' *Le Donk & Scor-zay-zee* (2009) was made for £50,000 in just five days, using two digital cameras running constantly over four days, allowing a fifth day for re-shoots and editing. He found this approach exciting and challenging at the editing stage, signalling post-production becoming an enhanced focus of 'craft' in the culture of digital film-making. Terence Davies' *Of Time and the City* (2008) included digitised archive footage as a key element of its aesthetic approach, with the rest of the film shot with a medium-definition digital camera and then transferred to 35mm. The result is a stunningly evocative visual homage to Liverpool in which shots of the past and present deliver a powerful montage that exemplifies Davies' poetic style. Stephen Ball's *The War on Television* (UK, 2004) experimented with the glitches, distortions and fragmentation that often occur when the digital television signal is weak. His short video is a collage of 'digital disobedience', assembled from images derived from such interference, randomly processed and manipulated through layers of scratch techniques that exaggerate the 'stuttering fragmentation of the pristine digital veneer, the authority and reliability of the always on twenty-four hour news channel fucked-up, becoming abstracted into a flow of jarring noise and stammering incoherence' (Melbourne Cinémathèque programme notes, 2011). In this way the aesthetic expectations of high-end digital towards seamless perfection are subverted as well as offering a political critique of the similarly distorted capitalist news media machine (Ball 2010).

Two of Britain's most pre-eminent directors, Danny Boyle and Michael Winterbottom, have been pioneers of digital technology. Danny Boyle chose to shoot *28 Days Later* (2002) on digital, the convenience of which enabled a particular location – central London with no cars or people – to be shot in a way that might have been difficult if conventional 35mm cameras had been used. He used multi-cameras, filming for up to two minute slots during the brief moments when the traffic was held back by his crew. He claimed that the spectacle of a deserted London helped to sell the film (Boyle 2003). While it is probably the case that the same shots could have been obtained with film, it was nevertheless Boyle's choice to go digital and such examples are typical of the at times defensive discourse around its deployment at this time when criticised for being of lower quality than film. The cinematographer working with Boyle was Antony Dod Mantle who has been a significant figure in the development of digital cinematography. Prior to *28 Days Later* he was central to the early films of the Dogme 95 movement, including *Festen* (1998), and has worked with Lars von Trier on many occasions. Boyle also chose digital for *Slumdog Millionaire* (2008) which was shot on a 2K digital camera by Dod Mantle. It was the first digitally photographed film to win an Academy Award for Best Cinematography, although it should be pointed out that the film was shot using multiple formats which included 35mm and digital stills. Michael Winterbottom's films frequently use digital cinematography in titles that include *24 Hour Party People* (2002), *In This World* (2002), *9 Songs* (2004), *The Road to Guantánamo* (2006), *A Mighty Heart* (2007) and *Genova* (2008). In these films digital facilitates an edgy, loose, drama-documentary style which Winterbottom has developed since his breakthrough feature film *Wonderland* (1999). As with Danny Boyle, the partnership with a particular cinematographer has been influential in Winterbottom's approach to digital film-making, in this case working on many occasions with Danish cinematographer Marcel Zyskind who worked as camera operator with Dod Mantle on *28 Days Later*.

Billie Eltringham's first feature film, *This Is Not a Love Song* (2003), was streamed on the web at the same time as its cinema premiere. Having previously worked in 35mm, for this film she found it advantageous to shoot quickly on digital, without lights and on a low budget. As for look, she aimed to exploit what she considered to be elements specific to DV such as 'weird leak-out' effects and a frenetic sense of movement created with hand-held cameras, rather than attempt to replicate 35mm (Gilbey 2002: 17). For subsequent films she has reverted to more conventional approaches using film. Tracey Emin's *Top Spot* (2004) consisted of a mixture of DV footage, Super 8 and Betacam to achieve a deliberately uneven look which suited the experimental, personal nature of the film. Popular television serials such as *Cranford* (2007–, BBC), *Lark Rise to Candleford* (2008–, BBC) and *Wallander* (2005–, Sweden; 2008–, UK) are also originated on digital cameras. The work of animation companies such as Aardman has been greatly assisted by new technologies, even if the pixel has not yet completely replaced the pencil.

Taking the lead from natural history films and car crash safety trials, experiments with high-speed digital video permit an extreme slowing-down of movement and the capturing of unpredictable events that was previously difficult, costly and not always possible with 35mm film (Schonfelder 2010). In the same spirit of using digital as a platform for innovative approaches to expansive notions of the film frame Peter Greenaway and Mike Figgis have been identified with exploring 'a desktop aesthetic' (Willis 2005: 39). Greenaway's *The Tulse Luper Suitcases* consisted of three films released in 2003 as part of an extensive multimedia project that included DVDs, a television series, a website and gallery exhibitions. Mike Figgis' *TimeCode* (2000) showed four different viewpoints of a narrative situation on a single screen divided into four quadrants, while on occasion drawing the viewer's attention to a particular quadrant with slight sound amplification. As well as the usual theatrical and DVD release, Figgis exhibited *TimeCode* to audiences as a 'performance' of different combinations of sound and image (ibid.: 40). In these ways the 'desktop aesthetic' was realised by both film-makers in their creation of multiple streams of visual information across different platforms, requiring the viewer to be more than usually active in attempting to decode any particular element.

Before its closure in 2010 the UK Film Council's emphasis on modes of production which related to budget and nationality did not neglect low-budget, domestic film-making. Short digital films were encouraged by specific schemes such as the New Cinema Fund's partnerships with organisations in each region of the UK, to enable film-makers to make innovative shorts using digital technology. Their claim to innovation is up for debate since, as we have seen, just because the technology is available there is no guarantee that it will be deployed differently. Although many films showcase visually arresting techniques such as speeding-up shots, shooting in reverse or multiple dissolves, the same levels of frenetic activity cannot be easily sustained outside of the short film, advertising or music video markets. A high-resolution aesthetic arguably favours less camera mobility, slowness and an emphasis on *mise en scène* or the hyper-pictorialism evident in high-definition 'quality' television. The nature of the film industry is such that success is a value-laden judgement that favours the repetition of proven conventions, and this can apply as much to artists' films as to genre production. On the other hand, such initiatives can be seen to boost styles of production with which British film-making is often identified, such as the realist approaches of Ken Loach or Shane Meadows. While 'high-end' production is dominated by high-definition/resolution, as we have seen with Sally Potter's *Rage*, if the extent of manipulation possible during post-production is given full rein, a film shot on a relatively low budget can equally bear the markers of quality as they relate to 'high-end' production. If one looks at a sample of shorts funded by the New Cinema Fund it is clear that while some directors have not progressed far beyond their first digital short, others have gone on to feature films. These include Mat Whitecross who wrote and directed the digital short *Job Street* (2005). He has since collaborated with Michael Winterbottom in co-directing *The Road to Guantánamo* (2006) and *The Shock* (2009), and has also directed *Sex and Drugs and Rock and Roll* (2009).

Image delivery and digital projection

The relatively short route from theatrical release to DVD and Blu-ray has had a major impact in extending the range of content available for educational use in schools, colleges and universities. Gone are the days of paying hire costs for damaged prints, often only available in 16mm and with a limited range of titles. 'Streaming' titles in downloadable forms to computers and hand-held devices also has profound implications for the ways in which we watch films. Faster broadband speeds are hastening this development which is generally seen as less prone to piracy than DVDs which can easily be copied. Increasingly, there are multiple means of experiencing moving image content with less emphasis on viewing a title in its entirety. Trailers are often viewed on mobile phones after a film's theatrical release and for pure interest in trailers as a genre/form, thus divorcing them from their original advertising context with less stress on being seen before a film is viewed in a cinema. Extracts from films can be 'grabbed' and presented as part of alternative content as an aesthetic of assemblage and reuse becomes a common artistic form. Copyright issues are complex around this use of moving image material and are difficult to regulate in a market that increasingly veers towards open access. Boundaries between 'high' and 'popular' art are being eroded by such trends and there is also a move towards digital access broadening selection in terms of theatrical release.

Delivering top-quality high-resolution images depends on more than having a state-of-the-art camera. Resolution is dependent on projection and the audience sitting at the optimum distance from the screen. A large and well-advertised part of the 'Digital Britain' platform has been the inauguration of the Digital Screen Network (DSN), a scheme launched by the UK Film Council in 2005. One of the main drivers was to facilitate increased access to 'specialised' films via digital copies and equipment replacing expensive 35mm celluloid prints. The initiative cost £12 million to equip 240 screens in 210 cinemas across the UK with digital projection technology. There are many persuasive arguments for equipping cinemas with digital projectors. Prints are cheaper and can be beamed by satellite, thus eliminating transportation costs. A digital release print is not as subject to scratches or visible damage as is often the case with film, and other advantages include the durability of prints. Satellite projection has some interesting consequences in that it facilitates the exhibition of a wider range of content in cinemas such as theatrical productions, opera, directors introducing new films, music and sport. By expanding the range of available content such cinema 'event screenings' extend expectations of what one can see in a cinema, almost taking us back to the multiple uses of public entertainment spaces in the history of early cinema.

In 2007 South West Screen announced that nineteen cinemas across the region were to receive digital film projectors funded by the UKFC. In exchange for the equipment the cinemas agreed to provide more screening time to showing a greater selection of more specialised (non-Hollywood), classic, experimental and foreign language movies. While the Independent Film Parliament, a public forum launched in 2003 that was initiated by *Vertigo*, a magazine that promoted 'independence, innovation and diversity across the whole moving image culture', welcomed the DSN initiative, concern was expressed about the need for longer-term structures to be put in place to ensure the extension and maintenance of the equipment, as well as the importance of promoting specialised films to audiences by means of festivals and educational events so that more diverse taste cultures can be visible and flourish (2006: 10–11). While the DSN may be a way forward, it is uncertain whether it will result in a growth of specialised film and a re-education of taste. In the long term, it could simply represent a realignment of screening technology and the end of celluloid (Hanson 2007: 370–83). While it might be the case that the availability of digital has had an impact in boosting the exhibition sector (admissions for 2010 were 169.2 million, a 2 per cent decrease on 2009, but there was an increase of 5 per cent in box-office receipts), the transition has been far from smooth or total (British Film Institute 2011: 9–11). Independent exhibitors fear that once the major companies – Odeon, Cineworld and Vue – move completely into digital exhibition, it will be too costly for them to compete as projectors become more expensive. Independents also argue that distributors who have most to gain from digital exhibition should contribute substantially towards purchasing projectors, a view hardly welcomed by the distribution sector (Macnab 2009: 46–7). Yet there is no doubt that digital exhibition is on the march, particularly in multiplex cinemas. The number of multiplexes has risen steadily from 1,624 in 1999 to 2,767 in 2010, whereas the number of 'mixed-use'/traditional cinemas has fallen from 1,134 in 1999 to 904 in 2010 (British Film Institute 2011: 84). By 2010 the UK had 1,415 'high-end' digital screens (75 per cent of these were 3D enabled), over half the number in 2009 (642) and an increasingly high number in relation to the total number of screens (3,671) in the UK (ibid.: 92), that is nearly 50 per cent and increasing fast.

For some time there was a delay in cinemas switching to digital projection and the DSN was criticised for being expensive to maintain, with exhibitors bearing the brunt of these costs after the Film Council's initial financial assistance ran out. Film projectionists are worried about deskilling due to the uptake of digital projection; once installed in a venue there is little need for specialist projection skills. Projectors also need to keep pace with new technical developments and a lack of agreed standard of luminosity means there is much variation in quality. As Fossatti points out, 'Although digital projectors today can approach film projection quality, there are still large differences in the representation of color as the color depth per pixel is still inferior to that of film projection' (2009: 54). A positive step has been the recommendation of standard specifications by the Hollywood-based organisation Digital Cinema Initiatives in 2007, but there is a long way to go before the most difficult problems are overcome, or the full complexities around a major change to the ways in which we publicly watch films are addressed. The quality of digital projection is improving, but cinemas still generally maintain projectors for 35mm film. As we have seen, even though titles such as *Rage* were shot and post-produced using digital technology they are often printed back onto a 35mm film print for projection. Again we find a historical precedent since there were debates in the past about the desirability of standardising the luminosity of cinema projection in order for a print to be screened with the highest-quality result, particularly for colour. Digital is similarly creating pressure for standardisation in projection as resolutions increasingly get higher. The Film Council hoped that the DSN would facilitate a wider range of 'specialised' films being shown, including restored classics. In this enterprise there is a link with restoration projects which tend to favour the auteurs preferred by their sponsors. This perpetuates a particular hierarchy of 'important' film titles – many films which are not well-known are not given restoration treatment, so there is a tendency to revert to older canons of what counts as 'good' cinema.

Restoration and preservation

In the preface to Paolo Cherchi Usai's *The Death of Cinema*, Martin Scorsese notes the work of digital technology in film restoration: 'Digital technology is certainly not a substitute for motion picture stock when it comes to the preservation of the original cinematic experience and the conservation of the film artefact, but it surely can help in facilitating the work of those who attempt at bringing back the moving image to its original glory' (Cherchi Usai 2001: ii). The restored *Caesar and Cleopatra* (1945) released on DVD contains dramatic 'before and after' images which emphasise this point. Digital's tendency towards mimicry noted earlier is very pertinent concerning these questions. As Ian Christie points out in connection with the recent high-profile restoration of *The Red Shoes* (1948):

> What has now been created is essentially an ingenious copy or simulacrum of the 1948 film, even to the extent of retaining the original circular cue marks that signalled the end of each reel for the projectionist. Just as digital photography has been calibrated to mimic the look of the earlier photochemical process – like a computer being taught to 'act human' – so a digital restoration is also an act of reconstruction. (2009: 37)

The wonders of restoration are a key marketing ploy for the theatrical and DVD release of such titles.

While these are of course laudable sentiments and Scorsese has been at the forefront of restoring the films of Powell and Pressburger, it is not a straightforward case of digital constituting a timely technical intervention in the history of film restoration. Charlotte Crofts has expressed concern around this area in that there appears to be a lack of a clear policy that includes questions of preservation, recommending

> the need for a coherent, well-thought-out strategy for digitisation, and an understanding of the separate purposes of online access, digital distribution, and preservation sub-masters, including some sort of international agreement on standard formats for each. Without further international debate and collaboration on this, the project of digitising existing archive material could become a costly white elephant as the codes, formats, and compression rates are rapidly superseded by new

improved versions, and different territories digitise to different formats, undermining the possibility of joining up archives globally in future. (2008: 19–20)

Candidates for restoration are most often selected on the basis of notoriety or for authorial interest. In many cases previous restorations had been undertaken before digital technology was available, as with Powell and Pressburger's films restored by the British Film Institute in the 1980s and currently receiving Scorsese's attention funded by high-profile organisations including the Hollywood Foreign Press Association, the Louis B. Mayer Foundation and the Film Foundation. In 2008 the British Film Institute announced the theatrical release of restored versions of the first ten films directed by David Lean that had been completed in partnership with Granada International and Studio Canal and funded by the David Lean Foundation. The restoration of *This Happy Breed* (1944), a film shot in Technicolor, utilised digital technology to scan negatives at high resolution that had been particularly affected by mould and water damage. The spots were then manually removed from the digital files frame by frame and the files laser-recorded to film stock (Genaitay 2008). This example shows that in current restoration projects a number of approaches will be combined, only some of which will involve digital work. But with the soundtrack a full digital restoration was undertaken because of the bad condition of the original sound negative. As well as the film being released theatrically in print form, the digital files enabled screenings on the DSN as well as a DVD release.

It is very important to note that digitisation does not necessarily mean preservation. As Ian Macdonald argues: 'Recent film processes involve making a digital intermediate copy rather than an internegative, and the disappearance of the data on such copies has resulted in serious damage to at least one major film' (quoted in Crofts 2008: 11). It is dangerous if everything is digitised and no master negatives or copies are stored. Digital invariably seems to be less messy or organic, or subject to visible deterioration than film (ibid.: 11). Yet digital is *not* indestructible. Content cannot always be accessed after a certain length of time and digital assets are more costly to store than film. Many film archivists are anxious about questions of digital storage, especially when it is feared that the production of film stock will be discontinued. The EYE Film Institute Netherlands, for example, considers any film preserved in a format different from film as a copy for access. At the same time, digital data files need to be preserved as long as possible as a key means of maintaining our moving image heritage. When Arianna Turci surveyed the use of digital restoration within European film archives in 2005 she found that overall restorers were most concerned about respecting the original film versions:

> They are prepared to experiment with digital technology as long as the original version is respected... Archives are wary of storing films in digital formats, because they do not think that current digital technology offers a stable base of support for preservation work... Technical obsolescence is a central issue for preservation and an important concern for its economic impact on large digital collections. (2006: 121–2)

Restoration projects tend to be a negotiation between various 'versions' of films, from deteriorating nitrate prints to incorporating the aims and aesthetics of previous restorations. This complicates notions of 'authenticity' since digital projects must engage with previous incarnations, a notion that questions the very existence of an 'original'. The BFI's recent (2010) restoration of *The Great White Silence* (1924) looked to a number of previous sources including the director Herbert G. Ponting's own colour instructions scratched into sections of leader, as well as previous restorations (found in Amsterdam, France and London), and photographs. Whereas previous restorations tended not to prioritise colour, the BFI was concerned to try to incorporate some of Ponting's intentions (as far as they could be discerned from fragmentary evidence) while producing a film that would be received positively by today's audiences eager for footage about Scott's fated polar expeditions which took place a hundred years ago and continue to generate enduring fascination.

Another high-profile restoration project, Claude-Friese Greene's *The Open Road* (1925), shows some of the problems and benefits of resuscitating films from the archive for contemporary release. *The Open Road* was 26 short films of a motor tour of Britain from Land's End to John O'Groats. On first exhibition the films were stymied by a technical fault that was connected with 'Natural Colour', the two-colour additive process used by Friese-Greene. The main problem was 'time parallax' whereby if an object changed position during the time it took to expose the records these appeared misaligned when projected, resulting in colour fringing around the moving object. When the British Film Institute restored the films that were subsequently released on DVD in 2006 they decided to reduce the faults which had contributed to Natural Colour's rapid demise (Genaitay and Dixon 2010: 138–41). The historic value of the travelogue was considered to be important enough for the images to be made more visually acceptable, using digital and other methods of restoration, to the viewing public. On one level the DVD is an inaccurate record of what contemporary audiences would have seen. It does, however, permit us to judge whether rapid movement was avoided in order to detract from any fringing which might occur, as well as appreciate the many 'showcase shots' commented on in reviews. Some slight instances of 'fringing' were retained to convey something of the technical difficulties of early film colour processes. The BFI's approach to restoring *The Open Road* has at least enabled the images to be seen with ease nearly a hundred years after they were shot. By retaining some of the technical flaws that were clearly visible in the 1920s, the restoration maintains a crucial link with the technical problems grappled with by Friese-Greene and other contemporary colour inventors that clearly influenced their approach to filming movement and shot construction.

There are many related issues regarding authenticity as a greater number of digitised images are easily reproduced alongside others and often in contexts far removed from their origins. There needs to be a coherent approach to 'image ripping', the re-presentation and assemblage of content and attendant copyright issues, since on YouTube, for example, there are often different versions of older films available but without comment or contextualisation given about the source of the footage. Once again the complexities of the transitional moment confound many specialists wishing to see a clear way forward with digital technology.

The coexistence of analogue and digital is likely to persist for some time ahead, so much so that the term 'Digital Britain' is an aspiration rather than a fact. Current film-making and exhibition practices are most certainly affected by new technologies. As we have seen, this ranges from the availability of lightweight cameras capable of filming longer and more cheaply than with conventional film stock, to the installation of digital projectors all over the country. The question is to what extent is the economic, cultural and aesthetic landscape being changed in the UK? If we are living in a 'digital age' what are its characteristics and consequences? Because of the transitional nature of much digital work, often used in combination with film and needing to mimic the latter in order to be commercially viable, the potential for innovation is arguably limited. As with the introduction of earlier technological innovations the turn to digital has not been complete, or necessarily resulted in new aesthetic approaches or themes. The lines of debate engage with familiar theoretical issues concerning the relationship of moving images to 'the real' as well as their ability to exceed human perception and experience. The attempt to harness technology to conventional norms rather than exploit its potential for innovation is also a historical paradigm which has been demonstrated on many occasions.

So there is evidence here for Winston's observation that technologies are made to 'fit' society. The development of high-definition television and high-resolution cameras serves two intertwined economic and cultural imperatives. Increasingly complex cameras, projectors, domestic televisions and hand-held devices are all symptomatic of product differentiation following saturation of the market after the first phase of digital consumer goods. As such they represent a typical paradigm of capitalist development. The preference for sharper, more clearly defined images can be related to the highly polished, crisp and line-driven aesthetic associated with advertising. While digital technology is capable of facilitating shots of 'the real' in low light-levels and enabling anyone to shoot a film using their mobile phone, there are brakes on the extent to which this will fundamentally change mainstream film-making. Since, as Rodowick notes, 'every medium consists of a variable combination of elements', digital media is caught between exploring the limits of its own specificities and demonstrating that it is no different from film which remains the benchmark for quality (2007: 86). What digital can deliver is a product that looks the same but is cheaper. This fundamental driver acts as a limit on its potential for formal experimentation, even though in the area of post-production this clearly can take place to a major extent and is positively demanded in certain generic contexts. There is also evidence from many of the examples cited in this article that digital film-making is providing an exciting creative space for many people who would formerly have had limited access to professional, quality image-making.

Blithe Spirit (1945), one of the British films recently restored using digital for part of the picture and for the soundtrack, was seen by the majority of viewers on a digital projector. In keeping with the film's premise our experience of new technologies is indeed both spectral and spectacular, on occasion obtrusive while for a good part of our viewing an experience invisible. Digital developments connect to the ways in which previous technologies have been showcased, negotiated and absorbed into the market and culture. What is perhaps most remarkable is the extent to which digital technologies are becoming ever-present in our daily lives so that what is happening in film and television is connected to a much bigger picture and experience of technology. The full impact is not yet entirely clear to us as we live through a period when the old and the new coexist as they always have done, awaiting the time when dominant forms replace residual and the ghost in the 'post-human', digital machine is a benign one called celluloid.

Note

1. A 2K digital cinema means an image container of approximately 2,000 pixels across (2,048 × 1,080 or 2.2 million pixels). A 4K projector, used for large screens, doubles these dimensions (4,096 × 2,160 or 8.8 million pixels).
2. Warp X website, http://www.warpx.co.uk/about-us.asp.
3. RED website, http://www.red.com/experience.

References

Ball, S. (2010), Presentation to 'The Idea of Digitality in a Post-Digital Age', University of Westminster, http://www.flaxton.btinternet.co.uk/KTWest.htm.

Boyle, D. (2003), *28 Days Later*, DVD audio commentary, 20th Century-Fox Home Entertainment.

Branigan, E. (2006), *Projecting a Camera: Language-Games in Film Theory*, London and New York: Routledge.

British Film Institute (2011), *Statistical Yearbook 2011*, London: British Film Institute.

Brown, W. (2009), 'Men without a movie camera – movies without men: towards a posthumanist cinema?', in W. Buckland (ed.), *Film Theory and Contemporary Hollywood Movies*, London and New York: Routledge, pp. 66–85.

Cherchi Usai, P. (2001), *The Death of Cinema: History, Cultural Memory and the Digital Dark Age*, London: British Film Institute/Palgrave Macmillan.

Christie, I. (2009), 'Seeing red', *Sight and Sound*, 19: 8, pp. 36–8.

Crofts, C. (2008), 'Digital decay', *Moving Image*, 8: 2, pp. xiii–35.

Deakins, R. (2009), Interview with Roger Clarke and Edward Lawrenson in 'Talking Shop', *Sight and Sound*, 19: 4, pp. 18–24.

Flaxton, T. (2011), Conversation with author, 13 July.

Fossatti, G. (2009), *From Grain to Pixel: The Archival Life of Film in Transition*, Amsterdam: Amsterdam University Press.

Genaitay, S. (2008), 'Restoration: *This Happy Breed*', *Sight and Sound*, 18: 7, pp. 41–3.

Genaitay, S. and Dixon, B. (2010), 'Early colour film restoration at the BFI National Archive', *Journal of British Cinema and Television*, 7: 1, pp. 131–46.

Gilbey, R. (2002), 'Reasons to be cheerful', *Sight and Sound*, 12: 10, pp. 14–17.

Hanson, S. (2007), '"Celluloid or silicon?" digital cinema and the future of specialised film exhibition', *Journal of British Cinema and Television*, 4: 2, pp. 370–83.

Independent Film Parliament (2006), *Report to the Department of Culture, Media and Sport*, London: Independent Film Parliament.

Macnab, G. (2009), 'The big switch', *Sight and Sound*, 19: 9, pp. 46–7.

Meadows, S. (2009), Quoted in the *Guardian Film Blog*, 26 June.

Misek, R. (2010), 'The "look" and how to keep it: cinematography, postproduction and digital colour', *Screen*, 51: 1, 404–9.

Petrie, D. (2002), 'British low-budget production and digital technology', *Journal of Popular British Cinema*, 5, pp. 64–76.

Potter, S. (2009), Blog, 22 April, http://www.sallypotter.com/money.

Rodowick, D. N. (2007), *The Virtual Life of Film*, Cambridge, MA and London: Harvard University Press.

Schonfelder, A. (2010), Presentation to 'The Idea of Digitality in a Post-Digital Age', University of Westminster, http://www.flaxton.btinternet.co.uk/KTWest.htm.

Turci, A. (2006), 'The use of digital restoration within European film archives', *Moving Image*, 6: 1, pp. 111–24.

UK Film Council (2009), *UK Film: Digital Innovation and Creative Excellence*, London: UK Film Council.

UK Film Council Statistics (2009), http://www.ukfilmcouncil.org.uk.

Uricchio, W. (2002), 'Old media as new media: television', in D. Harries (ed.), *The New Media Book*, London: British Film Institute, pp. 219–30.

Willis, H. (2005), *New Digital Cinema: Reinventing the Moving Image*, London and New York: Wallflower.

Winston, B. (1996), *Technologies of Seeing: Photography, Cinematography and Television*, London: British Film Institute.

Sarah Street is Professor of Film at the University of Bristol. Her publications include *British National Cinema* (1997, second edition 2009), *Transatlantic Crossings: British Feature Films in the USA* (2002) and *British Cinema in Documents* (2000). She has also co-authored with Tim Bergfelder and Sue Harris *Film Architecture and the Transnational Imagination: Set Design in 1930s European Cinema*. Forthcoming publications are *The Negotiation of Innovation: Colour Films in Britain 1900–55* and the volume *Colour and the Moving Image* co-edited with Simon Brown and Liz Watkins.

Blurring Borders: Scottish Cinema in the Twenty-First Century

Jonathan Murray

More and more often, to watch and think about twenty-first-century Scottish cinema is to be transported beyond a single set of territorial and cultural borders. Yet, from the late 1970s, academic discussion of Scottish film traditionally saw the representation and reformation of national identity by indigenously based film-making talent, the creation of 'alternative discourses... adequate to the task of dealing with the reality of Scottish life' (McArthur 1982: 3), as an evolving local production sector's main *raison d'être*. Such priorities undoubtedly cast helpful light upon the defining characteristics of earlier eras within Scottish film history. They also provide a valuable reminder of a vibrant national cinema's capacity to engage domestic audiences in shared processes of discussion and self-definition. Yet with each passing year, the idea of a deliberate, dominant and didactic focus on the question of nation seems less and less applicable to more and more of the cinema which contemporary Scotland produces. This is not to say that belief in Scottish cinema's capacity 'to play an important role at the heart of a revitalised national culture in reflecting the diversity of contemporary Scottish experience' (Petrie 2000a: 226) ought to be junked overnight. It is, though, to argue that criticism must be prepared to acknowledge and explore the full range of contemporary Scottish film-makers' creative and cultural ambitions. The latter both include *and* extend beyond the desires of an inwardly focused celluloid commentariat.

Journal of British Cinema and Television 9.3 (2012): 400–418
DOI: 10.3366/jbctv.2012.0097
© Edinburgh University Press
www.eupjournals.com/jbctv

Compared to the 1990s, the twenty-first century's opening decade saw levels of Scottish feature production increase only modestly. The same period, however, saw the range of genres inhabited and issues explored by Scottish film-makers expand rapidly. For instance, many Scottish writers and directors whose careers began at home during the local production upsurge of the late 1990s (for more detail, see Petrie 2000b) went on to spend much of the 2000s examining societies and working within film industries located outside Scotland's borders.[1] The contemporary Scottish cinema of *The Magdalene Sisters* (Peter Mullan, Ire/GB, 2002), *The Last King of Scotland* (Kevin Macdonald, GB, 2006), *Summer* (Kenny Glenaan, GB/Ger, 2008) or *We Need To Talk About Kevin* (Lynne Ramsay, GB/USA, 2011) is one defined by international migration and exploration on the part of local artists. Alternatively, one might acknowledge the marked rise of low-budget genre production within Scotland during the last decade. A determinedly populist Scottish cinema, one created by film-makers who choose (or are compelled) to remain locally based, either rejects outright detailed interrogation of native society and identity in ostentatious detail, or does so in oblique and novel ways. The contemporary Scottish cinema of *Wild Country* (Craig Strachan, GB, 2005) and *Outcast* (Colm McCarthy, GB/Ire, 2010) subjects council estate teenagers to all manner of unlikely lycanthropic travails; the *Outpost* (Steve Barker, GB, 2008) franchise produces unapologetically outré fantasies of undead Nazi *Einsatzgruppen* lurking in abandoned central European Second World War bunkers; *The Purifiers* (Richard Jobson, GB, 2004) turns nocturnal Glasgow into an anonymous dystopian metropolis of the proximate future, a hostile and perilous space controlled by dictatorial corporate interests and policed by vigilante gangs who fuse cyberpunk and Asian martial arts cinema aesthetics in their appearance and behaviour.

One could easily list several other important twenty-first-century trends which complicate traditional conceptions of Scottish cinema as a collective creative endeavour that is geared primarily or exclusively towards an examination of the meaning and identity of 'Home'. Indeed, this essay will go on to examine two such movements within 2000s Scottish film-making. The first involves a decade-long process of strategic collaboration with Scandinavian counterparts; the second relates to local film-makers' recent interest in themes of ethnic and racial diversity, conflict and exploitation, whether domestically or globally framed, past or present day. In the case of both movements, I identify and analyse the work of particular individuals and institutions that proved exceptional with regard to the amount of feature work

401

which they produced during the early 2000s. At the same time, however, I also suggest that these individual success stories are also markedly representative case studies: they illustrate some of the main directions in which early twenty-first-century Scottish cinema has developed as a whole. With regard to Scottish-Scandinavian co-production, a great deal of my discussion explores the output of Sigma Films, a Glasgow-based independent production company established in 1997 by producer Gillian Berrie, actor Alistair Mackenzie and director David Mackenzie. In the years since the company's feature-length debut, *The Last Great Wilderness* (David Mackenzie, GB/Den, 2002), Sigma has acted as lead or co-producer on no fewer than seventeen further feature projects, a record unmatched by any other Scottish independent. In the case of films exploring questions of ethnicity and race, the work of screenwriter Paul Laverty is singled out for special attention. The most prolific Scottish screenwriter of the late 1990s and early 2000s, Laverty made his feature debut with the script for the English director Ken's Loach's *Carla's Song* (GB/Sp/Ger, 1996); since then the pair have collaborated on another eleven projects, the most recent of which, *The Angel's Share* (Ken Loach, GB/Fr, 2012), is in post-production at the time of writing.

The combined example of Sigma and Laverty, not to mention that of the other films and film-makers examined below, illustrates an argument I have advanced elsewhere (Murray 2007: 90). This is the idea that contemporary Scottish film criticism needs to go where contemporary Scottish film-makers have already gone. We must learn to see explicit and extended representation of nation as but one of many creative possibilities to explore from a local perspective. A more traditional view of Scottish film criticism, as a vehicle used to canonise what Blain (2009: 776) calls a leftist and realist 'central spine... attached to the notion of a characteristically Scottish film and television product' and to a national cinema reductively equated with 'Bill Douglas' *Trilogy*, the [Peter] McDougall/[John] Mackenzie and Loach/Laverty partnerships, and the developing career as director of Peter Mullan' (ibid.: 776), today seems undesirable and unfeasible in equal measure.

It is certainly the case that a self-consciously inclusive (and often internationally focused) imperative has defined much of the most significant Scottish cinema scholarship published in recent years. Duncan Petrie (2004: 206) perhaps started a collective process of critical recalibration by stressing 'the crucial dialectical interplay of the indigenous and the international, the specific and the general, the local and the global' which he increasingly saw at work within

Scottish moving image cultures. David Martin-Jones (2009: 1) built on this insight by professing a desire to 'not focus solely on films made by Scots, about Scots, for Scots' within his tellingly titled monograph *Scotland: Global Cinema*. Of the 22 post-1990 features which Martin-Jones' book discusses, more than one-third are mobile, rather than indigenous, productions, and more than half are directed by non-resident overseas film-makers. Elsewhere, Sarah Neely (2008: 161) discerns 'a recent trend in Scottish cinema, where issues of national identity are dealt with more tentatively', and argues that 'the opening-up of modes of discourse within Scottish film-making should also be reflected in [Scottish] film criticism' (ibid.: 162). Most recently, Simon Brown (2011) has suggested that 'transnationalism... offers a broader, more inclusive approach to New Scottish Cinema, [one which] encompasses, rather than eclipses, the national' (see also Street 2009). The present essay echoes the overarching tenor of these critical interventions by identifying and examining the two important strands of 2000s Scottish film-making singled out for analysis above.

A still ongoing process of collaboration between individuals and institutions working within the Scottish and Danish production sectors represents perhaps the most visible example of contemporary Scottish cinema's systematic move beyond a single set of national borders in both industrial and representational terms. Something like one in five of the early twenty-first-century fiction features produced with a significant element of Scottish financial and/or creative input emerged from what Mette Hjort (2010: 46) terms a strategic process of 'milieu-developing transnationalism' overseen from opposite sides of the North Sea. Early co-production initiatives at the start of the 2000s, such as *Aberdeen* (Hans Petter Moland, GB/Nor/Swe, 2000) and *The Last Great Wilderness*, instigated a fertile tradition of transnational cooperation, one which has regularly involved other Scandinavian and European film industries over and above those of Scotland and Demark. The result has been a relatively large number of Scottish-set but internationally co-produced features: *Wilbur (Wants to Kill Himself)* (Lone Scherfig, Den/GB/Swe/Fr, 2002), *Skagerrak* (Søren Kragh-Jacobsen, Den/Swe/GB/Sp/Ger/Fr/Swi, 2003), *One Last Chance* (Stewart Svaasand, GB/Nor, 2004), *Red Road* (Andrea Arnold, GB/Den, 2006), *Donkeys* (Morag McKinnon, GB/Den, 2010) and *Perfect Sense* (David Mackenzie, Ger/GB/Swe/Den, 2011).

As Robin MacPherson (2010) notes, the cornerstone of recent Scottish-Scandinavian collaboration has been a long-term working relationship built by the two central production companies behind *The Last Great Wilderness*, Glasgow-based Sigma Films and

Copenhagen-based Zentropa Entertainments. Speaking in 2004, producer Gillian Berrie, co-founder of Sigma, was unapologetically direct in acknowledging the extent to which her company sought to learn from and emulate the example set by its internationally successful Danish counterpart, arguing that 'all I'm doing is what they did in Denmark' (Phelan 2004). Of the eight Scottish-Scandinavian features noted above, only two (*Aberdeen, One Last Chance*) were produced without either Sigma or Zentropa's involvement. Sigma participated, moreover, in a further eight non-Scottish-set co-productions with Zentropa: *Dogville* (Lars von Trier, Den/Swe/GB/Fr/Ger/Neth/Nor/Fin, 2003), *Brothers* (Susanne Bier, Den/GB/Swe/Nor, 2004), *The Judge* (Gert Fredholm, Den/GB, 2005), *Manderlay* (Lars von Trier, Den/Swe/Neth/Fr/Ger/GB/It, 2005), *Zozo* (Josef Fares, Swe/Cze/GB/Den/Neth, 2005), *1:1* (Annette Olesen, Den/GB, 2006), *After the Wedding* (Susanne Bier, Den/Swe/GB/Nor, 2006), *When Children Play in the Sky* (Lorenzo Hendel, It/Den/Ice/GB/Ire, 2006). Of course, these features, by virtue of their narrative settings and/or the national identity of their writers/directors/characters, have no immediately obvious substantive connection to Scotland. Yet this generally overlooked aspect of Sigma's output is not irrelevant to the development of Scottish cinema in the 2000s.

For one thing, five of the eight projects noted immediately above are concerned with issues of increasing ethnic diversity within small northern European nations and/or evince a deepening local awareness of the relationship between those societies and complex, because globalised, networks of neo-colonial economic exploitation and military conflict. Contemporary Scottish film-makers' deepening interest in just such themes constituted a significant element of that country's early twenty-first-century cinematic output. Sigma's involvement in a range of non-Scottish-set international co-productions represents, then, an additional facet to the contemporary domestic turn towards questions of race and racism. For another, the extensive experience of European co-production which Sigma's Danish connections facilitated helps explain the company's striking success in maintaining a rolling slate of feature projects over the last decade. In addition to Sigma's direct involvement in the fourteen transnationally financed projects listed above, the company produced or co-produced another five Scottish-set features during the same period: *Young Adam* (David Mackenzie, GB/Fr, 2003), *Dear Frankie* (Shona Auerbach, GB, 2004), *Hallam Foe* (David Mackenzie, GB, 2007), *You Instead* (David Mackenzie, GB, 2011) and *Citadel* (Ciaran Foy, GB/Ire, 2011). In this respect, Sigma represents easily the most substantive achievement of a key aspiration voiced at the end of the late-1990s indigenous production boom. Film-makers and policy-makers alike started to propose that Scottish cinema's long-term industrial security and expansion would be dependent upon indigenous independents' success in developing rolling slates of production, rather than a fragmented and unpredictable series of one-off feature projects (Hunter 1999, 2000). Sigma's collaborative endeavours with Zentropa helped to mould a Scottish independent with the international experience and profile necessary to undertake a range of feature productions over and above those which involved Danish colleagues.

Scandinavian involvement within 2000s Scottish cinema also exerted a marked degree of influence over representational trends during the period. Locally set co-productions with Nordic partners contributed substantially to a wider contemporary qualification or circumnavigation of national identity's traditional pre-eminence within Scottish film-making. More than half – *Aberdeen, Skagerrak, Wilbur* . . . , *One Last Chance, Red Road, Perfect Sense* – of the eight 2000s Scottish-Scandinavian co-productions located in Scotland were, for example, written and/or directed by overseas film-makers. The notable presence of such artists within 2000s Scotland can perhaps be ascribed to an overarching commercial, rather than cultural, agenda. From certain Nordic perspectives, Scotland appeared an alluringly convenient beachhead from which to consolidate post-Dogme Scandinavian cinemas' provisionally expanded foothold within Anglophone theatrical markets. In late 2002, for instance, Zentropa President Peter Aalbæk Jensen argued that, 'today it is impossible to package a film with a budget exceeding $3m, if you insist on shooting it with Danish dialogue . . . foreign financiers will never place their money in a Danish-language film. We would have made [*Wilbur* . . .] in Danish, had the costs not been so high' (European Film Promotion 2002). Foreign film-makers' understandably limited knowledge or experience of Scottish cultural minutiae entailed that, for the most part, questions of national identity were not prioritised within the work which they produced on Scottish soil. During the 2003 Edinburgh International Film Festival, *Wilbur* . . . co-writer Anders Thomas Jensen argued of his film that 'I don't know if the film is Scotland . . . for me it's the way [director] Lone [Scherfig] and I think Scotland is' (Script Factory 2003).

Such pronounced disinterest in accurate or politically engaged local nuance is worth noting, as Jensen's attitude finds numerous echoes within the corpus of 2000s Scottish-set Scandinavian co-productions.

The titles of many of the films in question, for instance, deploy place names in a deliberately misleading manner. The monikers of such works seem at first sight to promise the pleasures of rooted location within a specific and stable physical and cultural milieu; yet the films in question instead transport their viewers to a series of far more diffuse and diverse interior spaces, ones associated with the displaced and distressed psyches of often mobile and non-native central protagonists. Thus the eponymous Skagerrak of Søren Kragh-Jacobsen's 2003 feature is not a remote rural region of Denmark, but a Glaswegian garage inexplicably named after the former. An attendant sense of carefully cultivated displacement is amplified by the work's convoluted tale of mistaken identity and misplaced desire played out between three Irish, Danish and American incomers to Scotland (two female best friends, one male). *Skagerrak*'s carefree cosmopolitanism is essentially that of the raucous foreign females at the movie's heart. Tellingly, this central pairing adopts Eurythmics' 'Sweet Dreams (Are Made of This)' – a song co-written and sung by a Scotswoman, but narrated by a peripatetic protagonist who endlessly 'travel[s] the world and the seven seas' – as their personal anthem, playing or performing the track at numerous points across the narrative.

The title of writer/director Andrea Arnold's *Red Road* also proves to be a red herring. Instead of close engagement with local specificity – Red Road is a Glasgow street address – this film's name refers primarily to the idea of a place, and a personal journey one takes to reach it, conceived in terms psychological, not physical. Arnold notes, for instance, that:

> I started from the character and [her] emotional place, so I'd say the story is about Jackie and her journey . . . it could be universal . . . I didn't know Glasgow . . . as I was writing I was incorporating what I was seeing and the Red Road flats came into the story . . . the film shows a certain side of Glasgow and not [the city's] whole self. (Rowin 2006)

The developmental process which the film-maker describes here is perhaps reflected in the fact that almost eighteen minutes of the movie's narrative elapse before the titular tower blocks of dilapidated Glaswegian public housing are explicitly shown and named. Yet before that point, bereaved central character Jackie (Kate Dickie) sees, or is seen against, no fewer than ten examples of red-hued *mise en scène* (a symbolic motif which persists throughout the work's duration). Of these early instances, eight are clearly linked in some way to ideas of sexuality and procreation. These central aspects of human experience are precisely what Jackie has tried to divorce herself from, in an act of perverse self-preservation provoked by the unexpected loss of her partner and child in a motor accident a decade previously. The 'red road' which a partially healed main protagonist chooses to traverse by the film's conclusion does not refer, then, to a public domicile. Rather, it offers a metaphorical understanding of the unpredictable individual life journey which Jackie's renewed openness to the possibility of intimate emotional and physical contact with others will entail.

Andrea Arnold's creative priorities, speaking as they do of a desire to circumvent or downplay questions of cultural specificity and national representation, do not appear to have been a phenomenon which emerged over time as local film-makers acquired enhanced experience of collaborating across European borders. This kind of artistic agenda seems, in fact, to have been built into 2000s Scottish-Scandinavian cinema from the movement's very outset. A symptomatically deceptive use of place names is present, for instance, within the decade's earliest Scottish-Scandinavian co-productions. *The Last Great Wilderness* represented the first collaboration between Sigma and Zentropa, and the Glaswegian company's first involvement in a feature-length project. David Mackenzie's film names itself after a popular way of describing the Scottish Highlands, and takes knowing advantage of a narrative device familiar from innumerable twentieth-century Scottish-set but overseas-produced works: the idea of strangers crossing the border into Scotland and finding themselves radically transformed by their immersion within a quasi-magical national sphere (Murray 2005: 15). This aspect of the work undoubtedly opens it up to the possibility of readings which stress issues of national identity and representation. Thus David Martin-Jones interprets the film as a post-devolution allegory, one in which

> the Englishman [central protagonist Charlie (Alastair Mackenzie)] firstly comes to terms with the separate identity of the Scottish, and then accepts his own status as part of a newly independent nation ... the knowledge that he takes with him on departure [from Scotland is] of England's ability to function independently of Britain. (2005: 233)

Yet when *The Last Great Wilderness* is set alongside other 2000s Scottish-Scandinavian co-productions rather than a longer British/Hollywood tradition of incomer narratives, a non-nationally specific reading seems both more obvious and plausible. Like *Skagerrak* or *Red Road*, Mackenzie's film is self-consciously concerned with psychological questions – understanding the transformations which take place within characters – rather than with national ones – commenting upon the identity of the place within which individual metamorphoses unfold.

407

Near the work's conclusion, one protagonist, a deeply unconventional Scottish psychotherapist, points towards his own heart, observing that, 'the last great wilderness is not 'out there'... it's in here.' In this and other ways, *The Last Great Wilderness* sets a template followed in time by most other Scottish-Scandinavian features, interested primarily in the exploration of psychological hinterlands as opposed to physical Scottish Highlands.

Finally, one might argue something very similar of Hans Petter Moland's *Aberdeen*, a co-production that predated *The Last Great Wilderness* by some two years, and which, unlike the latter film, was written and directed by Scandinavian, not Scottish, artists. Kaisa (Lena Headey), a promiscuous, cocaine-addicted young corporate worker in the City of London, is unwillingly reunited with Tomas (Stellan Skarsgård), her estranged alcoholic Norwegian father. The pair endure a constantly interrupted and diverted journey from Norway to Aberdeen, where Helen (Charlotte Rampling), Tomas' ex-wife and Kaisa's mother, is dying of cancer. On the one hand, the nature of *Aberdeen*'s plot and Kaisa's periodic utterances about the importance of reaching the Scottish city of that name – 'I want to leave straight away – for Aberdeen' – appear to signify the centrality of place within this work. Yet this assumption is complicated by several different factors. Firstly, as David Martin-Jones (2009: 64) notes, *Aberdeen* is a road movie where 'many scenes take place in unidentified or anonymous locations, including airports, a caravan park, a cathedral ruin... no attempt [is] made to integrate characters and locations'. Secondly (and perhaps more fundamentally), the film suggests that Kaisa's need to return home represents an emotional, rather than literal, longing. *Aberdeen* opens with archive Super 8 footage that documents happier times within a later broken family. An infant Kaisa joyfully welcomes Tomas home from an offshore stint on a North Sea oil rig; Chet Baker's version of the Hoagy Carmichael standard 'I Get Along Without You Very Well' plays on the soundtrack. These images then briefly reappear some 20 minutes into the film's narrative, by which time the now middle-aged Tomas' addictive self-degradation has been made abundantly clear. As a result, both the presence and significance of a physical detail easy to overlook during the first appearance of the Super 8 shots become pointedly apparent: in the mid-distance behind embracing father and prepubescent daughter, an Aberdeen place name sign hangs. The practical difficulties which Kaisa and Tomas each precipitate as they try to reach the northern Scottish hospital where Helen lies dying therefore perform a number of different narrative functions. As well as generating suspense, they illustrate the elusive (but therefore seductive) nature of the place which traumatised Kaisa truly yearns to revisit: 'home' in the sense of a functional family unit, rather than a particular city or country in which three people once shared a roof.

The collaboration with Scandinavian counterparts was of pronounced significance for Scottish cinema during the 2000s which, as the decade wore on, increasingly transcended nationally exclusive or essentialist concerns, both industrial and representational. Of comparable importance in this regard was the turn by local film-makers towards an exploration of questions of ethnicity and race. In stark contrast to late twentieth-century English cinema (see, for example, Pines 2008; Korte and Sternberg 2008), representation of ethnic diversity proved conspicuously absent from Scottish film-making of the 1970s, 1980s and 1990s. Writing in 1982 about an early 1950s Scottish film, *The Gorbals Story* (David MacKane, GB, 1950), John Hill argued that a work notable and novel for its inclusion of a Scots-Pakistani protagonist ultimately 'signifies cultural and ethnic difference . . . only to go on and deny it under an umbrella of universalised humanism' (106). The terms of Hill's microcosmic analysis could, perhaps, be modified to offer one speculative macrocosmic explanation for the near-total whiteness of Scottish cinema before the new century's dawn. Prior to this point, a dominant umbrella of universalised *nationalism* – the dominant principle, whether articulated by film critics, film-makers or film funders, of indigenous feature production as a vehicle for national representation and self-expression – held sway. Such hegemony encouraged the production – whether on the silver screen or the printed page – of totalising assertions about a Scottish identity and society conceived in the singular. Explorations and articulations of sub-national cultural heterogeneity were marginalised as a result.

During the early twenty-first century, however, a significant proportion of contemporary Scottish cinema has seen local film-makers tackle questions of ethnic diversity and conflict directly and in detail. This important turn has complicated Scottish cinema's traditionally asserted umbilical link to domestic issues of national identity, and this is so in a number of different ways. Firstly, many of the movies concerned – *Gas Attack* (Kenny Glenaan, GB, 2001), *Yasmin* (Kenny Glenaan, Ger/GB, 2004), *Tickets* (Abbas Kiarostami/Ken Loach/Ermanno Olmi, It/GB, 2005), *Cargo* (Clive Gordon, Sp/GB/Swe, 2006), *True North* (Steve Hudson, Ger/Ire/GB, 2006), *Trouble Sleeping* (Robert Rae, GB, 2008), *Outcast* – examine the experience of non-Scottish protagonists, whether newly arrived in that country or located outwith its borders. Secondly, several of the films in question – *Yasmin*,

Cargo, True North, The Last King of Scotland–are wholly or mostly set outside of Scotland. Finally, even when set within Scotland, a large proportion of these works–*Gas Attack, Ae Fond Kiss* (Ken Loach, GB/Bel/Ger/It/Sp, 2004), *Nina's Heavenly Delights* (Pratibha Parmar, GB, 2006), *Trouble Sleeping*–are explicitly concerned to acknowledge modern Scotland's increasingly multicultural make-up. In such ways, films of this ilk call definitive and/or comprehensive prescriptions of a single overarching Scottish culture and identity into serious question.

Gas Attack, Kenny Glenaan's debut feature, examines the traumatic and socially deprived experience of many within Scotland's refugee communities by narrating a fictional account of a racially motivated anthrax attack on Kurdish immigrants housed in a Glaswegian tower block. For Glenaan, 'immigration is the big story of the twenty-first century' (Drew 2003). *Gas Attack* diagnoses some of the contradictions and hypocrisies inherent within Scottish governmental policy towards immigration, underscoring the extent to which cities like Glasgow were willing to 'welcome' significant numbers of political refugees to Scotland at the turn of the century, not as a matter of principle, but due to the financial attraction of large European Union grants offered in support of such action. Glenaan's next feature, *Yasmin*, tackled closely related subject matter. That film's eponymous central character is a young Northern English-Pakistani woman forced, by a British state-sponsored post-9/11 upsurge in Islamophobia, to renegotiate the already conflicted terms of her bifurcated cultural heritage and identity. Glenaan noted that his aim here was to highlight the existence of 'an invisible war happening in Britain which British Caucasians may or may not see ... for the Muslims of our country, it's similar to being Irish in the '70s and '80s–guilty until proven innocent' (Jennings 2005).

Several other post-2000 Scottish features echo Glenaan's perception of immigration into contemporary Scotland/Britain as a vehicle through which fear of the Other can be mobilised for reactionary ends and with inhuman consequences. *True North* tells the story of a Scottish father-and-son fishing trawler, the ironically named *Providence*, fighting a losing battle to meet monthly mortgage repayments. The unending financial worries endured by Sean (Martin Compston), the son of the boat's unnamed skipper (Gary Lewis), lead the young man into people trafficking. Sean's decision to conceal a group of Chinese migrants in the boat's hold and smuggle them from the Belgian port of Ostend to Scotland has disastrous consequences for all concerned. As this brief plot summary might suggest, *True North*'s most audacious ideological decision involves the film's deliberately one-sided focus on, and consequent alignment of audience identification with, the perspective of Scottish smugglers rather than the smuggled Chinese. For writer/director Steve Hudson, 'there have been several very strong films that have told illegal immigrants' stories from their point of view. What really interested me, though, was to make a film from the point of view of people smugglers' (Pinto 2007). The *Providence* and its small native crew therefore come to function as a metaphor for hegemonic Scottish (and, indeed, Western European) attitudes towards the issue of mass migration. Establishing shots of the boat at sea and docking at Ostend during the film's opening titles highlight not only the vessel's name, but also the proximity of a painted St Andrew's Cross to this. The political perspectives on display within a microcosmic version of Fortress Scotland/Europe range from the clueless (the ship's cook) though the compromised (Sean) to the downright callous (the skipper). *True North*'s deliberate dehumanisation of its mostly unseen migrant cargo can be understood as an attempt to emphasise, rather than obscure, the routine inhumanity that characterises much party political and media discourse around the subject of immigration. Domestic viewers are challenged to ask themselves whether, in an ideological sense, their personal beliefs and prejudices place them in the same boat as the misguided crew of the *Providence*.

A closely related set of narrative and political strategies to those at work in *True North* can be discerned within *Cargo*, a Spanish-British-Swedish co-production scripted by the Scottish screenwriter Paul Laverty. Chris (Daniel Brühl), a young white German man, stows away beneath deck on the *Gull*, a cargo ship sailing back to Europe from an unnamed African port city. His illicit presence quickly discovered, Chris is offered free and safe passage by Brookes (Peter Mullan), the vessel's taciturn, enigmatic captain, in return for unpaid labour during the voyage home. But that journey proves to be no pleasure cruise. Chris is not the ship's only unauthorised passenger: the crew hunt down and throw overboard desperate African stowaways who also secreted themselves in the hold. Brookes invites a morally repulsed Chris, who by now knows too much, to join the crew and save his skin. Chris first succumbs, pushing a female stowaway overboard to her apparent death, then repents, leaping after her and drowning in the ocean's waters. A distraught Brookes (who had seen Chris as a possible surrogate replacement for his own dead child) orders the crew to abandon ship and 'save your miserable souls'. The jettisoned stowaway manages to clamber back on board and strikes out in a lifeboat for the European coast now visible on the horizon.

Chris's exposed situation throughout *Cargo*'s narrative acts as an empathy-inducing proxy for the comparably powerless position

411

of penniless and illegal Third World would-be migrants. In this way, the film encourages viewers to identify with non-white, non-European characters and human experiences which are defined by systematically policed and preserved economic disadvantage. Equally counterintuitive to Chris's unlikely status as a cipher for African experience is the extent to which *Cargo*, a work centrally concerned with themes of neo-colonial economic exploitation and inequality, pursues little direct investigation of the contemporary geopolitical mechanics which underpin such phenomena. The closest the movie comes in this regard is, perhaps, an unanswered question posed sneeringly and in passing by Brookes. The *Gull*'s legitimate cargo is African cocoa, and the ship's captain asks Chris if the young man has ever considered why European shops are not full of chocolate bars which are manufactured and sold by companies owned within the same continent where the raw materials necessary to make such confectionary products are found. Instead of following up such detailed lines of questioning, *Cargo* instead adopts a parable-like approach to its central political conundrum. Lead actor Peter Mullan, for example, presents the film as 'one great big allegory about globalisation and what it does to people. The ship is very much the symbol of the rotting vessel of capitalism trundling through the waters destroying any weakness that it sees' (Archibald 2005). Paul Laverty's script certainly proceeds by metaphor rather than manifesto, a fact indicated by the Biblical source (Luke's Gospel) of the enigmatic graffito which Chris encounters while scrubbing the ship's toilets: 'for nothing is secret that shall not be made manifest'. Ultimately, the 'secret' which *Cargo* makes 'manifest', the obscured truth which Chris uncovers within the *Gull*'s dark hold (and Brookes pointedly persists in asking the young man if he knows yet what lurks unseen within that shadowy space), is not a comprehensive, fact-based understanding of a colonialist global economic system's material workings. Rather, it is what Brookes terms, in a Conradian-cum-Darwinian voice-over monologue which begins the film, 'the filth of it all': the animalistic and perhaps innate aspects of human nature which allow the species to first construct, then subsequently countenance, grossly exploitative socio-economic relations among individuals, nations and entire continents.

The work of Paul Laverty seems especially important to mention in the context of contemporary Scottish cinematic explorations of ethnic diversity and colonial conflict. More than any other local film-maker, Laverty has returned time and again to such territory over the last decade and a half. Perhaps key in this regard is the writer's script for Ken Loach's *Ae Fond Kiss*, a romantic melodrama charting the course of a true love which runs anything but smooth. Romance is a troubled affair within this film precisely because its creators aimed to acknowledge and anatomise the existence and effects of a range of complex conflicts between – and, just as importantly, *within* – different cultures and communities which coexist uneasily within early twenty-first-century Glasgow. Like Kenny Glenaan's *Yasmin*, the genesis of *Ae Fond Kiss* stemmed from a troubled awareness of rising levels of racial tension and prejudice within post-9/11 British society. Laverty noted how:

> One of my friends from a traditional Muslim background told me her niece, who was born in Glasgow, was scared to go out. That really got to me... it made me want to examine what was going on... when Catholics first came to Scotland 150 years ago they were seen as aliens with a loyalty to something foreign to the indigenous population. (Mottram 2004: 23)

Thus in Laverty's script Casim (Atta Yaqub), the early twenty-something son of first-generation Pakistani Scots, starts a relationship with Roisin (Eva Birthistle), a white, Roman Catholic Irish immigrant who teaches music at a local secondary school. The couple move in together and Casim is estranged from his family as a result. Meanwhile, Roisin loses the chance of a permanent teaching post at her school: the local Catholic priest, who has learned of her affair with a Muslim, refuses to provide her with the necessary official Church confirmation of good character. Despite these and a range of other obstacles, *Ae Fond Kiss* ends with Casim and Roisin happily united in her flat. As John Hill (2009: 102) notes, the film actively attempts to 'embrace[...] the continuing possibility of living with new, hybrid forms of cultural identity... Casim and Roisin... represent a new kind of social settlement in which a variety of forms of cultural identification and social inheritance may coalesce' within contemporary Scotland and further afield.

It is worth noting the extent to which *Ae Fond Kiss* appears to have consolidated the overarching trajectory of its screenwriter's creative practice. The majority of Laverty's scripts immediately pre- and post-*Ae Fond Kiss* take the long-term consequences of colonialism, both the traditional form practised by sovereign nation states and the modern counterpart essayed by mobile multinational capital, as a narrative and ideological starting point. This is so regardless of whether any given project has been Scottish-set or not, or written for Ken Loach or another director. *Bread and Roses* (Ken Loach, GB/Fr/Ger/Sp/It/Swi, 2000) follows the struggle of low-paid immigrant Latin American workers for union rights in modern-day Los Angeles; Loach and

Laverty's segment of the 2002 portmanteau documentary *11' 9" 01* (Various, GB/Fr/Egy/Jap/Mex/USA/Ir, 2002) links the American 9/11 of 2001 to the Chilean 9/11 of 1973, the US-endorsed *coup d'état* that overthrew the democratically elected Allende government; Laverty's script for *Cargo* is discussed briefly above; *The Wind that Shakes the Barley* (Ken Loach, Ire/GB/Ger/It/Sp/Fr/Bel/Swi, 2006) examines the early twentieth-century Irish War of Independence; *It's a Free World . . .* (Ken Loach, GB/It/Ger/Sp/Pol, 2007) highlights endemic exploitation of migrant workers within modern Britain; *Route Irish* (Ken Loach, GB/Fr/It/Bel/Sp, 2010) delves into the murky world of private security contracting in post-Saddam Iraq; *Even the Rain* (Icíar Bollaín, Sp/Mex/Fr, 2010) juxtaposes the April 2000 Bolivian Water War with the arrival of Columbus's Spanish colonists in the Americas several centuries previous. Laverty's position within a twenty-first-century Scottish cinematic turn towards questions of race and ethnicity is not unlike that of Sigma Films in relation to the contemporaneous rise of systematic Scottish-Scandinavian creative and financial collaboration. The relatively small size of a cinema such as Scotland's raises the possibility that especially prolific individual *oeuvres* create the illusion of wider industrial and representational trends which in fact possess little or no material substance. In both cases discussed above, however, it seems that the movements in question cannot be reduced to no more than one or two isolated career trajectories.

This essay has argued that Scottish cinema became markedly more diverse during the 2000s than was the case in earlier decades. But if that is really so, then any act of criticism is, by definition, one story about, not the story of, its object of study. Other ways of understanding and engaging with contemporary Scottish film-making abound, some suggested or implied by this piece, others lying beyond its scope. Yet I would argue that any remotely comprehensive or responsive study of Scottish cinema must be open to a number of overarching precepts. Firstly, that a maturing indigenous sector is now firmly embedded within transnational networks of financial and creative exchange. Of the 28 features supported by indigenous sources of public finance between 1983 and 2000 which Duncan Petrie (2000a: 227–8) lists, less than half (ten) were international co-productions. But of the 43 post-2000 films identified above as incorporating a degree of Scottish financial and/or creative involvement, the corresponding figure rises to 33. This in turn points to a second precept: Scottish cinema in the twenty-first century routinely incorporates work made by overseas artists working in Scotland and by Scottish artists working overseas. Twenty of Petrie's 28 indigenously supported features between 1983 and 2000 are locally set; of the 43 post-2000 films cited by the present discussion, the equivalent figure is but seventeen. Eighteen of Petrie's late twentieth-century sample were directed by film-makers who are Scottish by birth; the same is true of only eleven out of the 43 works surveyed within these pages.

Of course, any choice to understand contemporary Scottish cinema as something which 'exists in the midst of, and interjects in various ways with, the increasingly decentralised flows of film production and distribution that circulate the globe' (Martin-Jones 2009: 11) poses a vexed, but potentially productive, fundamental question. What might one today recognise as 'a Scottish film', and with what critical purposes in mind? Robin MacPherson (2011) cautions, for instance, against an anything goes form of 'journalistic boosterism' which he sees at work within recent press identification of *Wuthering Heights* (Andrea Arnold, GB, 2011) as a 'Scottish' movie purely because its director (Andrea Arnold) and producer (Douglas Rae) happen to have shot and set earlier feature projects in that country. From such a perspective, many of the films which the present discussion cites as Scottish may well cause eyebrows to be raised.

Two points may be made in response to such scepticism. Firstly, Scottish cinema has by 2012 attained a level of critical mass sufficient to render pragmatic questions of how best to create, consolidate and grow a fragile indigenous production sector just one of several important agendas which critical analysis needs to pursue. One of the latter involves documenting the extent to which the significant gains of the late 1990s gave birth to a substantial nucleus of local film-making talent which spent the next decade entrenching and enhancing individual careers by working both at home and abroad. Of course, the precise nature and significance of the forces which drove that development are open to question. Director Paul McGuigan, for example, proposes that the internationalisation of his *oeuvre – Gangster No. 1* (GB/Ger/Ire, 2000), *The Reckoning* (GB/Sp, 2003), *Wicker Park* (USA, 2004), *Lucky Number Slevin* (Ger/USA, 2006), *Push* (USA/Can, 2009) – in the decade since his debut feature, *The Acid House* (GB, 1999), is a symptom of local cinematic failure, not success. For McGuigan, key public bodies such as Scottish Screen 'decimated' a fledgling local production culture during the 2000s, signally failing to foster an 'industry that creates home-grown entertainment and at the same time makes money and creates jobs in Scotland' (Anon. 2009). Elsewhere, the director complains that 'it sometimes seems that the younger generation have ... to move away ... get a career somewhere else, which is a fucking shame because ... [film production] can make a lot of money for Scotland' (Bodsworth 2010). Although it is outside the present article's scope, a debate does need to take place around the points that McGuigan raises. That process would take in a large number of vexed issues, including changing levels of public finance available for Scottish film production over the last decade and a retrospective assessment of the strategic priorities which moved key funders of the period (such as Scottish Screen) to distribute the monies at their disposal in the precise ways that they did. Yet for the specific purposes of the discussion presented here, the main point to determine is not whether McGuigan's analysis is 'right' or 'wrong'. Rather, it is to understand that his individual career trajectory, like those of most of the native Scottish film-makers discussed above, illustrates the extent to which, given the way in which Scottish cinema has developed over the last decade, we blind ourselves in one eye if we refuse to accept that both indigenous and international components of increasingly globalised creative careers ought to be explored in tandem. The comparative absence of significant works such as *Housekeeping* (Bill Forsyth, USA, 1986) or *Comrades* (Bill Douglas, GB, 1987) from Scottish cinema literature could at one time be explained away by protestations that artists such as Bill Forsyth and Bill Douglas were, by virtue of their cosmopolitan professional histories, glaring exceptions to a general rule. Such a position is increasingly hard to cleave to today.

The second point to make about the nucleus of local talent which emerged during the late 1990s is that it necessarily diversifies the various types of film-making career which Scottish cinema scholars ought to be interested in following. A near-exclusive traditional focus on the activities of directors is potentially as blinkered a critical approach as the one which prefers to admit only films shot and set on home soil to the Scottish cinematic canon. Instead, the analysis presented here has traced directing, scriptwriting and producing careers in its identification of a broad range of early twenty-first-century feature work which can, in a variety of ways, be justifiably understood to be Scottish in some significant way. Yet fully detailed accounts of important Scottish producing – Gillian Berrie, Andrea Calderwood, Andrew Macdonald, Chris Yong – writing – Andrea Gibb, David Kane, Paul Laverty, Jack Lothian – and acting – Gary Lewis, Ewan McGregor, Peter Mullan – careers which have flourished since the mid-1990s are still be written. As suggested above, the new century's first decade witnessed a welcome and unprecedented proliferation of modes within Scottish film-making. To document that phenomenon, Scottish film criticism must first prove willing to duplicate it.

Note

1. In this journal we do not normally give films' countries of origin, nor the name of the director of every film cited. In this case, however, these details are crucial to the article's argument [eds].

References

Anon. (2009), 'Film quango slammed for lack of vision', *The Scotsman*, 1 August, http://www.scotsman.com/news/film_quango_slammed_for_lack_of_vision_1_1355047.

Archibald, D. (2005), ' "Knocking on the door of Moronville": interview with Peter Mullan', *The Drouth*, 18, Winter, http://www.thedrouth.org/storage/The%20Drouth%2018.pdf.

Blain, N. (2009), 'The Scottish dimension in film and television', in K. Veitch (ed.), *Scottish Life and Society: Transport and Communication (A Compendium of Scottish Ethnology, Vol. 8)*, Edinburgh: Birlinn, pp. 768–92.

Bodsworth, R. (2010), 'Paul McGuigan on *Sherlock*', 21 July, http://www.reelscotland.com/exclusive-interview-paul-mcguigan-on-sherlock/.

Brown, S. (2011), ' "Anywhere but Scotland?": transnationalism and new Scottish cinema', *International Journal of Scottish Theatre and Screen*, 4:1, http://erc.qmu.ac.uk/OJS/index.php/IJOSTS/article/view/109/pdf.

Drew, J. (2003), 'Aftermath of an anthrax attack', *European Voice*, 27 March, http://www.europeanvoice.com/article/imported/aftermath-of-an-anthrax-attack/47064.aspx.

European Film Promotion (2002), 'Spotlight on Nordic cinema', *EFP Promotion*, 5 (special issue), http://www.efp-online.com/pdf/newsletter_no5.pdf.

Hill, J. (1982), ' "Scotland doesna mean much tae Glesca": some notes on *The Gorbals Story*', in C. McArthur (ed.), *Scotch Reels: Scotland in Cinema and Television*, London: British Film Institute, pp. 100–11.

Hill, J. (2009), ' "Bonnie Scotland, eh?" Scottish cinema, the working class and the films of Ken Loach', in J. Murray, F. Farley and R. Stoneman (eds), *Scottish Cinema Now*, Newcastle: Cambridge Scholars Publishing, pp. 88–104.

Hjort, M. (2010), 'Affinitive and milieu-building transnationalism: the *Advance Party* initiative', in D. Iordanova, D. Martin-Jones and B. Vidal (eds), *Cinema at the Periphery*, Detroit, MI: Wayne State University Press, pp. 46–66.

Hunter, A. (1999), 'Declaration of independence', *Screen International*, 1221, p. 12.

Hunter, A. (2000), 'Gabriel, Bronco secure Scottish Screen loans', *Screen Daily*, 10 November, http://www.screendaily.com/gabriel-bronco-secure-scottish-screen-loans/404192.article.

Jennings, T. (2005), 'Same difference?', *Variant*, 23, http://www.variant.org.uk/23texts/Jennings.html.

Korte, B. and Sternberg, C. (2008), 'Asian British cinema since the 1990s', in R. Murphy (ed.), *The British Cinema Book*, third edition, Basingstoke: Palgrave Macmillan, pp. 387–94.

McArthur, C. (ed.) (1982), *Scotch Reels: Scotland in Cinema and Television*, London: British Film Institute.

MacPherson, R. (2010), 'Is bigger better? Film success in small countries: the case of Scotland, Ireland and Denmark', http://researchrepository.napier.ac.uk/3752/1/Is_bigger_better..._R_MacPherson_31May2010.pdf.

MacPherson, R. (2011), 'What is a Scottish movie? *Wuthering Heights* and the wittering *Herald*', 11 September, http://robinmacpherson.wordpress.com/2011/09/11/what-is-a-scottish-movie-wuthering-heights-and-the-wittering-herald/.

Martin-Jones, D. (2005), 'Sexual healing: representations of the English in post-devolutionary Scotland', *Screen*, 45: 2, pp. 227–33.
Martin-Jones, D. (2009), *Scotland: Global Cinema*, Edinburgh: Edinburgh University Press.
Mottram, J. (2004), 'In the mood for love', *Sight and Sound*, 14: 3, pp. 22–3.
Murray, J. (2005), 'Straw or wicker? Traditions of Scottish film criticism and *The Wicker Man*', in B. Franks, S. Harper, J. Murray and L. Stevenson (eds), The Wicker Man: *Film and Cultural Studies Perspectives*, Dumfries: Crichton University Press, pp. 11–36.
Murray, J. (2007), 'Scotland', in M. Hjort and D. Petrie (eds), *The Cinema of Small Nations*, Edinburgh: Edinburgh University Press, pp. 76–92.
Neely, S. (2008), 'Contemporary Scottish cinema', in N. Blain and D. Hutchison (eds), *The Media in Scotland*, Edinburgh: Edinburgh University Press, pp. 151–65.
Petrie, D. (2000a), *Screening Scotland*, London: British Film Institute.
Petrie, D. (2000b), 'The new Scottish cinema', in M. Hjort and S. MacKenzie (eds), *Cinema and Nation*, London: Routledge, pp. 153–69.
Petrie, D. (2004), *Contemporary Scottish Fictions: Film, Television and the Novel*, Edinburgh: Edinburgh University Press.
Phelan, S. (2004), 'Girl on film', *Sunday Herald*, 1 February, p. 8.
Pines, J. (2008), 'British cinema and black representation', in R. Murphy (ed.), *The British Cinema Book*, third edition, Basingstoke: Palgrave Macmillan, pp. 118–24.
Pinto, V. (2007), 'Interview with Steve Hudson', http://cineuropa.org/2011/it.aspx?t=interview&lang=en&documentID=78434.
Rowin, M. J. (2006), 'See, saw: an interview with Andrea Arnold, director of *Red Road*', *Reverse Shot*, 19, http://www.reverseshot.com/article/interview_andrea_arnold.
Script Factory (2003), 'A conversation with Lone Scherfig and Anders Thomas Jensen', http://scriptfactory.co.uk/go/Training/Extract_194.html.
Street, S. (2009), 'New Scottish cinema as trans-national cinema', in J. Murray, F. Farley and R. Stoneman (eds), *Scottish Cinema Now*, Newcastle: Cambridge Scholars Publishing, pp. 139–52.

Jonathan Murray lectures in Film and Visual Culture at Edinburgh College of Art. He is the author of *Discomfort and Joy: The Cinema of Bill Forsyth* (Peter Lang, 2011) and *The New Scottish Cinema* (I. B. Tauris, forthcoming).

'The Desert and the Dream': Film in Wales since 2000

Kate Woodward

A young woman stands still, calmly and silently, statue-like against a thatched cottage. She is clad in a traditional Welsh costume and wears a tall black hat tied with a black bow under her chin, a shawl around her shoulders and a flannel bed-gown. She slowly begins to brush the floor with her broom. Suddenly, a mobile phone rings in her apron, and the stillness of this portrait-like shot is broken, its heritage film connotations and historical specificity destabilised. This rich and provocative opening sequence from Marc Evans' *Patagonia* (2010) provides an early suggestion that tired symbols of Welshness will have no place in this contemporary exploration of the historical relationship between Wales and Patagonia. Here, it transpires that Gwen (Nia Roberts) is literally part of a historical re-enactment at a museum, while the news – brought by a symbol of global culture and digital communication technologies – places her own future in doubt. Her journey to Patagonia, beyond the historical period she inhabits at the museum as well as the geographical borders of Wales, is to find her future.

In 1997, the election of New Labour saw the establishment of a constitutional path to devolution in Wales. Since the referendum on devolution in September 1997, and the subsequent establishment and opening of the National Assembly in 1999, there has been an increasing sense of nation-building in Wales. One of the main architects of devolution, former Secretary of State for Wales Ron Davies, famously described it in 1999 as 'a process, not an event' (Davies 1999), successfully illustrating how the idea of the nation as 'relational, processual, dynamic and eventful' (Brubaker 2004: 11) is particularly resonant in

Journal of British Cinema and Television 9.3 (2012): 419–435
DOI: 10.3366/jbctv.2012.0098
© Edinburgh University Press
www.eupjournals.com/jbctv

419

Wales. The referendum on devolution in 1997 resulted in the most marginal of majorities voting in favour of devolution, following a clear rejection of similar proposals in 1979. The creation of the Assembly has seemingly boosted Welsh self-confidence. The official transmission of authority in May 1999 was widely celebrated as if it marked the coming into being of a liberated nation (Aaron and Williams 2005: xv). The images associated with that evening's concert–a red dragon aflame over Cardiff Bay, Shirley Bassey clad in the Welsh flag–appeared to many to be symbols of a regenerated Wales. This was seemingly a new nation embarking on a new mode of existence promising greater national self-determination in spheres not just restricted to the political (ibid.: xvi). The rock group Manic Street Preachers' millennium concert, held with 57,000 revellers at the newly completed Millennium Stadium in the heart of Cardiff, appeared to function as an emblem of a newly energised nation, just as a new millennium dawned.

In this article, I will trace developments in film in Wales during the first decade of the new millennium, a decade which coincides with a period of unprecedented nation-building, bookended by the official opening of the National Assembly for Wales in 1999 and the referendum of 2011 on increased further powers for the Assembly which resulted in a resounding 'Yes' vote. I will argue that film production in Wales in the first decade of the twenty-first century, despite its piecemeal, sporadic, uneven and erratic nature, has culminated in a film that attempts to forge the image of an inclusive, forward-looking Wales whose culture thrives both at home and beyond. According to John Osmond, devolution has meant that 'Britain has changed and continues to change. It no longer provides the essential lens through which Wales and what it means to be Welsh has been viewed... Welsh identity is no longer to be nationalised within Britain' (Osmond 2005: 54). I will argue that the film *Patagonia* demonstrates a shifting of horizons: from Wales being defined in opposition to its English neighbour and by its junior position within the UK towards a wider gaze that looks beyond the geographical borders of Wales. I will indicate the way the film, while engaging with and interrogating aspects of the nation's past, engages in a peripheral form of transnationalism that befits a more autonomous Wales that is keen to project a presence beyond its borders.

Issues of representation

The unprecedented degree of self-governance conceded to Wales has fuelled a new debate, specific to the post-devolution movement, about what today's Wales might have in common with the experience of postcolonial societies elsewhere in the former British Empire. This debate is schematically framed as the question of how the 'post-devolution' condition compares to the 'postcolonial' one. The cinematic tradition attached to Wales has undoubtedly tended to exemplify an outsider's tourist gaze rather than creating an identifiably independent vision (Urry 2002). In his review of the first hundred years of cinema and film in Wales, *Wales and Cinema*, David Berry suggested how the work of incoming film-makers – particularly from the US and England – had resulted in superficial portrayals of everyday life that meant 'national identity' had 'been surrendered too often to outsiders in the past' (Berry 1994: 436). Writing in relation to film and media in Wales, Kevin Williams has also complained how '[b]eing locked inside someone else's misrepresentation of your life or community can be a withering experience' (1997: 61) with the result, as Osmond suggests, that there has, historically, been a 'lack of cultural confidence' within Wales (1995: 118). In such a situation, postcolonial theory suggests, the means to 'release' or 'liberate' involves a process of 'mental decolonisation' whereby there is a process of disengagement from those characteristics that have been assumed, or imposed, as a result of the oppressive 'other' (Childs and Williams 1997: 69).

The year 1997 saw the release of three very different films that seemed to suggest that a new film culture was being established in Wales and that a process of 'mental decolonisation' was beginning to occur. In quick succession, *Twin Town*, *House of America* and *Darklands* – with their Welsh settings and distinctively Welsh concerns – seemed to herald a new era of film of, and about, Wales. *Twin Town*, in all its expletive-strewn swaggering confidence, ensured, for the first time in decades, that a film about contemporary Wales was seen in cinema multiplexes. Its trailer, beginning with the line 'Rugby. Tom Jones. Male Voice Choirs. Shirley Bassey', concludes with the words 'If that's your idea of thousands of years of Welsh culture, you can't blame us for trying to liven the place up a little, can you?' and boldly claims that this film will present a new version of Wales for the cinema screens. Director Julian Richards similarly claimed that *Darklands* was the 'first indigenous Welsh horror film', that it explicitly addressed Welsh identity, and that it used 'cultural, political, social and economic issues in Wales' to discuss 'Celtic cultural angst'.[1] Ed Thomas, the ubiquitous darling of the pro-devolution campaign, and author of both stage and film versions of *House of America*, declared in the *Observer*: 'Old Wales is dead and new Wales is already a possibility, an eclectic self-defined Wales with attitude'

(1997: 18). But the three films, in many respects, proved a false dawn. Despite Steve Blandford's contention that they 'presented a Wales to the world that is as far from male voice choirs and rugby as *Shallow Grave* and *Trainspotting* were from the 'Tartanry and Kailyard' of the once dominant filmic representations of Scotland', their enthusiasm for exploding stereotypes prevented them from seeing how their foundations, in all their subversive glory, were built on the very stereotypes they sought to explode, and thus inadvertently reinforced them (Blandford 2007: 94). Marc Evans, director of *House of America*, qualified his original assumption that his film was the first of a new wave of films about Wales, later conceding, 'I thought we were making something very modern, if not post-modern, whereas we were having an argument about the past' (2002: 259). In addition, if these films had Wales as their subject matter, they certainly were not brought about by significant Welsh funding. *Twin Town* was funded by Polygram, and although *Darklands* and *House of America* received small amounts of Lottery funding through the Arts Council of Wales, they were predominantly funded by Metrodome, and British Screen and the Dutch Film Board respectively. The question raised, therefore, was whether a newly devolved, seemingly confident Wales would be able to develop and sustain an indigenous film culture, with both the infrastructure and the ability to address the complex hybridity of contemporary national identity.

Post-devolution institutions and opportunities

To understand film-making in Wales between 2000 and 2010 it is crucial to understand the institutional context and the resources, opportunities and constraints governing cultural production. In April 1997, at the premiere of *Twin Town* in Swansea, its director, Kevin Allen, took the opportunity to launch a scathing attack on Welsh cultural life, declaring that there was 'no talent in films and television in Wales at the moment' (Risoli 1997: 1). He described Wales as 'a hotbed of mediocrity' and claimed that it was seen by the rest of the UK as a 'backwater' (ibid.: 1). Berwyn Rowlands, the newly appointed Chief Executive of the new Sgrîn: Media Agency Wales (replacing the Wales Film Council and Screen Wales), strongly refuted these comments.[2] But five years after devolution and the establishment of Sgrîn, *Twin Town*'s main star Rhys Ifans was still vocal in his criticism of the Welsh Assembly Government (WAG), accusing it of driving talent out of Wales and depriving the sector of money (Anon. 2002: 3). Two months later, during the International Film Festival of Wales, Berwyn Rowlands once again declared that '[o]ur Film Industry has never been in better shape' (Rowlands 2002: 14). Days earlier, the Minister for Culture, Sport and the Welsh Language, the Liberal Democrat Jenny Randerson AM, had said that WAG was in the process of setting up a Film, Television and New Media Fund which she hoped 'to announce next Spring' (Roberts 2002: 15). Sgrîn had, in name, taken over the distribution of £1 million of Lottery funds previously distributed by the Arts Council of Wales. Pierce Brosnan and Halle Berry were filming the closing scene of *Die Another Day* (2002) at Penbryn Beach, Ceredigion, while Angelina Jolie was filming in various locations in Snowdonia for *Lara Croft Tomb Raider: The Cradle of Life* (2003). Richard Attenborough had declared, in his role as chair of Dragon International, that he planned an enormous £330 million film complex on a former open-cast mine in Llanilid, near Bridgend. Already dubbed 'Valleywood', the twelve state-of-the-art sound stages and TV studios, the type of which had 'not been seen for decades throughout the world', would, it was claimed, make South Wales 'a centre of the UK film industry'[3] and would be the 'crowning glory' of Attenborough's career (Pritchard 2002: 15). Despite these developments, Rowlands' optimism did not prove to be justified. By 2003, WAG's much-anticipated Film Fund had been shelved; by 2006, Sgrîn had closed its doors and, by 2008, administrators had been called into Dragon Studios.

Following the resurgence in support for the Labour Party in the second election to the National Assembly of Wales in 2003, Alun Pugh, a Labour AM, was appointed Minister for Culture, Sport and the Welsh Language, which resulted in the shelving of the much-promised Film Fund to which his predecessor had agreed. The reasons given for this decision were 'other priorities' and the belief that it was 'too risky' (Evans 2003: 8). The director Marc Evans called the decision 'depressing and baffling', and declared 'as it stands, that [film] industry is as invisible as many others in Wales and Welsh films are as scarce as pithead wheels' (ibid.: 8). The original plan was to be the cornerstone of a far bigger vision; the £3 million investment would have brought in another £14 million of funding from the European Union as well as other private and public investors. Pugh's decision was a significant blow to Sgrîn, which had expected to oversee the initiative in partnership with Finance Wales (a subsidiary of WAG) and the Welsh Development Agency, although a number of critical reports were soon to make its position untenable. The first report, commissioned by Sgrîn itself, raised concerns over the competence of its management and asked a number of negative questions regarding its internal management structure, its lack of focus and lack of strategy, and the perception of the agency as an 'outsider' rather than an 'insider to the industry'.[4] The second report, commissioned by WAG, concluded that Sgrîn's role 'as both a cultural and economic development agency, as well as its New Media remit, had resulted in a lack of clarity in its relationship with the sector', and that its activities did not meet the future needs of creative business (WAG 2004: 23). Sgrîn was attacked yet again in a report by the Arts Council of Wales, which argued that the agency lacked the 'business savvy' to see many of its big screen projects completed, claiming that it struggled to sell projects to partners and had a 'historical shortage of completed projects'.[5] Over 200 short films had been completed, but of a total of 27 feature films that were awarded funding through the Arts Council and Sgrîn between 1995 and 2005, only fourteen were completed, and only two, Amma Asante's *A Way of Life* (2004) and Sara Sugarman's *Very Annie-Mary* (2001), had received a general release. Sgrîn closed its doors in March 2006.

Duncan Petrie, in his examination of the relationship between film economics and culture in Scotland, rightly says that film-making must be concerned with 'more than questions of economics' and that the way initiatives relate to the issue of cultural need must be addressed (Petrie 2000: 162). It could be argued that WAG embraced an economic conception of film as primarily a commodity at the expense of important cultural considerations. The first major development after devolution was the launch of a single national body to promote Wales as an attractive and competitive film location in November 2002. The Wales Screen Commission was established to promote the facilities and locations on offer in Wales to the international film industry. Later, the first strategy for the creative industries in Wales, *Creative Success*, unveiled in 2004, demonstrated unequivocally its financial imperatives. The strategy was 'directed at commercial creative businesses who compete globally in the 'tradable services sector' and make an important contribution to modern economies' with the aim of supporting 'Wales-based creative businesses that can make a significant contribution to the economy in Wales' (WAG 2004: 23). The main focus of the strategy was on intellectual property (IP) and it addressed the sectors of film, music, new media and television, for which it was felt there was an urgent need to develop solutions. Although the strategy acknowledged that 'Wales' bedrock of creative and technical talent' had 'been shaped by the unique cultural characteristics of its people' and 'enhanced by its language and its art', and also recognised 'the inter-linkages between culture and the creative industries', it was clearly focused on commercial businesses and not the subsidised sector (ibid.: 16). Its flagship initiative was a £7 million Wales Creative IP Fund aimed at boosting the sector in Wales, launched, tellingly, by the Enterprise, Innovation and Networks Minister, Andrew Davies. Managed by Finance Wales, the IP Fund aimed to fill the funding gap in projects that were also capable of attracting private sector investors and became operational in April 2005. The fund was open to any creative business whether UK or internationally based looking to invest in projects in Wales, and would make 'upfront' investments of between £50,000 and £700,000 in creative IP in return for a share of future royalty streams, as well as proactively seeking out more commercial financial deals (ibid.: 7).

The first feature to be backed by the new fund was *Big Nothing* (2006) starring US actor David Schwimmer and English actor Simon Pegg. The fund took a minority stake in the film for £300,000, and was to receive a share of box-office takings. The film was partly shot on location in Barry. Among other films to receive investment were Steve McQueen's *Hunger* (2008), which received £120,000, which it spent at the post-production facility Dragon DI near Bridgend. An equity stake of just over £360,000 was taken in *Mr Nice*, an adaptation of the best-selling autobiography by Howard Marks, starring Rhys Ifans. It was claimed that the production company had spent a month filming in Cardiff and the Vale of Glamorgan, resulting in a direct economic benefit to the region of around £600,000 (Blake 2009: 8). Citing Section 43 of the Freedom of Information Act, the Fund has consistently refused to disclose the amount of cash returned on its investments. But, by March 2010, it had invested £10 million in 26 projects, including a £700,000 investment in a film about Dylan Thomas, *The Edge of Love* (2008), which returned only £70,000 following the collapse of the film's sale agent (WAG 2010: 16). According to one report, returns equalled 21 per cent of the sums invested, at odds with initial WAG hopes that the fund would achieve 'evergreen' or self-sustaining status (ibid.: 15). In the second review of the Creative Industries, *The Heart of Digital Wales* (conducted by Ian Hargreaves and published in March 2010), it was recommended that Wales' support for a film industry should be reorganised in a way which 'maximises its economic impact and efficiency' (ibid.: 40). The report suggested that there should be an orderly transition from the Creative IP fund to a new and broader Creative Industries Fund. The long-term benefit of funds of this nature are unclear, particularly in view of the fact there is a scarcity of companies in Wales compatible with such funding initiatives. So far, the fund has focused heavily on the intrinsically short-lived, single-project inward investment approach, as its key spend criterion has been 'Welsh spend' as opposed to criteria which insisted on Welsh talent or companies.

Out of the ashes of Sgrîn Cymru Wales came Film Agency Wales (FAW), established in July 2006 as the lead agency for film in Wales, with a remit to ensure that the economic, cultural and educational aspects of film are effectively represented in Wales, the UK and beyond. Although it is still early days for this young, lean agency, it seems to be punching above its weight. It aims to facilitate the emergence of a viable and sustainable Welsh film industry and to promote a vibrant and dynamic film culture. It finances films with Welsh talent, be it writers, directors or producers, at the helm. Its tightly focused remit contrasts heavily with Sgrîn's rather cumbersome involvement in broadcasting, new media, film and television archives, international marketing and a number of short film projects. In a relatively short amount of time, FAW has played a part in many successes, most notably Richard Ayoade's *Submarine* (2010) and Gideon Koppel's *sleep furiously* (2008). By February 2010 it had co-financed 22 feature films and provided development funding for 59. The £600,000 per annum of Lottery funding available to support development and production compares starkly with the Creative IP Fund's £10 million (with the majority of that spent on film). As such, FAW's economic clout is necessarily curtailed. It could be argued that in light of the (however naive) confidence expressed about Welsh film in the late 1990s some redressing of the balance needs to take place to promote indigenous production and to counter disillusionment with the lack of production since devolution.

Importantly, broadcasting was not devolved, with S4C, the Welsh-language fourth channel in Wales, remaining with the Department of Media, Culture and Sport (DCMS) in London. S4C had been a keen film producer since its establishment, and had succeeded – at least in Hollywood terms – in receiving Academy Award nominations in the Best Foreign Language Film category for both *Hedd Wyn* (1992) and *Solomon and Gaenor* (1999). Despite the fact that the channel adopted a 'theatric policy' enabling it to release films theatrically before showing them on television, none of its films have received a general release. Between 2000 and 2010, the number of films produced by S4C declined dramatically. A change in policy seems apparent as a new Programme Strategy in 2004 resulted in the channel producing extended versions of their most popular dramas and comedies for the Christmas slot that was traditionally dedicated to film.

Following the burst of activity that occurred in 1997, three films released since 2000 seem to characterise the attempts to create a film culture in Wales. The first, *Rancid Aluminium* (2000), was directed by Ed Thomas, the author of *House of America*. It came to be considered as one of a number of disastrous attempts to emulate the success of *Lock, Stock and Two Smoking Barrels* (1998). One review in the national press called it 'the worst film ever made in the UK' and it was held up as an example of all that was wrong with the British film industry during the New Labour years.[6] On a smaller scale, Euros Lyn's *Diwrnod Hollol Mindblowing Heddiw* (*A Totally Mindblowing Day Today*) (2000) was a film influenced by the Danish Dogme group. Despite its small budget, its young inexperienced actors and handheld camera aesthetic, it succeeded in exploring identities in contemporary Wales, with the young characters travelling the length of the country from their home on Bardsey Island to Cardiff and back. In 2004, Amma Asante's *A Way of Life* was one of only two films that Sgrîn funded to receive a general release. Funded largely by Lottery money and by HTV Wales, it is a harsh and raw depiction of racism in contemporary South Wales. The film opens with a brutal, bloody and fatal beating of a Turkish man by a group of young people. The main perpetrator is Leigh-Ann Williams (Stephanie James), a white teenage single mother who is struggling, by dint of her social and economic situation, to create a life for herself and her daughter. Racial tensions in South Wales had been explored before in *Solomon and Gaenor*, Paul Morrisson's heritage film. But the starkness and devastating violence in *A Way of Life* succeeded in challenging ideas of Welsh identity, and pleading for inclusiveness and hybridity in Welsh experience.

Patagonia *(2010) and transnational cinema on the periphery*

In the wake of attempts to reconceptualise the idea of national cinema, the concept of the 'transnational' and how it relates to cinema has recently been the subject of considerable debate (Higbee and Lim 2010). Some have argued that the idea of the transnational has always been implicit in film history and practice, citing cinema's global reach since its earliest years. Nevertheless, transnationalism has emerged as a dynamic and diverse field of enquiry, described by Tim Bergfelder as a 'new turn in European film studies ... a reconceptualisation of the field, which has significantly paralleled and been motivated by the wider process of political integration' (2005: 316). Is has also been argued that this 'new turn' involves a recognition of the decline of national sovereignty and the weakening of the nation-state. Andrew Higson (2000) has gone so far as to reject the notion of the 'national' in considering the contemporary politics of world cinema, arguing that it is inherently limiting and that it is destabilised by the dynamics of modernity and transcultural contact. What is rarely acknowledged in such arguments is that, far from heralding the death-knell of the nation-state, the age of globalisation has also been the age of nationalist resurgence (Castells 2010: 79). As such, national cinema is not necessarily a site of defiant essentialism, but a political project that attempts to resist 'the totalising logic of a 'global film culture" through the use of transnational strategies (Ďurovičová 2010: xi). So, rather than contradicting the 'political integration' that Bergfelder discusses, devolution in Wales only represents devolution from the British state; it is also an expression of a desire for an increase in the internationalism of Welsh identity and an opportunity to emphasise global connections. Ulf Hannerz has usefully argued that transnationalism consists of phenomena 'which can be of quite variable scale and distribution even when they share the characteristic of not being contained within a state' (1996: 6). Thus, while *Patagonia* maintains a number of features of transnational cinema – such as the diversity of its production base, funding sources, origin of production personnel and actors and the variety of locations (Street 2009: 142) – it also maintains culturally specific features, themes and subject matter.

Marc Evans' *Patagonia* is the first Welsh film to be set outside Wales post-devolution. In the film, the representations of Patagonia employ a transnationalist rhetoric that casts Wales's global presence as key to the country's future. The languages of the film, Welsh and Spanish, here represent a dynamic but decentred form of transnationalism, born at the edge of empire and reinvented as supra-national and local entities (i.e. the European Union and a self-governing body for Wales). A Wales/Argentine co-production, the film's premise is based upon the historical relationship that has existed between Wales and Patagonia since 1865, when the *Mimosa* set sail from Liverpool for Argentina. On board were 163 Welsh men, women and children, fleeing the low wages of the coal mines and the poverty of their hill farms. They hoped to find a promised land, where they would be free to speak their own language and prosper. Two months later the Welsh came ashore in Patagonia, a far-off territory inhabited only by small tribes of the nomadic Tehuelche people, where they faced a barren, inhospitable desert and endured many years of suffering. They laboured to irrigate the land and eventually, aided by the Tehuelche, they conquered the surrounding desert. A 150-year-old utopian endeavour, the Welsh settlement and the Welsh language survive there to this day. Conceived at the periphery of the expansionist projects of both Britain and Argentina, Patagonia is a colony that Wales as a sub-nation-state continues to celebrate.[7] *Patagonia* is not the first example of a film exploring contemporary Welsh identity being set, or partially set, on foreign soil. The device has been used in both Karl Francis' *Milwr Bychan/Boy Soldier* (1985) and Ceri Sherlock's *Branwen* (1994) in which the directors attempted to articulate contemporary Welsh identity through juxtaposition with the Northern Irish 'Troubles'. The politics of Thatcherism and its effect on Wales cast long shadows across both films, and powerful parallels are drawn between the peripheral status of Wales and Northern Ireland within the United Kingdom, underscored by the use of the Welsh and Gaelic languages. Later, in Endaf Emlyn's *Gadael Lenin/Leaving Lenin* (1994) a group of sixth-formers from the South Wales valleys visit St Petersburg. As traditional belief-systems collapse in the early 1990s, the fate of young people in post-Thatcher Wales and post-Soviet Russia are juxtaposed, raising questions about personal and national identity, and the role of politics and art in the construction of those identities. Language again has a pivotal role, but this time the Welsh language is placed alongside two of the great imperialist languages of the world, ensuring that a local situation – the destruction of the valleys as a result of Thatcherism – resonates powerfully in a global context (McLoone 2009: 355).

Patagonia is a film that, in the words of Higbee and Lim, is 'keenly aware of power relations between centre/margin, insider/outsider, as well as the continual negotiation between the global and local that often extends beyond the host home binary in transnational or diasporic cinema' (2010: 9–10.) Set in the present day, it has two disconnected narratives. Cerys (Marta Lubos), a partially sighted elderly Argentine woman, travels from Patagonia to Wales with her young neighbour Alejandro (Nahuel Pérez Biscayart), hoping to find the farm where her mother grew up, armed only with an old black-and-white photograph. A young troubled Welsh couple, Rhys (Matthew Gravelle) and Gwen, are travelling in the opposite direction as Rhys, a photographer, works on his dream commission to photograph the Welsh chapels in the desert.

When Gwen and Rhys' relationship breaks down shortly after arriving in Patagonia, Gwen falls into the arms of Mateo, the Welsh-speaking gaucho guide. In some ways, it could be argued that the dynamics of this romance replicate those of tourism between more and less affluent countries. Kamal Kempadoo has discussed 'romance tourism' in the Caribbean as a phenomenon in which relationships between European women tourists and resident men pass as romance but have a fundamentally economic subtext. In a sense, these relationships replicate the power imbalance of colonial situations even though a hyper-masculine stereotype assumes the role of the once-feminised colonial subject (1999: 3–33). Gwen and Mateo's brief

involvement might well be read as a romance whose dynamics resonate
with those of first-versus-third world encounters. After all, it seems that
for Gwen, the attraction is purely physical, and her sexual involvement
with Mateo is a temporary distraction from the recent news that she
is unable to bear children. But the film attempts to circumvent such
a reading. Firstly, explicit links are made between Gwen and the story
of Blodeuwedd (Face of Flowers), which appears in *The Mabinogion*.[8]
In the myth, Blodeuwedd is made out of flowers to be a wife for
Lleu Llaw Gyffes, but embarks on an affair with another man. She is
punished, banished and turned into an owl, destined to live in enmity
and isolation. In *Patagonia*, Gwen reads Saunders Lewis' dramatisation
of the myth, where contrary to the original, Blodeuwedd is treated
sympathetically as the victim of fate and sexual passion. Gwen makes
the link between herself and Blodeuwedd explicit by leaving the copy
of the play for Mateo, inscribing her name on it and drawing a picture
of an owl. Her true infatuation in the film is with the landscape of
Patagonia itself, its endless starry skies and dusty roads. It could be
argued that these power relations are again complicated by the casting
of Matthew Rhys, clearly the film's biggest 'name', as the indigenous
gaucho. But despite his Californian credentials, having appeared in
the glossy television drama *Brothers and Sisters* (ABC, 2006–11), pre-
publicity for the film aggressively aligned his persona with that of
Mateo's. He was frequently quoted expressing his strong affinity with
Patagonia, and his month-long journey on horseback, riding from the
Atlantic to the Andes accompanied by 30 descendants of the region's
original settlers, was given much attention, with an accompanying
television documentary and book (Booth 2011; Price 2011).[9]

The second way in which the film derails its parallels with typecast
tourist encounters and their attendant colonial resonances is by
insisting on the common, as well as the contrasting, experience of
its Welsh and Patagonian protagonists. It inverts Gwen and Mateo's
liaison through the development of a parallel romance in Wales
between Alejandro and the Welsh, Spanish-speaking girl Sissy (Duffy).
In the younger characters many contemporary versions of Welshness
collide, especially as a chance encounter results in their shared
experience of both the urban capital and the rural north. Having
arrived in Cardiff, Alejandro is coerced into joining three Eastern
Europeans in sampling the capital's nightlife. In a club, he briefly
meets the cosmopolitan, trilingual Sissy, whom, it transpires, is equally
at home in the stillness of rural Gwynedd as she is in the young capital's
vibrant nightclubs. She can effortlessly transcend the boundaries of
the urban sophisticated Welsh capital as well as the slower traditions

of rural Wales, allowing *Patagonia* to articulate distinct but compatible versions of Welshness, as well as mapping for the twenty-first century a Wales with a renewed transnational presence.

Despite these contemporary romantic and sexual Welsh-Argentinian relations, the relationship between Rhys and Martin (Rhys Parry Jones), an Argentine Falklands veteran, teems with tension, terror and paranoia. A tempestuous snooker match between the pair turns into a re-enactment of the Falklands war, with a drunk and unhinged Martin declaring 'I was there' before firing make-believe shots at Rhys with his snooker cue. He attempts to steal Rhys' photography equipment, as if trying to deny him the traditional Welsh 'tourist gaze' of the Patagonia of chapels and tearooms, and forces him to confront a darker Welsh and Argentine history. Later, Martin reveals the war's destructive effect on him. Seeing Rhys as the enemy, he says to him, in Welsh, 'I would have killed you, you know. No, not last night. The Falklands, during the war. Maybe you would have killed me. Maybe you did.' For Rhys, the war is a piece of history – 'I don't even remember that war. I was nine years old at the time' – but, for Martin, the war will continue to define him. He is the embodiment of the grim history of the Malvinas conflict, which was a particularly difficult episode for Patagonia's Welsh descendants such as Martin, who were obliged to support the Argentine cause and in some cases fight in the Argentine army, despite the significant presence of Welshmen among the British troops (Roberts 2003: 13). It is possible, therefore, that Welsh-speaking Argentinians were fighting Welsh-speaking Welshmen. While the other characters travel in search of a home, schizophrenic Martin is fated to travel forever, the bitter irony being that the war destroyed for him the very concept of home and homeland. From a Welsh point of view, not only was there no acknowledgment of the 'Welsh dimension' in the Malvinas conflict, but the British victory elevated Thatcher to great heights, for which Wales' heavy industries and communities would pay a significant price (ibid.: 11).

Following their arrival in Wales, Cerys and Alejandro travel the length of the country to visit three farms of the same name as the farm of her ancestors, 'Nant y Briallu' ('Stream of Primroses'). Cerys quickly dismisses the first two, claiming, despite her poor sight, that 'she will know' when she arrives at the correct farm. Alejandro discovers, through Sissy, that the farm was in fact drowned in 1965, as part of the flooding of the village of Capel Celyn, to create a reservoir to supply water to Liverpool. As Sissy's Uncle Wil (John Ogwen) vividly recalls bodies being exhumed from the village graveyard to be reburied close by, Cerys is shown among the moss-covered gravestones, finding and tracing the names of her ancestors with her fingers. The erasure of place, as it is presented here, is keenly associated with the postcolonial concept of exile which 'involves the idea of a separation and distancing from either a literal homeland or from a cultural and ethnic origin' (Ashcroft et al. 2007: 75). The drowning of Capel Celyn was one, but certainly not the first, instance of the appropriation of land for the benefit of England or Britain at the expense of a Welsh-speaking community, and it was seen by nationalists at the time as a colonisation of Welsh land and an attack on the Welsh language. Symbols of perceived disregard, or undervaluation, by the London government of the rural Welsh and their culture – the forests, reservoirs and military ranges – are numerous, and they have become powerful and immediately evocative Welsh nationalist tools. Many have long taken the position that Wales had, for many centuries, been subjected to colonial exploitation of its human and economic resources, and subsequently caught up in the ideological apparatus of imperial expansion. As early as 1979, Raymond Williams called Wales 'a post-colonial culture' and spoke of the oppression of the Welsh by the English (quoted in Williams 2003: xxx). Post-devolution, there has been renewed interest in the extent to which this relationship has ever been colonial, leading to some heated debate, predominantly between historians who claim that such a notion is 'self-indulgent and potentially offensive' and theorists who claim that the concept is useful as a means of illuminating relations of power, resistance and complicity between different sites. George Lamming's work may usefully be drawn upon when thinking about Cerys, when he talks of exiles feeling 'a sense of exile by our inadequacy and our irrelevance of function in a society whose past we can't alter, and whose future is always beyond us' (1960:12). An unbridgeable distance lies between Cerys and 'Nant Briallu', since there is no possibility of return to the place of her ancestors which has effectively ceased to exist. In the film, the drowning of Capel Celyn is instilled with an importance that goes beyond the Welsh language community. Cerys is denied the possibility of returning, and in that denial Capel Celyn is given an importance beyond that of Wales, the effects of the drowning having rippled outwards, beyond Wales, gaining transnational significance.

In the context of debate on a possibly 'postcolonial' Wales, one might expect the idea of a Welsh Patagonia to sit rather uncomfortably; as legacies of colonialism are re-examined, the mid-nineteenth-century founding of a Welsh settlement in Patagonia might itself come under question. The Welsh term for both the settlement project and the areas of contemporary Argentina that it occupied is 'Y Wladfa' which translates as 'The Colony'. Nevertheless the paradox of presenting Wales as a nation that was simultaneously colonised and colonising has been averted, if not fully resolved, with tacit recourse to the always peripheral relationship of Wales to England and its expansionist endeavours. As Esther Whitfield (2011) has noted, in a rhetoric that pervades political and cultural practice in contemporary Wales, Welsh Patagonia is constructed as an alternative model of colonisation. The Welsh presence in Patagonia in the mid-nineteenth century stands as a challenge to each of the major narratives – the British and the Argentine – that sought to define the region at that time. The leaders of the movement to found a Welsh colony in Patagonia propagated a utopian vision of a new homeland, far from the repressive influences of the English language and British rule (ibid.).

Cerys' mother and her unborn child were exiled from Wales to Patagonia due to Cerys' very existence. As an elderly woman, she is exiled once again, and dies alone, far from Patagonia, on the shore of Llyn Celyn in proximity to a native place to which she cannot return (Said 1993: 407). She cannot return to a place she has never visited, a place that ceased to exist over forty years previously, a home from which her ancestors were forced to depart. Through Cerys, *Patagonia* therefore constructs a transnational relationship between two peripheral entities: Patagonia, at the limit of the imperial world and at the 'extreme south', as it is known, of present-day Argentina; and Wales, bordering on England but distant, and increasingly devolving, from its centre of power. In this articulation of transnationalism at the periphery, *Patagonia,* gazing outwards, celebrates the transnational reach of Wales, its colonial and colonised past, its postcolonial present, acknowledging a utopian endeavour that represents a rebirth of Welsh language and culture that chimes with a more autonomous Wales that is keen, in the twenty-first century, to project a global presence beyond its borders.

I would like to thank my friends and colleagues Paul Newland and Rhodri ap Dyfrig for taking the time to read and comment on an earlier draft of this work.

Notes
1. http://homepage.ntlworld.com/elizabeth.ercocklly/julian.htm.
2. Sgrîn Cymru Wales (Sgrîn) was funded to the tune of £3 million a year by its core funders, the Arts Council of Wales (ACW), the Welsh Development Agency (WDA), BBC Wales, S4C, Wales Trade International, HTV and the Film Council. Its remit was to promote and develop film, television and new media in Wales.
3. http://news.bbc.co.uk/1/hi/wales/south_east/4655682.stm.

4. http://www.walesonline.co.uk/business-in-wales/business-news/content_objectid=13527838_method=full_siteid=50082_headline=-Relevance-of-Sgrin-to-media-industry-questioned-name_page.html.
5. http://news.bbc.co.uk/1/hi/wales/south_east/4569601.stm.
6. http://www.guardian.co.uk/film/2000/may/26/1.
7. In the past, the term 'stateless nation' has been used to describe Wales, but this seems inappropriate nowadays, where substantial sub-state legislatures exists.
8. The Mabinogion is a collection of stories collated from medieval manuscripts.
9. *Patagonia, O'r Môr i'r Mynydd: Dyddiadur Matthew Rhys* (Boomerang for S4C, 2008); Rhys (2010).

References

Aaron, J. and Williams, C. (eds) (2005), *Postcolonial Wales*, Cardiff: University of Wales Press.

Anon. (2002), 'Actor wants to tell assembly pay up', *Western Mail*, 9 September, p. 3.

Ashcroft, B., Griffith, G. and Tiffin, H. (2007), *Postcolonial Studies: The Key Concepts*, London: Routledge.

Bergfelder, T. (2005), 'National, transnational or supranational cinema? Rethinking European film studies', *Media Culture and Society*, 27: 5, pp. 315–31.

Berry, D. (1994), *Wales and Cinema: The First Hundred Years*, Cardiff: University of Wales Press.

Blake, A. (2009) 'Fund hopes for a Nice return as fund takes a stake in new film', *Western Mail*, 8 April, p. 8.

Blandford, S. (2007), *Film, Drama and the Break-Up of Britain*, Bristol: Intellect.

Booth, H. (2011), 'G2: from Patagonia with love', *Guardian*, 3 March, p. 22.

Brubaker, R. (2004), *Ethnicity Without Groups*, Cambridge MA: Harvard University Press.

Castells, M. (2010), *The Power of Identity*, Oxford: Wiley/Blackwell.

Childs, P. and Williams, P. (1997), *An Introduction to Post-colonial Theory*, London: Prentice Hall.

Davies, R. (1999), *Devolution: A Process Not an Event*, Cardiff: Institute of Welsh Affairs.

Ďurovičová, N. and Newman, K. (eds) (2010), *World Cinemas, Transnational Perspectives*, New York: Routledge.

Evans, M. (2002), 'Looking forwards, looking back', in E. Thomas, *Selected Work '95–'98*, Cardigan: Parthian, pp. 259–93.

Evans, M. (2003), 'Popcorn, parties and premieres', *Western Mail*, 14 November, p. 8.

Hannerz, U. (1996), *Transnational Connections: Culture, People, Places*, London: Routledge.

Hargreaves, I. (2010), *The Heart of Digital Wales: A Review of Creative Industries for the Welsh Assembly Government*, Cardiff: Llywodraeth Cymru/Welsh Government.

Higbee, W. and Lim, S. H. (2010), 'Concepts of transnational cinema: towards a critical transnationalism in film studies', *Transnational Cinemas*, 1: 1, pp. 7–21.

Higson, A. (2000), 'The limiting imagination of national cinema', in M. Hjort and S. Mackenzie (eds), *Cinema and Nation*, London: Routledge, pp. 63–74.

Kempadoo, K. (1999), 'Continuities and change: five centuries of prostitution in the Caribbean', in K. Kempadoo (ed.), *Sun, Sex and Gold: Tourism and Sex Work in the Caribbean*, Lanham, MD: Rowman & Littlefield, pp. 3–33.

Lamming, G. (1995), 'The occasion for speaking', in B. Ashcroft, G. Griffiths and H. Tiffin (eds), *The Post-Colonial Studies Reader*, Routledge: London, pp. 12–17.

McLoone, M. (2009), 'Internal decolonisation: British cinema in the Celtic fringe', in R. Murphy (ed.), *The British Cinema Book*, Palgrave Macmillan/BFI: London, pp. 350–6.

Osmond, J. (1995), *Welsh Europeans*, Bridgend: Seren.

Osmond, J. (2005), 'Devolution in Wales: nation building and the national assembly', in J. Coakley, B. Laffan and J. Todd (eds), *Renovation or Revolution? New Territorial Politics in Ireland and the United Kingdom*, Dublin: University College Dublin Press, pp. 52–70.

Petrie, D. (2000), 'The new Scottish cinema', in M. Hjort and S. Mackenzie (eds), *Cinema and Nation*, London: Routledge, pp. 153–69.

Price, K. (2011), 'Patagonia calling', *Western Mail*, 25 February, p. 1.

Pritchard, J. (2002), 'Attenborough chases his crowning glory', *Western Mail*, 7 December, p. 15.

Rhys, M. (2010), *Patagonia: Crossing the Plain/Croesi'r Paith*, Llandysul: Gomer.

Risoli, M. (1997), 'Wales dubbed a hotbed of mediocrity', *Western Mail*, 1 April, p. 1.

Roberts, I. (2003), *Rhyfel Ni: Profiadau Cymreig o Ddwy Ochr Rhyfel y Falklands/Malvinas*, Llanrwst: Gwasg Carreg Gwalch.

Roberts, R. (2002), 'Single body to promote Wales as film location', *Western Mail*, 21 November, p. 9.

Rowlands, B. (2002), 'Our film industry has never been in better shape', *Western Mail*, 29 November, p. 14.

Said, E. (1993), *Culture and Imperialism*, London: Chatto & Windus.

Street, S. (2009), 'New Scottish cinema as trans-national cinema', in J. Murray, F. Farley and R. Stoneman (eds), *Scottish Cinema Now*, Newcastle upon Tyne: Cambridge Scholars Publishing, pp. 139–52.

Thomas, E. (1997), 'The Welsh: a land fit for heroes (Max Boyce excluded)', *Observer*, 20 July, p. 18

Urry, J. (2002), *The Tourist Gaze*, London: Sage.

WAG (2004) *Creative Success: a strategy for the creative industries in Wales*, http://wales.gov.uk/topics/businessandeconomy/publications/creativesuccess/?lang=en.

WAG (2010) *The Heart of Digital Wales*, http://wales.gov.uk/topics/businessandeconomy/publications/heartofdigitalwales/?lang=en.

Whitfield, E. (2011), 'Empire, nation and the fate of a language: Patagonia in Argentine and Welsh literature', *Postcolonial Studies*, 14: 1, pp. 75–93.

Williams, D. (ed.) (2003), *Who Speaks for Wales? Nation, Culture, Identity*, Cardiff: University of Wales Press.

Williams, K. (1997), 'Dear Ron', *Planet*, 123, pp. 61–4.

Kate Woodward is a Lecturer in Film Studies at the Department of Theatre, Film and Television Studies, Aberystwyth University. Among her research interests are issues around film and television fictions, nationhood and cultural policy. Her monograph tracing the development and productions of the Welsh Film Board will be published by the University of Wales Press in 2012.

A Wilderness of Horrors? British Horror Cinema in the New Millennium

Johnny Walker

I have seen the future, and it is a kingdom of horror. (A.J., *Heartless* (2009))

The past is a wilderness of horrors. (Sir John Talbot, *The Wolfman* (2010))

Conceiving the unimaginable

In the concluding section of the first edition of *English Gothic: A Century of Horror Cinema*, Jonathan Rigby stated that 'like all things, the British horror cinema emerged, flowered briefly, decayed and then died' (2000: 245). Although a number of independently produced, low-budget horror films, did emerge amid the success of *Four Weddings and a Funeral* (1994), *Trainspotting* (1996) and *The Full Monty* (1997), controversies surrounding the alleged *Child's Play 3* (1990)-inspired murder of James Bulger and the press furore sparked by the likes of *Crash* (1996) did not provide the most welcoming environment for indigenous horror production. As Steve Chibnall and Julian Petley have argued, no one in their right mind would have produced a British 'video nasty' equivalent at this time, 'and just *imagine* what would happen were a film company to even suggest making a film about, say, Fred and Rosemary West... or the Bulger murder' (2002: 7–8).

Despite the premature publication of its obituaries, however, horror has become one of the most prolific British film genres of the twenty-first century, with hundreds of films having been produced either in

Journal of British Cinema and Television 9.3 (2012): 436–456
DOI: 10.3366/jbctv.2012.0099
© Edinburgh University Press
www.eupjournals.com/jbctv

the UK or with the support of British finance and resources. There has been an array of films, including: the unprecedented national and international hits *28 Days Later* (2002) and *The Descent* (2005); the hugely popular horror-comedy *Shaun of the Dead* (2004); not so popular ones such as *Lesbian Vampire Killers* (2009), *Doghouse* (2009) and *Zombie Women of Satan* (2009); blockbusters such as *Sunshine* (2007) and *The Wolfman* (2010); regionally set (and occasionally regionally funded) films such as *Eden Lake* (2008), *Hush* (2008) and *Salvage* (2009); a string of independently produced 'cult' films such as *Dead Creatures* (2001), *Dog Soldiers* (2002), *Cradle of Fear* (2002) and *Colin* (2008); and a number of horror-themed hard-core porn videos like *Cathula* (2001) and *Zombie Nation* (2007). There has even been, in ironic answer to the rhetorical question posed earlier by Chibnall and Petley, a British film condemned for turning 'the crimes of Fred and Rosemary West into an exploitation film' (Tookey 2008a), *Mum & Dad* (2008),[1] the release of the British co-produced fifth instalment of the *Child's Play* series, *Seed of Chucky* (2004), and, though very far from being a horror movie, a film about a child who murdered another child, *Boy A* (2007).

The last decade, put simply, has marked the first sustained period of horror production in Britain since Hammer Films closed its doors in the mid-1980s. But even though Hammer has reopened for business with *Beyond the Rave* (2009), *Let Me In* (2010) and, more recently, *Wake Wood* (2010) and *The Resident* (2010), things have changed. The new films (up until the release of *The Woman in Black* in 2011), despite bearing the company's iconic moniker, indicate a definite break with the Gothic tradition and period set-pieces which have come to symbolise 'British horror, *tout court*', a paradigm which once posited horror as a genre which 'Britain can properly claim as its own' (Pirie 2008: xv).

Contrary to the epigraphs which begin this article, then, I am inclined to reassert the age-old consensus that it is British horror's past which remains the accepted 'kingdom of horror', when the old Hammer was waving its imperial genre flag. 'Wilderness', then, might be more easily attributed not just to the future but also to the present of British horror, where even the most vague sense of homogeneity has proven difficult to discern.

This article considers the diversity of the genre since 2000 while also drawing attention to those various cycles and trends which have materialised more cohesively during this period. To begin, I will chart the major developments in the genre from its millennial 'rebirth', outlining the economic and cultural factors which led to its resurgence at the turn of the century, as well as alluding to the key films which have featured most prominently within such discourses. Following this, several of the major themes and trends which have become prevalent in the genre in recent years will be considered, in particular the notion of class and the British social realist tradition, and how such elements function in a recent cycle of films which locate the horror within the milieu of what sociologists have termed the new British 'underclass'. In doing so, this article seeks to offer a sense of coherence to a genre now recognised as a 'considerably more varied and consequently less cohesive phenomenon' (Hutchings 2009a: 149) than it has been thought of in the recent past.

New beginnings

The establishment of tax breaks for British films in 1997 and the birth of the UK Film Council (UKFC) in 2000 looked towards 'the development, production and export of [British] films that attract audiences in the UK and all over the world' (UK Film Council 2000: 3). Significantly for horror's future within British cinema, international genre successes of the 1990s such as *Scream* (1996), *Ringu* (1998) and *The Blair Witch Project* (1999) backed up the largely forgotten claim that it was 'possible to produce horror films that are both affordable and travel well' (Minns 2001: 26), although it took a while for UK financiers and distributors to catch on to the genre's indigenous and global market potential. For instance, one of the first productions of the new millennium, Simon Hunter's slasher movie *Lighthouse* (completed in 1999 but not released until 2002), had been in development since 1996, as had Neil Marshall's werewolf film *Dog Soldiers*. *The Hole* (2001)–which had, at the time, the highest ever UK opening figures for a Lottery franchise film, had been optioned from its source novel as early as 1994. An examination of *Screen International* reveals that between 2000 and the release of the first major British horror success, *28 Days Later*, in 2002, almost 50 horror movies had the potential of being produced in the UK, the majority of which were never made. These include the scheduled DNA Films production *The Devil's Chamber* and the Hammer remakes of *The Day the Earth Caught Fire* and *Quatermass and the Pit*.

It is understandable that the newly invigorated British film industry would wish to play it safe with regard to the kind of material which it was willing to explore in its prospective horror films, a genre with such a tainted critical legacy in the UK (Hutchings 1993: 4–7; Petley 2002) and one which had made very little money in the previous decade. The first major genre efforts of the UKFC,[2] *The Hole* and

438

Fig. 1. UK quad poster for *Scream 3* (2000).

Long Time Dead (2002), indicate this cautious approach; the latter was produced – not insignificantly – by WT2, the low-budget subsidiary of *Four Weddings* and *Notting Hill* producers Working Title Films, who would also produce another nationally successful horror film of 2002, Marc Evans' *My Little Eye*.

Although the films' young, attractive casts and plots about a faceless killer would evidence their riding on the coat tails of the post-*Scream* slasher boom, *The Hole* and *Long Time Dead* did manage to retain an ounce of Britishness which was likely to be familiar to both national and international audiences. (For a scathing critique of *Long Time Dead*'s US slasher allusions, see Pirie (2008: 219).) *The Hole*, for instance, is set on the campus of a highly Gothic British school of the kind endemic both to the heritage dramas of Merchant Ivory and the *Harry Potter* (2001–11) films, while the 'hedonistic teenagers' arc of the slasher film indirectly echoes the likes of *Trainspotting* and *Human Traffic* (1999), which sought to bolster chemical escapism from the mundanity of everyday existence. However, the films' evident textual and marketing indebtedness to the new wave of American slashers (note the similarities in their posters in Figures 1 and 2) lays claim to a more pronounced condemnation of youth culture than, say,

Fig. 2. UK quad poster for *Long Time Dead.*

Trainspotting's ambivalence about drug-taking, which probably owes something to the influential, self-reflexive sequence in *Scream* in which horror-geek Randy explains the rules of the subgenre and the horrible fates which await hedonistic teenagers in these kinds of films (Harries 2002: 289). Therefore, although the respective taglines of *Long Time Dead* and *The Hole* – 'Play it to death' and 'Desperate to get in . . . dying to get out' – both echo the 'Choose life' sentiments of *Trainspotting*, it is the horrifying/moralistic consequence (or 'Choose death') which is given real nuance in the marketing materials.

Although these films had a presence at the UK box office and in certain other European territories (*The Hole* grossed £2.2 million in the UK while *Long Time Dead* made £1.6 million), it has been the international (or, rather, the American) theatrical success of new British horror that has really marked the generic resurgence of the last ten years. While at the UK box office *Shaun of the Dead* grossed £6.5 million, *The Descent* £2.6 million and *28 Days Later* £6.1 million, in the US they accrued $13.5 million (approximately £8 million), $39.5 million (approximately £24 million) and $26 million (approximately £16 million) respectively. This may go some way to explaining why *28 Days Later* and *The Descent* are the only British-produced horror films of recent years (outside of a popular franchise)[3] to have warranted a theatrically released sequel,[4] while the team behind *Shaun of the Dead* have moved on to produce commercially resilient comedy blockbusters (albeit with pronounced horror undertones):[5] *Hot Fuzz* (2006), which borrows elements from rural horror films such as *Straw Dogs* (1971) and *The Wicker Man* (1973); *Burke and Hare* (2010), which re-tells the story of two Irish grave-robbers in Scotland in the late 1800s; and most recently, the alien-invasion comedy *Paul* (2011). In North America the initial hopefuls *The Hole* and *Long Time Dead* have had to contend with direct-to-DVD releases which, although now a more commercially sustainable outlet for film distribution,[6] was at the time a fate which testified to the ambivalence of both distributors and audiences towards such films, and evidenced their not having truly fulfilled the global hopes of the bodies which funded them.[7]

Until its closure in 2011, the UKFC continued to show faith in the commercial prospects of the horror film, having had considerable input into targeting the genre's relatively small yet 'very defined audience' (Kuhn, quoted in Macnab 2005: 12). This input includes the distribution of Lottery money through its New Cinema Fund to assist in the production of innovative, lower-budget films such as *Exhibit A* (2007) (£9,999), *Tony* (2008) (£150,000), *Cherry Tree Lane* (2010) (£155,000), *Donkey Punch* (2007) (£445,000) and *Chatroom* (2010) (£700,000); monies also come from its Premiere Fund to assist bigger releases such as *Creep* (2004) (£1.25 million) and *Triangle* (2009) (£1 million). Furthermore, there has been considerable investment from its Distribution and Exhibition Fund in order to help distribute films (including international productions) in the UK, from which *Colin*, *Exam* (2009), *Mum & Dad* and *Cherry Tree Lane* have each received £5,000, *Heartless* £30,000 and *Chatroom* £200,000. Several local bodies have also invested in horror films (with the support of the UKFC), such as Screen West Midlands which helped fund *Tormented* (2009) and *The Children* (2008), EM Media which assisted with *Donkey Punch*, *Hush* and *Mum & Dad*, Screen Yorkshire which distributed funds to *Kill List* (2011), and Northwest Vision + Media which helped to fund *Salvage* through the Digital Departures Scheme. Meanwhile the Irish Film Board and Scottish Screen have dispersed funding (including Lottery money) to horror films such as *Freeze Frame* (2004), *Wake Wood* and *Clive Barker's Book of Blood* (2009), as well as the Ireland/UK co-production *Outcast* (2010).

It is largely agreed that the new wave of British horror films – or, rather, the willingness of investors to fund them – rides on a distinct shift in opinions of the genre. For example, the release of Simon Hunter's *Lighthouse* in 2002, which was featured as part of a double

Fig. 3. UK quad poster for *Lighthouse/The Evil Dead* double bill.

bill with an uncut print of one-time 'video nasty' *The Evil Dead* (1981) (see Figure 3), certainly suggested that the British attitude to horror was changing, just as was British horror cinema itself. Up until this point, the only successful attempts to screen any of the 'video nasties' theatrically had been in select runs at art house cinemas and film festivals, while *Lighthouse/The Evil Dead* had a nationwide, 20-screen multiplex release lasting eight weeks. This shift in attitudes signalled progress for a genre which had repeatedly faced condemnation from British critics and censors. Simultaneously, as one critic noted at the time, the double bill was 'as much to do with a nostalgia for a bygone era of horror than anything else' (Ide 2002), and many films and film-makers have followed suit in fusing nostalgia for horror cinema of the past with contemporary themes and ideas.

Textual allusions to both British and global horror are there in abundance in the countless array of zombie films which have emerged since *28 Days Later*; these include *Colin*, *The Zombie Diaries* (2006), *Zombie Undead* (2010) and *World of the Dead: Zombie Diaries 2* (2011). Similarly, backwoods American horror of the chainsaw massacre ilk is recalled in films such as *Gnaw* (2008) and *Mum & Dad*, both of which see innocent teenagers fall victim to cannibalistic families. British myth has merged with the teen slasher film in *Ripper* (2001); the vampire film has resurged in *Octane* (2005), *Vampire Diary* (2007) and *Perfect Creature* (2006); the ghost story in *Spirit Trap* (2005), *Reverb* (2005) and *Psychosis* (2009); the serial killer film in *Ted Bundy* (2003); and the occult film in *Snuff Movie* (2005) (with hundreds of crossovers in between). Many directors have also taken advantage of the relaxation in British censorship attitudes following the retirement of James Ferman, with increased emphasis being placed on gore and visceral effects. These films include 'torture porn' such as *Spiderhole* (2009) and *Bane* (2009), Alex Chandon's Gothic anthology *Cradle of Fear*, Jake West's homage to *The Evil Dead*, *Evil Aliens* (2005), and Adam Mason's body-horror *The Devil's Chair* (2007). Several films also recall potently the 'video nasties' panic of the 1980s, either by situating the home-video medium itself as a signifier of horror or by presenting horror films as addictive and corrupting; these include *The Last Horror Movie* (2003) and *Resurrecting the Street Walker* (2009) (for discussion of which see Walker 2011a).

There is a strong sense that many of the new British horror films are being made by fans for fans, and one of the most engaging aspects of many of these films is that they are indicative of what might be regarded as a certain 'commercial anarchy' within which horror has developed over the years, with an array of directors making and releasing films beyond the purview of (and, occasionally, out of spite for) the UKFC. For instance, Adam Mason and Simon Boyes' *Broken* (2006), shot for £6,000 over two years, was, according to Mason on the DVD commentary, allegedly made as a direct response to the UKFC's lack of support for upcoming British film-makers, and yet it has since secured the film-makers' careers in Hollywood. Horror-themed film festivals such as England's Fright Fest and Mayhem, and Wales' Abertoir have also played a pivotal role in helping to sustain this grass-roots output, providing a platform for film-makers to screen their horror films – such as *The 13th Sign* (2000), *Evil Aliens*, *Monsters* (2004), *Kill List* and *Little Deaths* (2011) – to an appropriate audience. This has led to many film-makers exploiting these means of exposure by casting actors likely to be recognisable to horror fans, including a string of international horror stars of the past such as the cult Italian regular Giovanni Lombardo Radice, who appears in the British exploitation film *Day of Violence* (2009), and classic British familiars such as Stephanie Beacham in *The Witches Hammer* (2006), David McGillivray (the scriptwriter of such films as *House of Whipcord* (1974) and *Satan's Slave* (1976)) in *Unhappy Birthday* (2010) and Honor Blackman in *Cockneys vs Zombies* (2011). The ultra low-budget *The Lost*

(2006) (a film shot for a mere £3,000) marks Peter Cushing's last screen role as 'the narrator' (although only his voice features, taken from a recording of Cushing reading Peter Kayne's poem 'No White Peaks', which was made in the early 1990s).

The 'new' Hammer(s)

Perhaps the most anticipated development in recent British horror is that of the 'new' Hammer Films. Although the old Hammer is largely regarded as a British institution, the company's new incarnation[8] finds itself caught between wanting to reflect on and respect its early triumphs while also wishing to distance itself from its anachronistic former self. In a recent interview, the company's CEO, Simon Oakes, commented that 'we are trying to bring the brand kicking and screaming into the 21st century, with films that are set in the present day' (quoted in Anon. 2010: 16). This would go some way to explain their decision not to release *Lesbian Vampire Killers* as the company's comeback venture, a film which presumably drew too heavily upon (and parodied) Hammer's former period Gothic style (with particular nods to *Twins of Evil* (1971)). However, the fact that *Let Me In* is a UK/US remake of a Swedish film (*Låt den rätte komma in/Let the Right One In*) which was released in 2008 and set in the 1980s problematises this. This paradox resonates throughout a sequence from Hammer's own US-shot *The Resident*, when Juliet (Hilary Swank) and her prospective love interest, Max (Jeffrey Dean Morgan), sit in his apartment, which is littered with candles, large antique furniture and shelves of classic literature. 'You like old things,' Juliet says, to which Max embarrassedly confesses that he is out of touch with Twitter and cell phones. 'It makes me feel safe, warm,' Juliet replies, 'It feels like home.'

On the one hand pertaining to the homely 'cosiness' for which Hammer is world-renowned and on the other underscoring its outmodedness, this sequence indirectly echoes the company's attempt to explicate its contemporariness by launching its comeback through the social networking site myspace.com with its serial *Beyond the Rave*. The lukewarm critical response (for example, Cockwell 2010) which greeted the series across the Internet in many ways anticipated the difficulties which the new Hammer would face in outstepping its former self, whereas the company's new animated logo (which flicks through a series of classic images – including posters for *The Mummy* (1959) and *One Million Years B.C.* (1966) – before forming 'HAMMER' in bold, red letters)[9] and Christopher Lee's cameo in *The Resident* would ultimately suggest that its identity and appeal rest more upon the old than the new.

The past decade has seen an upsurge in smaller production companies which, like the old Hammer, specialise in lower-budget genre pictures. These include the short-lived Paranoid Celluloid (*The 13th Sign*, *Dust* (2001)), Exploitation Pictures (*Sick Bastard* (2007)), *The Turning* (2011), Gatlin Pictures (*Forest of the Damned* (2005)), *When Evil Calls* (2007)), their sister company Black Robe Productions (*F* (2010), *Forest of the Damned 2* (2011)) and a subsidiary of Warp Films, Warp X (*Donkey Punch*, *Hush*, *Kill List*). Of particular interest is Black and Blue Films, a company which seems as much committed to recalling the classic era of British horror as it is to making films with a contemporary feel. Partially owned by horror enthusiast Jonathan Sothcott (whose previous credits include the setting up of TV's The Horror Channel), Black and Blue's first horror feature *Dead Cert* (2010) is, according to Sothcott himself, 'very much [a] homage to *Dracula AD 1972*' (quoted in Bryce 2010: 32). The company has also shot a remake of the British rape-revenge film *Exposé* (1976) (entitled *Stalker* (2010)) and were recently discussing potential remakes of *The Sorcerers* (1967), *Blood on Satan's Claw* (1970) and *The Asphyx* (1972). In essence, Black & Blue symbolises the convenience of the digital medium, upon which another company, Slingshot Studios, also predicates its success. 'If properly harnessed,' Slingshot's website reads, 'digital enables the making of more interesting movies, and permits new and better ways for those movies to find their audiences.'[10] When asked by the author in an interview on 4 February 2011 to clarify this statement, CEO of Slingshot, Arvind Ethan David, stated that digital grants a freer rein to produce a variety of genre films (not just horror films),[11] and to aim them at their specific audiences without the financial pressure to please everyone. More interesting movies can materialise because of this, in his view, because they do not have to conform to mass demands or to rely on star-studded casts. As Geoffrey Macnab has argued, even when horror films underperform, they 'tend to lose their investors less money than other films that have proved damp squibs at the box office' (2005: 11). Lower-end companies such as Black and Blue and Slingshot embody this ethos in an industry-savvy way, and in many respects confirm the viewpoint of Christian Colson, joint managing director of Celador Films (*The Descent*), when he says that 'a bad horror movie is always likely to look like a more attractive proposition [to film producers] than a good drama' (quoted in ibid.: 11).

A mirror for England?

With the exception of *Shaun of the Dead* and *Severance*,[12] none of the big British horror money-spinners has been promoted in any way for its 'Britishness'.[13] 'In fact, the simple attribution of 'British' has been considered increasingly problematic in light of the many co-productions which have materialised over the last decade, although of course this does not apply solely to the horror film but to British cinema production more broadly (Higson 2011: 56–66). As James Leggott (2008) notes, even in the case of those films with identifiable 'British' settings – such as the London underground in *Creep*, Big Ben and other landmarks in *28 Days Later* (see also Hutchings 2009b) and the M1 motorway in *Hush* – many were actually filmed partially or totally in continental Europe, including *Dog Soldiers* (Luxembourg), *Severance* (Hungary), *Creep* (Germany) and *Hush* (Sweden). Co-productions such as these, however, which often function to appeal to a transnational audience (*Creep*, for example, stars German actress Franka Potente), have not impeded the materialisation of British cultural specificity within other British horror texts. In fact, there has been a cluster of films which have foregrounded not just their 'Britishness' but, more specifically, their 'regionality', indeed more so than anything else.

Dog Solders and *Wild Country* (2005) are both set in the Scottish highlands and, according to David Martin-Jones, use the myth of the werewolf to 'playfully rewrite the monstrous return of a previously repressed Scottish national history' (2011: 115). 'The resonance of the Scottish wilderness,' he continues, 'when deployed as part of a horror film, has a regional, or local, flavour' (132). In a similar vein, the recent *Rising Tide* (2011) takes place within the specific locale of Holy Island/Lindisfarne, a North Eastern tourist attraction which can be reached only by causeway and which is cut off when the tide comes in, while *Dead Meat* (2004) and *Isolation* (2005) have drawn upon rural Irish traditions (Newman 2006). Setting the films within a specific and identifiable region, and also imbuing them with a markedly British social realist sensibility (Leggott 2008: 59; Rose 2009: 8), has thus been one of the many ways in which British horror continues to convey a sense of national and regional specificity. As Julian Richards explains in his commentary on the DVD of his film *Summer Scars* (2007), which is set around Barry in Wales, when he was casting the film, 'getting the locality, getting the accent, and getting a sense of being from a working-class, underprivileged kind of background' was imperative to the authenticity and believability of his vision. Such concerns have, of course, been typical of British cinema for years. As John Hill argues:

> Within the British cinematic tradition, [cinematic realism] has generally involved the working class. In so far as the working class is neither more nor less 'real' than other social groups, the idea that realism is linked to the representation of the working class derives in part from context, and specifically the perceived absence of (adequate) representations of this group within the dominant discursive regimes. (2000: 250)

The context within which British horror cinema has found itself recently is that of the moral panic about 'broken Britain', which Amelia Gentleman (2010) lucidly sums up as 'an accordion-like concept, stretching and squeezing to fit different definitions depending on what the major worry of the hour is – youth crime, teenage pregnancy or anti-social behaviour.' As such, the impoverished and economically deprived milieu of the 'chav', the new British 'underclass' – a social stratum which is the subject of considerable negative mythologising and stereotyping[14] and which is blamed by many in authority for the latest phase of Britain's alleged moral decline – has functioned as a potent allegorical backdrop against which the most interesting, and most controversial, British horror films have recently emerged.

Certain films have placed 'underclass' youth as the source of the narrative's horror, in a direct echo of contemporary media generalities surrounding gang crime, the hoodie/chav (terms used synonymously about British youth) phenomenon and, most recently, the English riots of August 2011. (For an alternative reading of 'underclass' youth in British cinema, see Monk (2000).) *Eden Lake* and *Cherry Tree Lane*, for example, place such 'hoodies' against well-to-do middle-class folk whom they hunt down and then torture. These films – grouped within critical circles under the umbrella term 'hoodie horrors' (Maher 2008; Graham 2009; Newman 2011: 477–8; Walker 2011b) – can be seen as the antithesis of what Leggott (2004) has recognised as the 'angelic' youth films of contemporary British cinema, which include *Ratcatcher* (1999), *Billy Elliot* (2000) and *Gabriel and Me* (2001). These films, which depict kids locating 'their own spaces of transcendent play, in flight from a home environment that is posited as traumatic' (168), differ from the 'hoodie horrors' in that the 'transcendent play' in the latter consists of drug abuse, rape and murder; however, both sets of films reveal their protagonists' home lives as being unstable and conflict-filled. The final sequence in *Eden Lake*, for example, sees Brett's father exerting the same peer-pressure on his friends to kill a middle-class girl as his son exerted on his fellow gang members earlier in the film.

Parents, when they appear in these films at all, are abusive, as in *Eden Lake*, or neglectful, as in *The Disappeared*, in which Matthew's dad (Greg Wise) – a single parent – has an affair on the same night that his youngest son is abducted and murdered. In *Heartless*, the good family life which Jamie (Jim Sturgess) once had is offered as a perfect contrast to the hooded demons who lurk in the streets and who fragment the family structure further by killing Jamie's mother in front of him. Thus Jamie finds solace in the aptly named figment of his imagination, Papa B (as opposed to his deceased father or, if you will, 'Papa A'), while in *Summer Scars*, we could read the kids' initial attraction to Peter (Kevin Howarth), the traveller in the woods, as being attraction to a father figure: he is experienced, worldly and, most significantly, willing to socialise with and listen to them (unlike, presumably, their own parents).

Such films are symptomatic of contemporary British cinema's penchant for generic hybridity, touching upon the quality which Samantha Lay argues stems from the 'socially purposive' nature of British social realism while also functioning as genre films designed for pleasure and entertainment (Lay 2002: 55; Graham 2009). The hybrid nature of these films has proven problematic in the public sphere, where the lines between cinema and actuality have become increasingly blurred. Chris Tookey's (2008b) review of *Eden Lake* is notable here, in which he commends the film for its 'accurate' portrayal of young people and their irresponsible parents, despite director James Watkins' protestations that it is not 'a social realist drama – it's an all-out genre piece' (quoted in Jones 2009: 32). In his review, Tookey overlooks the film's elements of generic convention when he states that the film is 'willing to say what other films have been too scared or politically correct to mention: the *true* horrors we fear day to day are not supernatural bogeymen or monsters created by scientists. They're our own youth' (emphasis added). Tookey's willingness to accept contemporary stereotypes as fact – or, as he puts it, as 'truth' – can be read alongside Homi K. Bhaba's theorising of the colonial stereotype and the 'force of ambivalence' which he sees as endemic to the stereotype's cultural longevity:

> It is the force of ambivalence that gives the colonial stereotype its currency; ensures its repeatability in changing historical and discursive conjunctures; informs its strategies of individuation and marginalization; produces that effect of probabilistic truth and predictability which, for the stereotype, must always been in *excess* of what can be empirically proved or logically construed. (1994: 66)

Fig. 4. Cooper is subjected to peer pressure by gang-leader Brett in *Eden Lake.*

All of these aspects can be applied to Tookey's comments on class and youth, as well as to both horror's and social realism's reliance on conventions: factors which ensure 'repeatability in changing historical and discursive conjunctures'. It is therefore possible to suggest that certain 'social realist' traits have functioned within British horror in such a way that, simply by having working-class settings and characters, certain films are considered as 'realist', regardless of the other genres and film styles which they recall. In *Eden Lake*, for instance, the appearance of British-cinema regular Thomas Turgoose as Cooper, the youngest and most impressionable hoodie, sets up certain audience expectations. Turgoose, by the time that the film was released, had garnered a moderate cult following for his sympathetic portrayal of an eight-year-old skinhead in Shane Meadows' *This Is England* (2006), and had also appeared as a young boy who leaves his working-class background in search of friendship in Meadows' follow-up, *Somers Town* (2008). *Eden Lake* knowingly embellishes Turgoose's screen persona in, for example, a sequence in which Steve (Michael Fassbender) is tortured by the gang and Brett (Jack O'Connell) peer-pressures Cooper to involve himself, despite his own reluctance and protestations from the others that 'he's only small!' (Figure 4). And, later, when an adrenaline-fuelled Jenny (Kelly Reilly) stabs Cooper in the neck with a piece of broken glass, the sympathy garnered as a result of this is testament to Turgoose's performance and the familiarity which his on-screen persona had already attained. The fact that he has a prominent billing in the film's opening credits, despite having very little dialogue or screen time, is testament to this, as is his billing as co-star in some of the promotional material for the DVD of the film, and his subsequent inclusion on the covers of *The British Cinema Book* (Murphy 2009) and the 2011 BFI report, *Opening Our Eyes: How Film Contributes to the Culture of the UK.*

The possibilities for audience identification offered by instances such as the above make defining these films as purely 'exploitative' and 'patronising' (The Sneak 2008) a problematic endeavour, although Tookey's enthusiasm for *Eden Lake* might initially suggest otherwise (Jones 2011: 131). Notwithstanding how the youths may explicitly resonate as stereotypes which are founded upon reactionary, middle-class fears, it could be argued that such texts utilise these stereotypes in a way which exaggerates such fears and creates a dialogue which conflates the 'truth' of the media with the formal properties of genres which are predicated on excess. The 'hoodie horror' film in particular can thus be seen to create a dialogue between traditionally opposing means of representation, whereby the news media are meant to constitute 'the truth' while cinema is meant to constitute fiction. The realist attributes of the hoodies in these films, I would argue, are self-consciously challenged by the constant aligning of the hoodies in the films with the sensationalist rhetoric of the contemporary news media.

This is explored in *F* (2010), where the hoodies' blacked-out faces make distinguishing their gender, age and even species an impossible endeavour. *Heartless* similarly explores media generalisations by presenting the demonic hoodies of the narrative as literal psychological constructions of Jamie, the protagonist, who, throughout the film, is repeatedly influenced by news reportage of gang crime. In an early scene, Jamie and his mum watch a news programme reporting the death of a father and son by 'a gang of youths wearing hoods', which, according to one interviewee, 'sounded like a bunch of wild animals'. This works to literalise contemporary Britain's alleged moral decline – especially in light of the August 2011 riots – at the hands of 'feral youths... running wild like a pack of wild animals' (Broadbent 2006: 9).[15] 'The only 'human' element of their persona which is retained in the film is their age, but even the term 'youth' is employed more as a means to identify their otherness than to trigger any collective notion of mature human empathy. The hoodie in *Heartless*, as in society, has become, to borrow a term from Fiona Bawden, 'visual shorthand for "broken Britain"' (2009: 2).

By encasing the fears of a 'broken Britain' within self-aware genre films, and by exploiting the notion of such generalisations in such a context, the 'hoodie horrors' and the other films discussed in this article revel in excess, not vouching for the social divisions which they realise but making them clearly apparent. In so doing, they discredit – or at least bring into question – the validity of bigoted stereotypes of the 'underclass'. *Cherry Tree Lane* is perhaps the ultimate subversion of this myth, presenting middle-class family life as neglectful and unstable and working-class family life as one of strong bonds. To say that these films are representations of attitudes to class schisms in contemporary British culture is completely different from claiming that they are simply products of class hate or, to refer to Owen Jones' excellent study of contemporary representations of the British working class, affirmations of 'chav-bashing' (2011: 5). These films foreground and react to these attitudes; they do not validate them.

Conclusion: beyond the wilderness

British horror cinema remains a complex site of identities, economics, people and ideas. This article has attempted to offer a fuller picture of what the British horror film is today, how the genre has responded to industrial, textual and social factors, and also how it continues to ask complicated questions about representation and nationhood.

The future for British horror looks eventful and, perhaps most importantly, sustainable. At the time of writing, the latest Hammer film *The Woman in Black* is the first of their new ventures to cast major contemporary stars (including Daniel Radcliffe) and to date stands as the highest-grossing British horror film of all time. Along with *The Wicker Man* sequel, *The Wicker Tree* (2011), and a string of films such as *Jane Eyre* (2011) and *Wuthering Heights* (2011), one could even anticipate a Gothic revival (although there is a danger of being premature in making such statements, as other writings on the British horror film have shown (Pirie 2008: 192)). However, as the release of *Kill List* has demonstrated, horror films which explore violent, controversial issues can still be deemed worthy of good reviews in mainstream circles (Bradshaw 2011; Robey 2011), and the revisionist hoodie horror/sci-fi *Attack the Block* (2011) – in which the hoodies are the goodies – would seem to confirm that there is still a sufficient interest in culturally specific British comedy-horror. The slew of independent productions which continue to be released on DVD and other media formats also suggests that the demand for genre films in the UK and beyond is as high as ever. And although it is unlikely that contemporary British horror will ever escape the shadow of the 'old' Hammer Films, for the film spectator, amid the wilderness, a kingdom of horrors awaits discovery.

I wish to thank Arvind Ethan David, Simon Hunter and Adam Mason for giving up their time to be interviewed. I would also like to express my gratitude to Andy Betts at Hassle Records, Sayle Screen, and Nick Maine at the UKFC for his help in retrieving the information that helped complete this article. Thanks also go to Steve Chibnall and I. Q. Hunter for offering invaluable comments on earlier drafts.

Notes

1. The recent British TV drama about Fred and Rose West, *Appropriate Adult* (ITV 2011), faced similar criticism. See Anon. (2011) for an example of this, as well as a response from the writer of the drama, Neil McKay.

2. Interestingly, Gabriel Films – who later produced the werewolf film *Wild Country* (2005) – were awarded £5,500 by the Film Council in 2001 to assist in making a genre film set in Edinburgh, *Blood Relative* (http://www.ukfilmcouncil. org.uk/awards). However, I have been unable to uncover any records to suggest that this film ever went into production.

3. Notable here is the *Resident Evil* (2002–12) series, based on the popular US video game, which has benefited from tax relief in the UK. Other films include *Alien vs. Predator* (2009), which is classed as 'British' by the UKFC's contentious 'cultural test', despite having only economic connections with the UK.

4. *28 Weeks Later* (2007) and *The Descent: Part 2* (2009). At the time of writing a sequel to *Dog Soldiers* – prospectively entitled *Dog Soldiers: Fresh Meat* – is being shot in the USA.

5. Simon Pegg and Edgar Wright's love of the horror genre, and the intertextual function which it has in their films, is discussed in Pegg (2010: 197–200), Blake (2008: 169) and, briefly, Rose (2009: 127–9). It is also important to remember that such intertextuality was also prevalent in their UK TV series *Spaced* (Channel 4, 1999–2001). This is also true of another other British TV comedy series, *The League of Gentlemen* (BBC, 1999–2002), which not only frequently borrowed from and parodied elements associated with horror cinema but would also have a comedy-horror film spin-off: *The League of Gentlemen's Apocalypse* (2005).

6. As an example of this, *Mum & Dad* was released simultaneously at UK cinemas, on DVD and on online platforms on 26 December 2008. This proved controversial in some industry circles as it breached the traditional seventeen-week period which had become the norm for the theatrical window. However, it also signified that for a horror film a cinema release is not necessarily as important as it was once thought to be, that the multi-platform release of the film was 'a small but additional way to garner wider audiences', and that it made business sense (Marciano, of distributors Revolver Entertainment, quoted in Anon. 2008). For a thorough insight into the significance of DVD releasing in UK see Henderson (2009).

7. This was particularly true for British films which went 'straight to video' in the UK. As Marc Evans, the director of the British horror *My Little Eye* – a film released theatrically in the UK but which went straight to video in the US – has commented: 'If [*My Little Eye*] had gone straight to [UK] video, I don't think I would have made another film. I think that's the way the [British film] industry works' (DVD extra,

'The Making of *My Little Eye*', 2002). However, the most successful years for horror in the UK on video and DVD were 2003 (the year that *28 Days Later* and *My Little Eye* were released on DVD and that *The Texas Chainsaw Massacre* remake was released at the cinema), which saw horror take 9.5 per cent of the rental sector and 5.2 per cent of sales (UKFC 2004: 63, 64), and 2005 (the year that *Saw II* and *Hostel* were released in cinemas), when the genre took 8.6 per cent of rentals and 6.7 per cent of sales (UKFC 2006: 65, 67).

8. The new Hammer is a production subsidiary of Exclusive Media, a company launched in 2008 by the Dutch-based investors Cyrte Investments BV. Despite these international connections, Hammer operates from offices in London.

9. This can be viewed at: http://www.youtube.com/watch?v=U_y_Ucgyjlk (accessed 5 September 2011).

10. http://slingshot-studios.com/ (accessed 9 September 2011).

11. The company have also made the rom-com *French Film* (2008) and the comedy *The Infidel* (2010).

12. *Shaun of the Dead*'s poster claimed that it was 'A romantic comedy. With zombies'. *Severance*'s UK DVD cover proclaims the film as '*The Office* meets *Deliverance*'.

13. This is more of a tendency in low-budget, direct-to-DVD fare such as *Vampire Diary* (2007), which is promoted on its DVD cover as an 'independent British film', and *The Last Man* (2009), which is hailed as 'the UK's answer to *The Blair Witch Project*'.

14. As Owen Jones argues: 'The chav caricature has obscured the reality of the modern working class. We are fed the impression of a more or less comfortable "Middle England" on the one hand, while on the other the old working class has degenerated into a hopeless chav rump' (2011: 139).

15. The word 'feral' has been used increasingly to describe working-class/'underclass' youth in British news media since around 2005, when the Bluewater Shopping Centre in Kent banned hooded sweatshirts in order to deter young people from disguising their faces from CCTV cameras. The term was again popular throughout reportage of the August 2011 riots. For a particularly hateful example of this, see Littlejohn (2011).

References

Anon. (2008), 'Revolver release policy in firing line', *Cinema Business*, 50, p. 38.

Anon. (2010), 'Hammer Films: back from the dead', *SFX*, special horror edition, p. 16.

Anon. (2011), 'Why do we glamorise serial killers yet forget victims?', *Daily Mail*, 17 March, available at: http://www.dailymail.co.uk/femail/article-1367069/Fred-Rose-West-TV-drama-Why-glamorise-serial-killers-forget-victims.html (accessed 24 September 2011).

Bawden, Fiona (2009), 'Hoodie-winked', *Guardian*, 9 March.

Bhabha, Homi K. (1994), *The Location of Culture*, London: Routledge.

Blake, Linnie (2008), *Wounds of Nations: Horror Cinema, Historical Trauma and National Identity*, Manchester: Manchester University Press.

Bradshaw, Peter (2008), '*Mum & Dad*', *Guardian*, 22 December, available at: http://www.guardian.co.uk/film/2008/dec/22/horror (accessed 18 August 2009).

Bradshaw, Peter (2011), '*Kill List*', *Guardian*, 1 September, available at: http://www.guardian.co.uk/film/2011/sep/01/kill-list-film-review (accessed 27 September 2011).

British Film Institute (2011), *Opening Our Eyes: How Film Contributes to the Culture of the UK*, London: BFI.

Broadbent, Peter (2006), 'Losing yob battle', *Herald Express*, 9 March.

Bryce, Allan (2010) 'There will be blood', *DVD & Blu-Ray World*, 85, pp. 28–33.

Chibnall, Steve and Petley, Julian (2002), 'The return of the repressed? British horror's heritage and future', in Steve Chibnall and Julian Petley (eds), *British Horror Cinema*, London: Routledge, pp. 1–9.

Cockwell, S. (2009), '*Beyond the Rave*', available at: http://www.eatmybrains.com/showreview.php?id=528 (accessed 3 September 2011).

'Eric' (2009), 'Steven Sheil talks *Mum & Dad*', available at: http://www.bloody-goodhorror.com/bgh/interviews/05/06/2009/steven-sheil-talks-mum-dad (accessed 3 September 2011).

Gentleman, Amelia (2010), *Guardian*, 31 March, available at: http://www.guardian.co.uk/society/2010/mar/31/is-britain-broken (accessed 31 March 2010).

Graham, Jane (2009), 'Hoodies strike fear in British cinema', *Guardian*, 5 November, available at: http://www.guardian.co.uk/film/2009/nov/05/british-hoodie-films (accessed 20 May 2011).

Harries, Dan (2002), 'Film parody and the resuscitation of genre', in Steve Neale (ed.), *Genre and Contemporary Hollywood*, London: BFI, pp. 281–93.

Henderson, Stuart (2009), 'From screen to shelf: perspectives on independent distribution', *Journal of British Cinema and Television*, 6: 3, pp. 468–80.

Higson, Andrew (2011), *Film England: Culturally English Filmmaking Since the 1990s*, London: I. B. Tauris.

Hill, John (1983), 'Working-class realism and sexual reaction: some theses on the "British New Wave"', in James Curran and Vincent Porter (eds), *British Cinema History*, London: Weidenfeld & Nicolson, pp. 368–70.

Hill, John (2000), 'From the "New Wave" to "Brit-grit": continuity and difference in working-class realism', in Justine Ashby and Andrew Higson (eds), *British Cinema: Past and Present*, Routledge: London, pp. 303–11.

Hutchings, Peter (1993), *Hammer and Beyond: The British Horror Film*, Manchester: Manchester University Press.

Hutchings, Peter (2009a), '*A New Heritage of Horror: The English Gothic Cinema*', review, *Journal of British Cinema and Television*, 6: 1, pp. 147–9.

Hutchings, Peter (2009b), 'Horror London', *Journal of British Cinema and Television*, 6: 2, pp. 190–206.

Ide, Wendy (2002), 'Mighty mouse: what's new pussycat? Stuart Little's nemesis gets his', *Sunday Herald*, 14 July, available at: http://findarticles.com/p/articles/mi_qn4156/is_20020714/ai_n12577984/ (accessed 6 July 2011).

Jones, Alan (1994), 'If I had a Hammer', *Shivers*, 10, pp. 19–21.

Jones, Alan (2009) '*Eden Lake*: paradise bloodied', *Fangoria*, 279, pp. 32–5.

Jones, Owen (2011), *Chavs: The Demonization of the Working-Class*, London: Verso.

Kerekes, David and Slater, David (2000), *See No Evil: Banned Films and Video Controversy*, Manchester: Headpress.

Lay, Samantha (2002), *British Social Realism – From Documentary to Brit Grit*, London: Wallflower.

Leggott, James (2004), 'Like father? Failing parents and angelic children in contemporary British social realist cinema', in Bruce Babington, Ann Davies and Phil Powrie (eds), *The Trouble With Men: Masculinities in European and Hollywood Cinema*, London: Wallflower Press, pp. 163–73.

Leggott, James (2008), *Contemporary British Cinema – From Heritage to Horror*, London: Wallflower.

Littlejohn, Richard (2011) 'So where are the parents? They are out looting too', *Daily Mail*, 12 August.

Macnab, Geoffrey (2005), 'Scare tactics', *Screen International*, 1565, pp. 11–12.

Maher, Kevin (2008), 'The kids are all frights', *The Times*, 26 June.

Martin-Jones, David (2011), *Scotland: Global Cinema – Genres, Modes and Identities*, Edinburgh: Edinburgh University Press.

Minns, Adam (2001), 'Gathering of evil in the UK', *Screen International*, 1335, p. 26.

Monk, Claire (2000), 'Underbelly UK: the 1990s underclass film, masculinity and the ideologies of "new" Britain', in Justine Ashby and Andrew Higson (eds), *British Cinema: Past and Present*, London and New York: Routledge, pp. 274–87.

Murphy, Robert (ed.) (2009), *The British Cinema Book*, third edition, London: BFI.

Newman, Kim (2006), 'Irish horror cinema', *Irish Journal of Gothic and Horror Studies*, 1, available at: http://irishgothichorrorjournal.homestead.com/kim.html (accessed 1 July 2011).

Newman, Kim (2011), *Nightmare Movies: Horror on Screen Since the 1960s*, second edition, London: Bloomsbury.

Pegg, Simon (2010) *Nerd Do Well*, London: Arrow Books.

Petley, Julian (2002), '"A crude sort of entertainment for a crude sort of audience": the British critics and horror cinema', in Steve Chibnall and Julian Petley (eds), *British Horror Cinema*, London: Routledge, pp. 23–41.

Pirie, David (2008), *A New Heritage of Horror: The English Gothic Cinema*, London: I. B. Tauris.

Rigby, Jonathan (2000), *English Gothic: A Century of Horror Cinema*, London: Reynolds & Hearn.

Robey, Tim (2011), '*Kill List*', *Daily Telegraph*, 1 September, available at: http://www.telegraph.co.uk/culture/film/filmreviews/8736144/Kill-List-review.html (accessed 27 September 2011).

Rose, James (2009), *Beyond Hammer: British Horror Cinema Since 1970*, Leighton Buzzard: Auteur.

Sneak, The (2008), '*Eden Lake*', *Sun*, 11 September, available at: http://www.thesun.co.uk/sol/homepage/showbiz/film/movie_reviews/article1676823.ece (accessed 20 July 2011).

Tookey, Chris (2008a) '*Mum & Dad*: this gorefest is just torture for the taxpayer', *Daily Mail*, 25 December, available at: http://www.dailymail.co.uk/tvshowbiz/reviews/article-1101734/Mum–Dad-This-gore-fest-just-torture-taxpayer.html (accessed 30 June 2011).

Tookey, Chris (2008b), '*Eden Lake*: a great movie (if you can stomach it)', *Daily Mail*, 11 September, available at: http://www.dailymail.co.uk/tvshowbiz/article-1054787/Eden-Lake-A-great-movie-stomach-it.html (accessed 30 June 2011).

UK Film Council (2000), *Towards a Sustainable UK Film Industry*, available at: http://www.ukfilmcouncil.org.uk/media/pdf/p/r/TASFI.pdf (accessed 7 January 2011).

UK Film Council (2004), *UK Film Council Statistical Year Book: Annual Review 2003–2004*, available at: http://www.ukfilmcouncil.org.uk/media/pdf/l/r/Final_Yearbook_0304.pdf (accessed 7 January 2011).

UK Film Council (2006), *UK Film Council Statistical Year Book 2005–2006*, available at: http://www.ukfilmcouncil.org.uk/media/pdf/l/r/Statistical_Yearbook_05–06.pdf (accessed 7 January 2011).

Walker, Johnny (2011a), 'Nasty visions: violent spectacle and contemporary British horror cinema', *Horror Studies*, 2: 1, pp. 115–30.

Walker, Johnny (2011b), '*F* for "frightening"? Johannes Roberts takes on hoodie horrors', *Diabolique*, 3, pp. 24–32.

Johnny Walker is a PhD student researching the cultural significance of the contemporary British horror film at De Montfort University, Leicester, where he has also taught on cult film and British and American horror. In March 2009 he co-organised with Steve Chibnall and I. Q. Hunter the international conference and film festival 'Bloodlines: British Horror Past and Present'.

'It's a Film': Medium Specificity as Textual Gesture in *Red Road* and *The Unloved*

Charlotte Brunsdon

British cinema has long been intertwined with television. The buzzwords of the transition to digital media, 'convergence' and 'multi-platform delivery', have particular histories in the British context which can be grasped only through an understanding of the cultural, historical and institutional peculiarities of the British film and television industries. Central to this understanding must be two comparisons: first, the relative stability of television in the duopoly period (at its core, the licence-funded BBC) in contrast to the repeated boom and bust of the many different financial/industrial combinations which have comprised the film industry; and second, the cultural and historical connotations of 'film' and 'television'. All readers of this journal will be familiar – possibly over-familiar – with the notion that 'British cinema is alive and well and living on television'. At the end of the first decade of the twenty-first century, when 'the end of medium specificity' is much trumpeted, it might be useful to return to the historical imbrication of British film and television, to explore both the possibility that medium specificity may be more nationally specific than much contemporary theorisation suggests,[1] and to consider some of the relationships between film and television manifest at a textual level in two recent films, *Red Road* (2006) and *The Unloved* (2009).

The transitions in the broadcast environment, which demand the recognition, as Bennett and Strange (2011) argue, of 'television as digital media', are simultaneous with parallel shifts from celluloid to digital in film production which have occasioned a substantial debate about 'the end of cinema' and a flourishing of moving image

Journal of British Cinema and Television 9.3 (2012): 457–479
DOI: 10.3366/jbctv.2012.0100
© Edinburgh University Press
www.eupjournals.com/jbctv

exhibition in non-theatrical spaces such as art galleries.[2] As the end of a media culture dominated by the traditions of British public service broadcasting accelerates, it is more possible to identify what has been specific to this culture.[3] What may now be needed is a more integrated history of the twentieth-century audio-visual landscape than the disciplinary and institutional divides between the study of film and the study of television always register. In 1986, at the beginning of an article in which he analyses cinema and broadcasting together, John Caughie observed that 'histories of British cinema and of British broadcasting serve to establish their separate chronicles and developments. What they often miss are the terms by which these separate developments and the ideological impulses behind them can be seen to belong to the same culture' (1986: 189). Caughie traced the role of 'independence' and 'public service' in the shaping of British cinema and British broadcasting. Twenty-five years later, each of these formations is more attenuated, while the shift to digital has substantially complicated what might be considered both constitutive of and distinct about broadcasting and cinema. Here, I will outline the ways in which the relationship between cinema and television in the British context is discussed, before analysing in more detail how some twenty-first-century texts negotiate this relationship. This will necessarily include a rather compressed argument, and I should state at the outset that I consider one of the problems with much discussion of convergence and the move to digital to be the implication that medium specificity used to be clear and now is not. On the contrary, I see the question of medium specificity, and the search for an artistic practice which is specific to the particular medium (however defined), as the dominant project of twentieth-century art. This is what modernist art is concerned with, and these concerns shape twentieth-century film and television, even in Britain.[4] Thus when, in the second part, I discuss the ways in which some twenty-first-century digital work defines itself as film rather than television, it should not be inferred that this distinction was simple in the twentieth century. The rhetorics of what is and isn't considered properly 'cinematic' and 'televisual' in twentieth-century Britain requires its own patient history.[5] But firstly, how is the scholarship on the audio-visual landscape patterned?

The first observation must be that to a certain extent, the study of British cinema and that of television have been constructed against each other. The study of British cinema has taken place between the Atlantic and the Channel, often yearning for Hollywood, but also attentive to the national-ness of 'European' cinema as a model for validating specifically British forms and genres. These cinematic interlocutors have taken precedence over television, despite the recognition, in nearly all accounts of British cinema, of the importance of British television in terms of both economic support and training.[6] The Britishness of British cinema (or its Englishness, or Scottishness), and its relation to British history have been shaping concerns, morphing into questions of how, and in what terms, the products of such a chronically unstable industry, often dependent on multinational funding, can be considered British at all. This is matched by the way in which the study of television has deliberately ignored consideration of film in its endeavour to establish a medium-specific discipline, and indeed, in its commitment to the popular, has been equivocal about 'serious drama' as part of the remit of television studies.[7] In turn, criticism of 'authored' television drama has had a tendency to ignore the broader televisual environment.[8]

Running through these divisions are the cultural resonances of film and television as media. My interest here is not so much in the distinction between the 'movie movie' and the 'TV movie' elegantly deconstructed by Martin McLoone (1996), but in the mode of attention which each medium is seen to merit. Despite the persistence of the 'glance/gaze' distinction, empirical research on how people watch television demonstrates that viewers can choose, in relation to a favourite programme, to watch with fierce attention, often arranging to avoid domestic distractions.[9] Conversely, it is clear that going to the cinema was often an activity in which film spectatorship was substantially subordinate to social and, frequently, sexual interest in other audience members.[10] However, the dominant characterisation of television in both everyday and scholarly literature is as a medium of distraction while cinema is one of concentration. To cinema is granted the possibility of aesthetic seriousness, while television – in blatant disregard of the history of much British television (and film) – is thought of as trivial.

This journal provides an interesting case history here, with its progenitors, firstly the newsletter of the *Society for the Study of Popular British Cinema* and then the Flicks Books-published *Journal of Popular British Cinema*, both excluding television, which appears in the title only with the move to Edinburgh University Press in 2004 when the 'popular' disappears. The original project is cinéphiliac rather than addressed to a popular culture which would include television. The assertion of the popular in the early titles is, at least in part, a precisely targeted assertion of the vibrant, unrespectable cinema championed by, for example, Steve Chibnall and Julian Petley, and is set against both British 'quality' and 'art' cinemas and, to abbreviate,

'BBC culture'.[11] 'B' movies were more interesting than bad (or even good) television.[12] The 'integrated' journal has created a significant space in which to address the British audio-visual landscape, but most individual articles focus exclusively (and for very good reasons – I'm not arguing for a facile inter-disciplinarity, or that these histories are not separate, as well as intertwined) on either cinema or television.

Coexisting with these disciplinary separations, there are certain topics on which film and television are addressed together. These are principally, the careers of individuals, Channel 4's involvement in film production, adaptation, and particular themes of representation. Studies of Alan Clarke, Stephen Frears, Tony Garnett, Verity Lambert, Mike Leigh and Ken Loach of necessity address both media, although often, as with Danny Boyle, the television work, if it is addressed at all, is conceived of as an apprenticeship.[13] The opening of Channel 4 in 1982, with a publisher rather than a producer model of broadcasting, a commitment to film investment and a public service remit which privileged catering to minority tastes, contributed to a flurry of discussion about 'convergence' between film and television during the 1980s. Christine Geraghty (2005) has usefully outlined the contours of this debate in relation to *My Beautiful Laundrette* (1986), a television-funded film which had a successful theatrical release and which in many ways epitomises the success of 1980s Film on Four. Particular topics of representation, such as Black Britain (Malik 2002), Scotland (Petrie 2004), Northern Ireland (McIlroy 1998; Pettitt 2000) and 'the North' (Russell 2004) have also crossed media, as does study of the adaptation of the work of, say, Jane Austen and Charles Dickens.[14]

In this context, there have been some interesting recent inclusions of television drama in work that defines itself as being about cinema. Thus the second edition of Friedman's *Fires Were Started* adds a chapter on *Boys from the Blackstuff* and *Threads* (O'Sullivan 2006), and Rosalind Galt's *The New European Cinema* (2006) concludes with *Our Friends in the North* (BBC, 1996). This 'slipping in' of television testifies to recognition of its importance to the British audio-visual landscape but, paradoxically, denies its specificity by annexing it to film.[15] The key argument against this view is found in John Caughie's *British Television Drama* (2000), where he argues for the significance of British television drama – rather than film – in understanding the engagement of British culture with modernism. This identification of the cultural centrality of mid-century British television is gaining depth in some of the recent work on the 1970s. Most notably, Dave Rolinson's analysis of 1970s television films allows a recasting of the debates about the decline of the television play (and, during the 1960s and 1970s, the debate among TV practitioners about using film),[16] while John Hill's 2011 book on Ken Loach situates the television work, and television as an institution, as both generative and determining. The 1970s might, indeed, prove particularly interesting here.

For example, a film such as *The Long Good Friday* (1980), made at the end of the 1970s, was principally funded through television money (Lew Grade's ITC films, through its subsidiary Black Lion Films), with a producer, Barry Hanson, who worked mainly for Thames Television (the Independent Television London weekday franchise in this period). Its director, John Mackenzie, who first worked for the BBC in the 1960s, directed the avant-garde *The Cheviot, the Stag and the Black Black Oil* (1974) which was written by John McGrath, as well as other notable 1970s television plays, but the television and film work is rarely referenced together. The look of the film, its grubby realist, late 1970s London, has close affinities with popular television series of the 1970s such as *The Sweeney* (ITV, 1975–8) and *Out* (ITV, 1978), which in turn were made for independent television by Euston Films, a wholly owned subsidiary of Thames.[17] This world, dominated by white working-class machismo and entrenched family loyalties, with cockney characters sharing a culture on both sides of the law, could also be found in 'high-end' BBC British television drama, such as G. F. Newman's *Law and Order* (1978), four films directed by Les Blair, in which, as with *The Long Good Friday*, the Irish war is shown to resonate on the mainland[18] and unlike in *The Sweeney*, the police can't be trusted to get the right man. In *The Long Good Friday*, though, the use of film and understated direction enter into a direct dialogue with the strategies of *The Sweeney*. These are all works emerging from the same mid-1970s London culture which can usefully be understood in relation to both film and television.

However, this more integrative critical and historiographical project is impeded by the connotational registers of film and television and the way in which film exudes a glamour never attained by the more domestic medium. Despite the distinguished record of, for example, BBC Pebble Mill or Granada in making high-quality British television drama,[19] still it is television that is the less prestigious partner in the film/television duo. But it is not just critical historiography that is affected by the meaning of the two media. For makers, too, the kudos has been with cinema, and these issues of cultural prestige – which many scholars have mapped over a derogatory 'feminising' of television – persist in a digital twenty-first century. The actual changes in British television in a multi-channel environment (the greater dependence on cheaper formats such as reality and game shows, the decline in the mixed schedule, the increased divide between prestige and banal television) in combination with increased digital production and single-screen delivery (to computer screens of one kind or another) means that it is now even more important for work which may well be funded by television to distinguish itself from – and it saddens me to say this – what 'television' now means.[20] It is with this 'gesture' of distinction that the rest of the essay will be concerned in relation to two films which inhabit their relation to television differently.

Desperate girls

Writing in the late 1990s, in an attempt to think across film and television, I discussed the 'desperate girls' who were the heroines of *Stella Does Tricks* (1996) and *Under the Skin* (1996), films by first-time female directors in the 1990s, Coky Giedroyc and Carine Adler respectively (Brunsdon 2000). These heroines, I suggested, were haunting shadows of the successfully achieving superwoman with which feminism was then associated in the popular media – young women who not only did not 'have it all' but actually had almost nothing, except their own considerable spirit and ingenuity, young women forced into commercial sex (Stella (Kelly MacDonald)) or expressing, through indiscriminate and damaging promiscuity, grief, anger and self-hatred (Iris (Samantha Morton)). If the 1950s in British culture had given us 'Angry Young Men', the 1990s, at the tail end of what had started in 1979 as the Thatcher government, had brought forth desperate girls. Since then, strikingly, their ranks have been increased, to considerable critical acclaim, by the eponymous heroine of Lynne Ramsay's second feature, *Morvern Callar* (2002), Jackie and Mia in Andrea Arnold's two features, *Red Road* and *Fish Tank* (2009), and Clio Barnard's Artangel-produced dramatisation of the life of Andrea Dunbar, *The Arbor* (2010). What is notable is that so many talented female directors working in the cinema are leading their work with 'fucked-up' heroines.

Considering the 1990s, I wanted to draw attention to the coexistence of these desperate girls within British subsidised cinema and their less unhappy sisters on mainstream British television. For the 1990s saw an expansion in the production of female ensemble dramas such as *Playing the Field* (BBC, 1998) and *Real Women* (BBC, 1998), written by Kay Mellor and Susan Oudot respectively, in which ensemble female casts dramatised the different ways of 'being a woman' that seemed to have become available. Serial television drama, as opposed to the single 90-minute feature, offered more space for equivocation about a woman's lot, and more chances for more characters to make more choices. Since then, of course, *Sex and the City*, which first aired in the US on the subscription channel HBO in June 1998, has made these characteristics of the female ensemble drama rather more widely recognised, and there is an extensive feminist and fan scholarship.[21]

By juxtaposing the desperate girls with the female ensemble dramas I was suggesting that there was some benefit to be gained by considering fictional femininities across film and television. This juxtaposition is informative about the way in which narrative modes currently conventional to film and television (the single feature and the episodic series) enable the telling of particular kinds of story. Each type of story (the enacting of the desperation of the desperate girl, the varied and representatively diverse feminine choices of the female group) bears witness to the paralysis which continues to attend the project of female subjects starring as agents in their own stories. At the same time, through these stories we may trace the reverberations of feminism in popular culture, the multiplication of prime-time fiction focused on women and the increased recognition of the attractions of the female audience. The transitions within, in particular, the institutions and structures of the television industry are also significant, with the shift to 'independent' production and its consequence for female career patterns. The consideration of film and television together gives us a richer understanding of particular work in each medium in a shared cultural context.

This argument could be continued into the decade which is the topic of this special issue, with the BBC's *Mistresses* (2008–) (in which four female friends fall in and out of love, jobs and marriages) as the most obvious post-*Sex and the City* ensemble drama for comparison with some of the films already mentioned. However, one of the characteristics of the changing broadcast environment is that national television is much less easy to specify, which in turn has methodological implications, restricting any simple recourse to 'national' readings.[22] Instead, what I want to do here is slightly different, in that I want to concentrate on two 'desperate girl' films, *The Unloved* and *Red Road*, and consider their relationship with television. Each was made with the participation of television, Channel 4 in the case of *The Unloved* and BBC Films in the case of *Red Road*. But it is not the financial contribution of the broadcasters that interests me but the manner in which each digitally shot film textually differentiates itself from the connotations of this source of funding. Hence my title: 'It's a Film'.

The Unloved: 'something a bit different'

The Unloved exemplifies the intimacy of British film with television and recalls the social ambition of British television drama, despite clearly being conceived by its producers as a film. Premiered on Channel 4 on 17 May 2009 and billed by the *Radio Times* as 'drama of the week', it received a theatrical release the following year. It is directed by Samantha Morton who had previously featured in the 1995 female ensemble drama *Band of Gold*[23] and starred in both *Under the Skin* and *Morvern Callar*. Morton's career, with performances in these and other films distinguished by a luminous vulnerability, has been accompanied by a continuous strand of publicity about the difficulty of her own childhood and she has made public statements about the inadequacies of the 'care' system for young people. *The Unloved*, which traces the plight of an 'at risk' eleven-year-old, Lucy Manvers (Molly Windsor), was developed by Morton, written by Tony Grisoni from Morton's material and produced by Kate Ogborn (producer of *Under the Skin* and *Stella Does Tricks*). Publicity for *The Unloved* declared that Morton chose television for a first screening because of the wider, domestic audience it would attract. In language that recalls justification for the mixed schedules of public service broadcasting in the last century, Morton speaks of wanting 'kids who normally watch *EastEnders* to find it on television and see something that feels a bit different'.[24]

For the television premiere, *The Unloved* formed the dramatic centrepiece of Channel 4's 'Britain's Forgotten Children' season.[25] Some of the ad-breaks within season slots included very short films about child neglect and abuse, which directed viewers to the Channel's website. *The Unloved* itself has a concluding title which refers to the number of children in Britain in care:

> 71,476 children are in care in the UK
> 36,405 children are on the 'at risk' register in the UK

The film was then given a very limited theatrical release by the Institute of Contemporary Arts (ICA) in February 2010, which then marketed it as an ICA DVD.

This exhibition history alone exemplifies the continuing complexity of the film/television distinction in the British context. On television, *The Unloved* came in at over two hours, with about twelve minutes of advertising per hour. As a theatrical feature, however, it runs at 103 minutes. Critical response to the film was spread over two years, responding to both the television and the film releases, and involves a wider range of commentators than would have been the case had there been only a television or film premiere. The film reviews in 2010, where *The Unloved* was juxtaposed not with the generic variety of television but with other, often higher-budget productions (most notably the Jeff Bridges vehicle *Crazy Heart*), tended towards the briefly sympathetic.[26] On the other hand, the earlier responses of television critics, while generally favourable, were marked by self-consciousness about the 'worthiness' of the film's topic, expressed most elegantly by Tom Sutcliffe in the *Independent* on 18 May 2009:

> Weighing in to a drama like this would be tantamount to saying that you don't give a damn about abandoned children or that you'd prefer it if Channel 4 had run a repeat of *A Place in the Sun*. It's one of those dramas that allow commissioning editors to hold their heads up when people start muttering about the public service remit... All of which is not the preamble to dissent, but a way of saying that although *The Unloved* was pretty much guaranteed a good review anyway, it really really deserved it on this occasion.[27]

The 'really really' in the last sentence captures the tension between the socially worthy and the aesthetically achieved which so often marks discussion of British cinema. This review installs British public service television at its core, suggesting that the perception of public money spent on television predisposes critical judgement in favour of the 'serious and sombre subject' handled non-exploitatively. The *Daily Telegraph* review by Michael Deacon on the same day, rather less kindly projects self-consciousness onto the drama, nominating its aesthetic as characteristic of 'BAFTA [British Academy of Film and Television Awards] Land':

> It was, from start to finish, powerful. Admiring it, though, required an ability to stomach not just the cruelty and ugliness, but also the setting: a place called BAFTA land. In BAFTA land, a lot of time is spent staring wordlessly out of windows and into the middle distance in grim towns. Mundane events, such as the riding of an escalator, or a walk through a shopping centre, are shown taking place in real time, even if they do nothing to advance the plot or give insight into character. There are frequent scenes in which a character, standing alone, gazes at a bleakly beautiful urban sight: dead leaves skittering across a pavement or a dew-heavy cobweb clinging to a wire mesh fence.

What I want to argue about *The Unloved* is that it makes a series of textual gestures which declare its aesthetic seriousness as cinema, even though it was part-funded by, and premiered on, British television.[28] It is on these textual gestures – characteristics of 'BAFTA land', if you will – which claim a certain mode of attention that designations of 'film' and 'television' will increasingly be based in the digital twenty-first century. Deacon identifies 'time spent staring wordlessly', the use of real time at narratively insignificant moments and 'bleak' urban beauty as significant strategies within the film to announce its award-readiness. His criteria implicitly demand sound-led, plot-driven *mise-en-scène*. He neglects the way in which the film's strategies give Lucy's drama a sense of place, of a real world, Nottingham, with its mixture of former factories, nineteenth-century civic buildings, shopping centres, terraced streets and green open spaces through which she must journey in search of care. Lucy's plight in the film is to be homeless. She starts off living with her father (Robert Carlyle), she is taken to a care home, she has previously had a foster home and she knows where her mother (Susan Lynch) lives. But in none of these places is she nurtured or safe. She is 'in care' but without care. While this impression is produced partly through what befalls Lucy in each of these places, it is also conveyed through her passages between them – with long, static shots as the small figure sets off away through early morning streets, caught against skylines, traipsing over rough ground. These long-held land- and city-scape shots emphasise how vulnerable, but also how intrepid, Lucy is. Their pace works within the film to demonstrate Lucy's labour, her effort to find succour, but also to demonstrate her situatedness. This child, in care and not in care, in a recognisable British city now – but also on television, where the look of the film indicates that it is 'something a bit different'.

While there are many reasons to suppose that title, pre-title and opening sequences of films are likely to have been made with particular care, these sequences have additional medium-specific demands put on them in the context of broadcast television flow. The broadcast environment of television is both busy with interstitial material such as ads and previews, and organised through repetitions which are often sound-led, such as announcers calling viewers to a favourite programme or theme tunes doing likewise. *The Unloved* was broadcast at 9.00 on a Sunday evening, traditionally the slot for less demanding drama than this on both the BBC and ITV, although it is often used as a film slot on Channel 4. It was preceded by a channel ident and, over the logo, the announcement that 'Now on Four the Britain's Forgotten Children strand continues. Samantha Morton directs Robert Carlyle in a film drama, *The Unloved*. With strong language, substance abuse and scenes which some viewers might find upsetting, we get a child's view of life in a children's home.' However, what comes next is nothing to do with a child's view of life in a children's home, but is instead an advertisement for Compare the Market.com, 'sponsors of drama

Fig. 1. Lucy in the first shot of *The Unloved.*

on Channel 4'. The film then immediately separates itself from this environment with a plain red title on black accompanied by birdsong. The film title fades to black and a child's voice intones: 'The Lord is my light and my salvation, whom shall I fear?', a prayer followed by the introduction of the ethereal, jangly music which will form Lucy's theme throughout the film and which continues over the first shot of the film, a high shot looking down on a young girl in school uniform (Lucy) lying at the foot of the staircase in a domestic hallway (Figure 1). This shot is held for fourteen seconds, and is followed by a closer, floor-level, eight-second shot of the back of the girl's head, cutting back to the first camera position which is then held for thirteen seconds while the passing of the day is signalled through changing light on the motionless figure.

This opening sequence is noticeably composed and formal. There is a narrative enigma available in the juxtaposition of the apparently fallen girl and her rhetorical question: 'Whom shall I fear?', but this is less important than the length of the shots and the refusal of any movement. This scene is organised through the opposite of classical cinema's cutting on action; it cuts on stasis. And so the viewer is held back from the scene and from involvement, tutored in an appropriate distance from what might follow. But the viewer is also tutored into paying attention in a way which is quite distinct from the huckster injunction to 'Compare the Market.com', a direct address which, paradoxically, necessitates disengagement from the screen. Here, the precise, modest, differentiated sound and the motionless images invite scrutiny. Through these textual strategies this drama declares that it is 'not television', even while it is on television, a point later made narratively with an excerpt from Vigo's *L'Atalante* (1934) shown on television in the children's home. This emphasis on the still image also suggests affinities with other strongly 'photographic' British films such as Gideon Koppel's *sleep furiously* (2007), Duane Hopkins' *Better Things* (2008), Anton Corbijn's *Control* (2007) and Steve McQueen's *Hunger* (2008), hinting at the increased importance of the unmoving camera to 'not being television' and to identifying art cinema.

Red Road

Red Road was Andrea Arnold's first feature film, although she had already won an Oscar for her short film *Wasp* (2003). It was the first of a proposed three-film suite to be made in Scotland under the Advance Party initiative, as a Sigma (Glasgow) and Zentropa Entertainments (Denmark) production, with additional funding from the UK Film Council, Scottish Screen, the Glasgow Film Office and BBC Films in association with Zoma Films and Verve Pictures. While this complex funding web has been typical of non-mainstream film-funding for some years, the innovative aspect of the Advance Party scheme is its attempt to develop a degree of continuity of character – and creative culture – across three films. The production notes describe this as follows: 'The idea behind Advance Party is that the same group of characters would be given to three different directors who would each have to develop a film around those characters. All the films would shoot for the same length of time in the same city, Glasgow.'[29]

Red Road, which premiered in 2006, was the first film in the trilogy to have been completed, with the film-makers Morag McKinnon and Mikkel Noergaard engaged for the other two and participating in the set-up discussions. At the time of writing, McKinnon's *Donkeys* has been screened in Scotland.[30] The Advance Party, to which Lars von Trier has given significant support, has its clearest connection with Dogme and its 'Vow of Chastity' through 'The Rules' drawn up by Lone Sherfig and Anders Thomas Jensen which stipulate the constraints within which all the film-makers must work and which include the demand that all of the characters, cast with the same actors, must appear in each of the three films, although they 'may be weighted differently as major or minor characters'.[31]

Mette Hjort (2010) has written in detail about the Advance Guard initiative as an example of what she calls 'affinitive and milieu-building transnationalism', exploring the relation between the Scottish and

Fig. 2. Jackie in front of the screens in *Red Road*.

Danish participants within this innovatory context which mobilises 'creativity with constraints' in order to develop and sustain the cinema of small nations. This production context suggests that it is easier to identify this 'culturally British' film as international art cinema than as straightforwardly Scottish or Danish, and also reveals an extreme self-reflexivity about the film-making process. This self-consciousness is manifest textually within the opening minutes of the film. Abstract, blurry images in the pre-title sequence become identifiable as screens, and their location is shown, after the title, to be a vast bank of monitors. The editing then cuts between the bank of monitors, with a woman (Jackie (Kate Dickey)) sitting at a control console, close-up images from individual monitors and extreme close-ups of Jackie's face as her eyes scrutinise and select images. She sits in front of the wall of screens, scanning the monitors and selecting individual images for close attention on a desk-top monitor. (Figure 2). The images which she selects, though, do not seem to be images of criminal acts in the night-time city but, instead, images of individuals – an office cleaner going to work, a man taking a dog for a walk – with which she seems to be familiar, smiling fondly and with amusement as she keys in the monitor number and uses the joystick to zoom into the image.

The film is, from its inception, explicitly self-reflexive, indicating that its story will be constructed through, and in relation to, a heroine who negotiates images for a living, sifting through myriad scenes for potential or actual significance and making narratives through the relations between screens. In the first few minutes, the viewer must

469

contemplate the almost indecipherable opening montage of degraded CCTV images, and then learn to negotiate the relationships between these multiple images of the Glasgow citizenry which collate their city and Jackie's gaze, mobilised through the joystick as she zooms in and out of scenes which catch her attention. Several different orders of image/reality relations are proposed: the real of the city, captured through the ubiquitous CCTV cameras, appearing mainly through grainy, barred images; Jackie's workspace, the conventional diegetic world of narrative cinema, constructed as a dark, studio-like space dominated by the huge bank of monitors, in which Jackie and her fellow-operatives sit in the dim light, scrutinising their city and its inhabitants; and, articulating the two, Jackie's attentive gaze, created through cutting between extreme close-ups of her face, her hand on the control and close-ups from zoomed-in selected images. Film direction is itself staged in the opening set-up of Jackie's world in *Red Road*: the silent world 'out there' and the animation of this out-there world through Jackie's interest in particular figures who recur in the vision-fields of different cameras. The narrative of the film explores the bringing together of these initially separate domains, finally demonstrating Jackie's redemption through her ability to participate in the out-there world. She achieves this integration through making a story happen to characters she finds in the city screens, which in turn reveals her story to the viewer and enables her to work through its trauma.

Jackie's job, as CCTV security officer, provides a contemporary form for what many reviewers recognised as a familiar, self-reflexive cinematic tale of surveillance, ranging from Fritz Lang's Dr Mabuse to James Stewart in *Rear Window* (1954) to Michael Haneke's more recent *Caché/Hidden* (2005).[32] CCTV technology, and most particularly the repeated banks of screens which characterise Jackie's workplace, City-Eye, are used here to draw attention to Glasgow as a 'seen' city, the cameras ceaselessly and impartially recording banal everyday life. In terms of narrative and character, Jackie's tender expression in relation to what the viewer soon learns are repeated characters in the sites which she regularly observes shows that she watches these myriad worlds with emotional engagement (the ailing, much-loved dog) and an eye for the quirky (the office cleaner dancing as she works). Jackie is shown to have humanity and humour in her dealings with the silent monitors. But the massed screens, the cupboards storing videotapes and the later plot developments which utilise the street cameras also work to shift the recognisable story of the cinematic surveillant-voyeur into a more dispersed diagnosis of a city under surveillance: a culture awash with images in which no action passes unrecorded. The film is set simultaneously in a real, location-shot Glasgow and a more abstracted city of screens and cameras. The setting of this story is a place of many images and it is thus imperative that the viewer is assisted in understanding the type of attention necessary. This, I propose, is enacted in the third scene of the film, when Jackie arrives home.

As she had left work, a friendly colleague had enquired whether she was going out as it was Friday night, and she replies with what is shown to be deadpan irony: 'You know me, Angus, party-animal'. As she walks home alone, silhouetted against revelry in the streets. Jackie is filmed letting herself into her flat, the frame as cramped as the corridor, while she juggles keys and the post she has picked up as she tries to turn on the light. There is a cut to a television screen, showing some kind of light entertainment, and Jackie opens her post as she waits for the microwave, the over-excited soundtrack of the game-show filling the flat as the camera moves into close-up of an envelope containing a wedding invitation. The extreme close-up moves down the white card of the invitation to pause on a handwritten exhortation at the bottom: 'Please, please come it's been too long', and then there is a cut to another extreme close-up of Jackie's face as she concentrates on the card. The camera then cuts back to the television, creating a contrast between Jackie's serious face, pale with only minimal make-up, and the television image of a high-production blonde woman, all gleaming teeth and shiny bouncy hair, being encouraged in an evidently amateurish basketball shot, the soundtrack rising to a crescendo. Jackie's hand moves into the image and abruptly turns the television off, and the camera lingers for a moment on the emphatically blank television screen in the sudden silence. The next shot returns to Jackie at the screen-bank of her work.

In many ways, this is a fairly straightforward 'single woman comes home to her flat' scene, an arrival marked, with earlier technologies, in films such as *Klute* (1971), by the protagonist entering her home and immediately turning on a telephone answering machine to listen to her messages, then opening the fridge to reveal appropriately low food stocks. The dependence on domestic technologies, rather than human beings, functions to underline the solitariness of the heroine. Here, the cut directly from her entry to the television screen suggests that one of Jackie's first actions on arriving home, before opening her post, is to turn on the television to produce some kind of broadcast conviviality. She may not be a party animal but, the scene suggests, she habitually seeks the illusion of electronic sociability. When she turns the television off, apparently better to concentrate on her post, her action intimates the seriousness, and the challenge, of this wedding invitation which she has received. So far, almost nothing has been disclosed about this character, except that she works in front of a bank of CCTV screens, she wears a wedding ring and she is not a party animal. The handwritten note on the invitation shows that she has had intimate connections that now seem in abeyance. The sudden silence, after the television is turned off, grants the invitation a problematic status at odds with the conventional associations of weddings.

So the brief appearance of live television in this scene, with its accompanying rather inane soundtrack, can be fully accounted for in relation to character and narrative development. The use of the television tells us that Jackie is used to living alone and that this wedding invitation is a big deal. However, I suggest that this brief blare of television also functions in another way. This third meaning is not derived from the world of the film, but instead concerns the ontological status of this unfolding fiction. It is about the film-ness of the film, and the use of television in this scene is a gesture which claims that the drama which we will be watching – on whatever type of screening device – is to be understood as a film, not as television. This scene is an example of what I am nominating medium specificity as a textual gesture rather than as any property of the audio-visual artefact itself.

My hypothesis is that as consumption of audio-visual fiction becomes increasingly 'platform indifferent', or, at least, 'platform unpredictable' – that is, film-makers and the makers of television drama can't predict the devices on which their fictions will be watched – then it is becoming correspondingly important for the work itself to prescribe textually the kind of attention which it requires. While part of this labour is typically performed by publicity, billing and scheduling, or through affiliation with movements such as 'slow cinema', this is also sometimes carried out, as here, through the rhetorical invocation of twentieth-century meanings of 'film' and 'television' within the text.

Within the world of *Red Road*, it is possible to speculate that Jackie turns off the television because its banal hysteria interferes with the impact of the wedding invitation. The invitation, so evidently a challenge to Jackie, is also a promise for the audience that, through the wedding, more will be disclosed about this quiet character who now lives by herself but evidently did once have close relationships. There is also a clearly signalled promise of realism in the contrast between the blonde television woman and Jackie's face framed with dark, nondescript dark hair: the contrast of the two modes of femininity. The sudden silence and the blank television screen when the game show is cut off provide a little quiet space in which the audience, as well as Jackie, can contemplate what might happen next. Evidently, what might happen next, the scene shows, will not involve the shouty, hyped-up, faked climax of the television game show, and will not be something that can be watched while you are also heating up a microwave meal for one and simultaneously opening your post. In this invocation of the bad, affect-less falsity of the television world, a world which one cannot watch, while simultaneously turning to it for company, the film demonstrates the kind of attention which it solicits. And this – serious, quiet, concentrated – is, for the reasons which I have outlined, most economically designated as 'not like watching television'. This is an instance of medium specificity as a textual gesture, when it is not the material support, or a set of conventions or protocols, or the institutional context which defines medium specificity, but the mode of attention invoked.

Conclusion

I began this article by considering the contours of scholarship on the British audio-visual landscape, and I want to conclude by returning to these matters. Lucy and Jackie are the protagonists of films which I have used to propose certain ideas about the conceptualisation of film and television in a digital age. The terrain which I have traversed in this piece has both international and national dimensions. Discussion of medium specificity, laments for the end of cinema and theorisation of post-cinema, post-television and the aesthetics of new media are international. In this international context, where discussion can take place at quite a high level of abstraction, I have argued for the importance of the national, the historical and the specific (particularly in its industrial, institutional and textual forms) in the conceptualisation of what we might mean by film and television. It is a particularly British heritage which brings the poetic social realism/social problem of *The Unloved* to Channel 4 at 9.00 on a Sunday night, funded by television but looking like art cinema. It is a strategy in 'the cinema of small nations' which engenders *Red Road* – which feels so much like a British film but was funded in Denmark and Scotland. In each case, I have argued that it is through textual gesture that the film declares its 'film-ness', and that this cleaving, within the text, to the category of film is a significant move in our understanding of medium specificity in a digital twenty-first century.

By publishing the article in the *Journal of British Cinema and Television*, I make a further argument. Through the history which I have sketched here, I believe that this journal is particularly well suited to developing a history and criticism of British cinema and television which traverses media, institutions, practitioners, critics, audiences and industries, in the ebb and flow of particularity and broader argument. This will entail scholarship which is sometimes about cinema, sometimes about television, and sometimes about movements between and across culture, media, forms and genres. This critical history will be made partly through a collage of different, separate projects over a longer period. But this particular, historical, nationally specific scholarship must not remain island-bound, and must engage with the broader theorisations of moving image media in an international context. Only in this conversation can a scholarship which is adequate to the changing conditions and manifestations of cinema and television be made.

As for Lucy and Jackie themselves, their stories are rather different. A child and a widowed mother – it is not really appropriate to link them together as 'desperate girls', but I hope that the 'girlification' of women which I have performed here will be forgiven in a larger argument about the noticeable persistence of an inconsolable femininity in the heroines of female-directed films. As the 'purchasing power' of post-feminism diminishes in the cash-strapped West, and as more and more studies show that it is women with caring responsibilities who are most hard hit by the cuts, perhaps this desperate femininity will extend its age range. Will it be better or worse to be speaking no longer of desperate 'girls'? But the point is perhaps a wider one in a special issue devoted to the first decade of the twenty-first century. British cinema and television have a long history of attention to ordinary lives and social deprivation – phrases that have become devalued in the contemporary marketing rhetoric which passes for politics nowadays – which means that they have the aesthetic resources to respond to the new age of austerity as triumphant neo-liberalism exacts its prices. Another way of looking at some of the films I have mentioned here, along with *Tyrannosaur* (2011), *Wuthering Heights* (2011), Shane Meadows' various revisitings of *This Is England* for television, but also low-budget genre fiction like *Attack the Block* (2010), is as contributors to a twenty-first-century audio-visual landscape of desperation. There is more to come – if only the funding can be sorted.

Earlier versions of this article were delivered to the 'Big Screen vs. the Small Screen' conference, Canterbury Christ Church University, February 2011, and as the Martin Walsh Memorial Lecture to the Film Studies Association of Canada at Congress, June 2011, Fredericton, New Brunswick. I am grateful to the organisers for inviting me, and for the useful discussion.

Notes

1. McLoone's 1996 discussion of medium specificity, which is attentive to national variation, is thus more germane than Carroll's (2003), although both emphasise contingency rather than essence.
2. The Anglophone literature alone is too lengthy to reference fully, but see, for example, on the post-medium condition: Krauss (1999); on television: 'The Ends of Television' conference at the University of Amsterdam, 2009; Lynn Spigel and Jan Olsson (2004); James Bennett and Tom Brown (2008); Graeme Turner and Jinna Tay (2009). On cinéphilia, the discussion includes: Paul Willemen (1994); Susan Sontag (1996); Marijke de Valck and Malte Hagener (2005), particularly the essay by Thomas Elsaesser; Laura Mulvey (2006); Christian Keathley (2006); Mark Betz (2010). On the aesthetics of new media, Lev Manovich (1999) has been influential, as have Bolter and Grusin (2000).
3. See Brunsdon (2008) for a more developed argument about the specificity of the British context in relation to television.
4. For differently inflected discussions of what modernism might mean in the British context in relation to television and film see Caughie (2000), Mulvey and Sexton (2007) and Orr (2010).
5. Andrews (2012) explores the importance of institutional nomination to the identities 'film' and 'television drama' in the British context.
6. See, for example, Auty and Roddick (1985: 27–30); Higson (2003: 113–18); Hill (1999: 53–70); Leggott (2008: 18); Petrie (2000: 123–47); Sargeant (2005: 248–51, 295–9); Street (2009: 28–30).
7. This is a complex argument which I am making too rapidly, and requires attention to the different institutional and disciplinary contexts in which television has been studied which include, using rather different paradigms, sociology and drama. Television studies, as a discipline, has tended to produce itself between these: see Fiske (1987) and, ten years later, Geraghty and Lusted (1998). Miller (2010) devotes nine pages (out of 189) to (UK and US) television drama.
8. See the shift between Brandt (1981) and (1993). But see also Cooke (2003), which combines television studies approaches with the study of television drama.
9. See Morley (1986); Gray (1992).
10. See Kuhn (2002).
11. See Petley's influential 'lost continent' chapter (1986) and Chibnall and Murphy (1999); Murphy (1998) and Street (1996) provide early accounts of what becomes the journal project. Cook (1996: 10–40), offers a germane feminist critique of British cinema historiography.
12. This sensibility has affiliations with what Jeffrey Sconce (1995) has identified as the enthusiasm for 'paracinema' and a contemporary manifestation in the DVD versions of low-budget mid-century British films marketed by the BFI as 'The Flipside'.
13. The Boyle of *Inspector Morse* seems unknown to many fans of *Trainspotting*.
14. Adaptation study, a burgeoning field, has its own well-documented issues in relation to medium-specificity. See, for example, Geraghty (2008). Higson (2010) includes

television in what he refers to as the 'Austen screen franchise', although the book is nonetheless titled *Film England*.

15. O'Sullivan (2006) is very attentive to the specificities of the use of film and videotape in *Blackstuff*, while Galt (2006) notes the serial structure of *Our Friends in the North*. This is not a point about what these authors say about these productions, but one about the post-1950s critical historiography of British audio-visual fiction which grants primacy to cinema, annexing television drama when it suits. Barr (1986) includes two essays on broadcasting and cinema which specifically address the relation and is not an example of what I am calling 'slipping in', even though the subtitle of his book is *90 Years of British Cinema*.

16. See Rolinson (2010), and also his 'Viewing Notes' for the 2011 DVD release of *Tales Out of School: Four Films by David Leland*. See also Cooke (2003: 90–127) and Andrews (2012) on *Penda's Fen*.

17. Alvarado and Stewart (1985) provide a rich account of this environment while Chibnall and Murphy (1999: 13) place *The Long Good Friday* in relation to television.

18. In *Law and Order*, IRA activity affects the price and supply of weapons. Lez Cooke (2003: 115–18) discusses the television programmes together.

19. See Lez Cooke's (2012) history of regional television drama which focuses on Granada between 1956 and 1982 and English regions drama between 1972 and 1982.

20. See Helen Wheatley (2004) for an argument about spectacular television in relation to 'ordinary' TV.

21. See, for example, Arthurs (2003) and Ball (forthcoming 2013).

22. See Turner (2009) for the general argument about national and television and Brunsdon (2010) for discussion of 'post-broadcast' interpretation.

23. *Band of Gold* (1995–7), written by Kay Mellor, was set in Bradford among women working as prostitutes, and Morton's part, a runaway working the streets underage, is that of a 'desperate girl'.

24. Interview with Samantha Morton, ICA press notes, February 2010, held at the BFI National Library.

25. *The Unloved* has a characteristic funding pattern for low-budget British cinema, drawing on both television and European funds, and being partly supported by Revolution Films. Production companies are listed thus: Film4 presents in association with EM Media and Revolution Films a Revolution Films Production. Developed with the support of Channel 4. Part funded by the European Regional Development Fund, co-financed by EM Media.

26. Xan Brooks, *Guardian, Film and Music*, 19 February 2010; *The Times*, T2, 19 February 2010.

27. See also Katherine Flett, 'Little girl lost – but who cares?', *Observer Review*, 24 May 2009; Sam Wollaston, 'Last night's TV', *Guardian Review*, 18 May 2009.

28. Arguably, a particular kind of British cinema, which, in an earlier moment, Christopher Williams (1996) characterised as a 'social art cinema'.

29. Production notes on *Red Road*, http://www.vervepics.com/redroad (accessed 17 July 2007).

30. *Donkeys* had a difficult production process which included casting James Cosmo instead of the late Andy Armour. See Jane Graham, 'The beast of burden of cinema', *Guardian Review*, 19 November 2011.

31. Production notes on *Red Road*, http://www.vervepics.com/redroad (accessed 17 July 2007).

32. Phillip French, 'Down and out in gritty Glasgow', *Observer Review*, 29 October 2006; Peter Bradshaw, 'Stars of CCTV', *Guardian Review*, 27 October 2006; Jonathan Romney, 'Sealed with a Glasgow kiss', *Independent on Sunday*, 29 October 2006; Hannah McGill, 'Mean streets', *Sight and Sound*, November 2006, pp. 26–8; Lake (2010).

References

Alvarado, Manuel and Stewart, John (eds) (1985), *Made for Television: Euston Films Limited*, London: BFI, in association with Thames Television.

Andrews, Hannah (2012), 'Public Service Cinema', unpublished PhD thesis, University of Warwick.

Arthurs, Jane (2003), '*Sex and the City* and consumer culture: remediating postfeminist drama', *Feminist Media Studies*, 3: 1, pp. 83–98.

Auty, Martyn and Roddick, Nick (eds) (1985), *British Cinema Now*, London: BFI.

Ball, Vicky (2012, forthcoming), 'The "femininization" of British television and the re-traditionalization of gender', *Feminist Media Studies*, 12: 2.

Ball, Vicky (2013, forthcoming), *Heroine Television: The Case of the British Female Ensemble Drama*, Manchester: Manchester University Press.

Barr, Charles (ed.) (1986), *All Our Yesterdays*, London: BFI.

Bennett, James and Brown, Tom (eds) (2008), *Film and Television After DVD*, London: Routledge.

Bennett, James and Strange, Niki (eds) (2011), *Television as Digital Media*, Durham, NC: Duke University Press.

Betz, Mark (ed.) (2010), 'In focus: cinephilia', *Cinema Journal*, 49: 2, pp. 130–66.

Bolter, Jay David and Grusin, Richard (2000), *Remediation: Understanding New Media*, Cambridge, MA: MIT Press.

Brandt, George W. (ed.) (1981), *British Television Drama*, Cambridge: Cambridge University Press.

Brandt, George W. (ed.) (1993), *British Television Drama in the 1980s*, Cambridge: Cambridge University Press.

Brunsdon, Charlotte (2000), 'Not having it all: women and film in the 1990s', in Robert Murphy (ed.), *British Cinema of the 90s*, London: BFI, pp. 167–77.

Brunsdon, Charlotte (2008), 'Is television studies history?', *Cinema Journal*, 47: 3, pp. 127–37.

Brunsdon, Charlotte (2010), 'Bingeing on box-sets: the national and the digital in television crime drama', in Jostein Gripsrud (ed.), *Relocating Television*, London: Routledge, pp. 63–75.

Carroll, Noel (2003), *Engaging the Moving Image*, New Haven, CT: Yale University Press, pp. 265–80.

Caughie, John (1986), 'Broadcasting and cinema 1: converging histories', in Charles Barr (ed.), *All Our Yesterdays*, London: BFI, pp. 189–205.

Caughie, John (2000), *British Television Drama: Realism, Modernism and British Culture*, Oxford: Clarendon Press.

Chibnall, Steve and Murphy, Robert (1999), 'Parole overdue: releasing the British crime film into the critical community', in Steve Chibnall and Robert Murphy (eds), *British Crime Cinema*, London: Routledge, pp. 1–15.

Cook, Pam (1996), *Fashioning the Nation: Costume and Identity in British Cinema*, London: BFI.

Cooke, Lez (2003), *British Television Drama*, London: BFI.

Cooke, Lez (2012), *A Sense of Place: Regional British Television Drama*, Manchester: Manchester University Press.

de Valck, Marijke and Hagener, Malte (eds) (2005), *Cinephilia: Movies, Love and Memory*, Amsterdam: Amsterdam University Press.

Fiske, John (1987), *Television Culture*, London: Routledge.

Galt, Rosalind (2006), *The New European Cinema*, New York: Columbia University Press.

Geraghty, Christine (2005), *My Beautiful Laundrette*, London: I. B. Tauris.

Geraghty, Christine (2008), *Now a Major Motion Picture*, Lanham, MD: Rowman & Littlefield.

Geraghty, Christine and Lusted, David (eds) (1998), *The Television Studies Book*, London: Edward Arnold.

Gray, Ann (1992), *Video Playtime: The Gendering of a Leisure Technology*, London: Routledge.

Higson, Andrew (2003), *English Heritage, English Cinema*, Oxford: Oxford University Press.

Higson, Andrew (2010), *Film England: Culturally English Filmmaking Since the 1990s*, London: I. B. Tauris.

Hill, John (1999), *British Cinema in the 1980s*, Oxford: Clarendon Press.

Hill, John (2011), *Ken Loach: The Politics of Film and Television*, London: BFI/Palgrave Macmillan.

Hill, John and McLoone, Martin (eds) (1996), *Big Picture, Small Screen: The Relations Between Film and Television*, Luton: John Libbey Media.

Hjort, Mette (2010), 'Affinitive and milieu-building transnationalism: the *Advance Party* initiative', in Dina Iordanova, David Martin-Jones and Belén Vidal (eds), *Cinema at the Periphery*, Detroit, MI: Wayne State University Press, pp. 46–66.

Keathley, Christian (2006), *Cinephilia and History, or the Wind in the Trees*, Bloomington, IN: Indiana University Press.

Krauss, Rosalind (1999), '*A Voyage on the North Sea': Art in the Age of the Post-Medium Condition*, London: Thames & Hudson.

Kuhn, Annette (2002), *An Everyday Magic: Cinema-going and Cultural Memory*, London: I. B. Tauris.

Lake, Jessica (2010), '*Red Road* (2006) and emerging narratives of "sub-veillance"', *Continuum*, 24: 2, pp. 231–40.

Leggott, James (2008), *Contemporary British Cinema*, London: Wallflower.

McGill, Hannah (2006), 'Interview with Andrea Arnold', *Sight and Sound*, 16: 11, p. 28.

McIlroy, Brian (1998), *Shooting to Kill*, Trowbridge: Flicks.

McLoone, Martin (1996), 'Boxed in? The aesthetics of film and television', in John Hill and Martin McLoone (eds), *Big Picture, Small Screen: The Relations Between Film and Television*, Luton: John Libbey Media.

Malik, Sarita (2002), *Representing Black Britain*, London: Sage.

Manovich, Lev (2001), *The Language of New Media*, Cambridge, MA: MIT Press.

Miller, Toby (2010), *Television Studies: The Basics*, Abingdon: Routledge.

Morley, David (1986), *Family Television*, London: Comedia.

Mulvey, Laura (2006), *Death 24x a Second*, London: Reaktion.

Mulvey, Laura and Sexton, Jamie (2007), *Experimental British Television*, Manchester: Manchester University Press.

Murphy, Robert (1998), 'Popular British cinema', *Journal of Popular British Cinema*, 1, pp. 6–12.

O'Sullivan, Sean (2006), 'No such thing as society: television and the apocalypse', in Lester D. Friedman (ed.), *Fires Were Started*, second edition, London: Wallflower, pp. 223–42.

Orr, John (2010), *Romantics and Modernists in British Cinema*, Edinburgh: Edinburgh University Press.

Petley, Julian (1986), 'The lost continent', in Charles Barr (ed.), *All Our Yesterdays*, London: BFI, pp. 98–119.

Petrie, Duncan (2000), *Screening Scotland*, London: British Film Institute.

Petrie, Duncan (2004), *Contemporary Scottish Fictions*, Edinburgh: Edinburgh University Press.

Pettitt, Lance (2000), *Screening Ireland: Film and Television Representation*, Manchester: Manchester University Press.

Rolinson, Dave (2005), *Alan Clarke*, Manchester: Manchester University Press.

Rolinson, Dave (2010), 'The last studio system: the case for British television films', in Paul Newland (ed.), *Don't Look Now: British Cinema in the 1970s*, Bristol: Intellect, pp. 163–76.

Rolinson, Dave (2011), Viewing notes for *Tales out of School: Four Films by David Leland*, Granada Ventures, Network DVD.

Russell, Dave (2004), *Looking North*, Manchester: Manchester University Press.

Sargeant, Amy (2005), *British Cinema*, London: BFI.

Sconce, Jeffrey (1995), 'Trashing the academy: taste, excess and an emerging politics of cinematic style', *Screen*, 36: 4, pp. 371–93.

Smith, Justin (2008), 'Glam, spam and Uncle Sam: funding diversity in 1970s British cinema', in Robert Shail (ed.), *Seventies British Cinema*, London: BFI/Palgrave Macmillan, pp. 67–80.

Sontag, Susan (1996) 'The decay of cinema', *New York Times Magazine*, 25 February, pp. 60–1.

Spigel, Lynn and Olsson, Jan (eds) (2004), *Television After TV*, Durham, NC: Duke University Press.

Street, Sarah (1996), 'What is popular British cinema?', *Society for the Study of Popular British Cinema Newsletter*, 1, pp. 1–3.

Street, Sarah (2009), *British National Cinema*, second edition, Abingdon: Routledge.

Turner, Graeme (2009), 'Television and the nation: does this matter any more?', in Graeme Turner and Jinna Tay (eds), *Television Studies After TV*, Abingdon: Routledge, pp. 54–64.

Turner, Graeme and Tay, Jinna (eds) (2009), *Television Studies After TV*, Abingdon: Routledge.

Wheatley, Helen (2004), 'The limits of television? Natural history programming and the transformation of public service broadcasting', *European Journal of Cultural Studies*, 7: 3, pp. 325–39.

Willemen, Paul (1994), *Looks and Frictions*, London: British Film Institute.

Williams, Christopher (1996), *Cinema: The Beginnings and the Future*, London: University of Westminster Press.

Charlotte Brunsdon's most recent book is a study of the controversial 1978 British television series, *Law and Order*. She is Professor of Film and Television Studies at the University of Warwick.

'If You Can't Make a Good Political Film, Don't': Pawel Pawlikowski's Resistant Poetic Realism

Claire Monk

[The resistance to making didactic films is] a kind of internal debate (for me) since I'm obsessed with politics... You can make a kind of personality-driven assault like Michael Moore, which I thoroughly approve of. But it's not filmmaking, it's closer to journalism. That needs to be done, but it's not what I'm good at... I believe that making a film where the characters are not stooges is itself a political gesture... Although *My Summer of Love* does not strike any political notes, I'm not dealing in staple characters and am going against the grain of the enormous media saturation that you find in Britain today... This was a political gesture of sorts, even if it was a negative gesture. (Pawlikowski, in Porton 2005: 41)

Introduction

The director and screenwriter Pawel Pawlikowski stands as one of post-2000 British cinema's most paradoxical key talents. Born in Poland in 1957, and resident in the UK since his teens, Pawlikowski studied Literature and Philosophy at Oxford to postgraduate level before building an early career as a maker of iconoclastic authored TV documentaries for the BBC, distinguished by their 'often surreal takes on Eastern Europe's past and present' (Barefoot 2006), before making the transition to drama and docudrama. He subsequently emerged as the acclaimed director of two of the last decade's most distinctive,

Journal of British Cinema and Television 9.3 (2012): 480–501
DOI: 10.3366/jbctv.2012.0101
© Edinburgh University Press
www.eupjournals.com/jbctv

debated and internationally acclaimed British features – *Last Resort* (2000) and *My Summer of Love* (2004).

At the date of writing, Pawlikowski had yet to complete or release a further British film. (*The Restraint of Beasts*, starring Rhys Ifans – based on Magnus Mills' 1998 debut novel, which derives chilling allegorical tragicomedy from tensions within the rural fencing business – was part-completed but then abandoned.) His recently released Euro-thriller *The Woman in the Fifth* (2011) should, however, be noted here for certain structuring affinities with *Last Resort*. Both films filter a defamiliarised, hostile culture – part-characterised by a transient multiculturalism – through the restricted subjectivity of a disoriented but relatively privileged white outsider: in *The Woman in the Fifth*, a mentally disordered US male academic adrift in Paris (played by Ethan Hawke), as opposed to *Last Resort*'s Russian female 'accidental' asylum seeker Tanya (Dina Korzun) adrift in Margate.

This article reappraises Pawlikowski's two completed British films of the 2000s: with reference to his avowedly anti-sociological and, at times, oblique representational strategies, but also situating them within a broader framework of issues manifested in and around post-2000 British cinema, contextual (socio-economic and geopolitical, discursive and interpretative) as much as textual (representational and aesthetic). Some of these issues can be felt with particular acuteness around the aestheticised 'poetic realist' strand which has found critical favour over the past decade, and with which critical responses to Pawlikowski's films have tended to align him. My analysis is centrally guided, however, by two propositions that intersect semi-autonomously with questions of realist or post-realist aesthetics. The first proposition is that an ethic (or underlying principle) of *resistance* is as critical to Pawlikowski's practice as notions of either realism or cinematic poetry, not merely as a facet of his self-projected public persona (in which Pawlikowski has long been vocal in resisted pigeonholing as either a realist or an issue-led director) but for apprehending the distinctiveness and – however elliptical and open-ended – the *politics* of his two post-2000 British films. The second proposition is that the particularities of both films (coupled, of course, with the case of Pawlikowski as a 'migrant' director) demonstrate the limitations and lacunae of 'the transnational' as an appropriate interpretative framework for post-2000 developments in British film, particularly in the light of the local specifics of history, economy and place, and the local and regional UK impacts and consequences of post-industrialisation and globalisation, that tangibly inflect *My Summer of Love* as much as *Last Resort*.

481

'Post-national' trends in the circulation and academic reception and interpretation of contemporary 'hybrid' or 'poetic' realist British films over the past decade or so prompt some critical concerns that, to date, have been little discussed. In a trend whose roots can be traced back to the 1990s (evident, for instance, in the repositioning of Mike Leigh as a European art-cinema auteur propelled by 1993's *Naked*), but which has become more marked since 2000, the films of contemporary British (or British-based) realist and poetic-realist directors have gained a welcome new international visibility. This has been facilitated in part, however, by a critical and reception discourse which understands and valorises these films centrally as the artistic or philosophical work of *trans*national or European auteurs, often at the price of an abstracted disengagement from (and, at times, even incomprehension of) sociological specifics, cultural nuances and British social and cinematic contexts – including the local consequences of the global (see, for instance, the specific argument advanced in Forrest (2010), or the strand of US monographs on Mike Leigh epitomised by Watson (2004) and Carney and Quart (2000)).

This changed circulation and reception context makes it pertinent to enquire what this – for some commentators 'new' – poetic realism in recent British cinema *consists of*, in relation to its politics of directorial self-positioning and critical celebration as much as its textual actuality. Allied to this question are the dangers of writing, and giving authority to, a reductive or historically amnesiac narrative of contemporary British cinema's hybridisation and evolution beyond the social-realist legacy – which, contrary to some recent accounts, is far from 'new' to the post-2000 decade. Moreover, *even while* – and *because* – the poetic, anti-sociological turn problematises the status of these films as social representations, events since 2000 have made the question of social representation itself – its form as well as its capacity for lucidity or obfuscation – newly urgent, at a time when the local and personal consequences of post-industrialisation, globalisation, economic po-larisation and social fragmentation spawned a 'hidden' social crisis in the UK – prior to the highly visible banking crisis (or crises) of 2008 onwards – yet only rarely received adequate engagement from British films. It is against this backdrop that I am keen to re-open consideration of Pawlikowski's two post-2000 British features as social representations – and to reconnect them with their local and British socio-economic and geographical as much as cinematic con-texts – albeit from a director who has complained that British cinema 'is drowning in sociology' (Foley 2004) and who prefers in his own films to eschew the 'social document' (ibid.) in favour of invoking 'a strange in-between land' (Pawlikowski, in Winter 2005: 24) and 'create a slightly abstract world' via performances that are 'believable, but strange, inflected' (ibid.: 26), to facilitate 'a poetry of cinema' (ibid.: 25).

While the frequent characterisation of Pawlikowski's films as 'poetic realist' is understandable, this label has accrued problematic associations in the light of a discourse which (counter to the earlier, historic suspicion of aestheticism within British film-critical culture) celebrates a broader poetic realist strand in post-2000 British cinema in terms of a (supposed) prioritisation of aesthetics, poetics and ambiguity *over*, and *abstracted from*, social or political engagement. (In accounts such as Forrest (2010), this 'new' poetic realism is associated not only with directors such as Lynne Ramsay and Andrea Arnold, but with a contentiously diverse longer list, ranging from Joe Lawlor and Christine Molloy to Shane Meadows, and from Steve McQueen to Joanna Hogg). In this contemporary climate – both within film culture/scholarship and as presented by the intensified neo-liberal turn in the wider political arena – the urge to eschew 'didacticism' and the 'sociological' takes on an ambiguous force. In which cases does it signal a recognition that 'straight' social-realist strategies have lost their freshness and effectivity for representing current social and political realities and may shut down certain representational possibilities, and in which is it merely an evasion of political engagement? In Pawlikowki's case, the distinctive qualities evident in his films and practice simultaneously fit the 'poetic realist' label *and* exceed or resist it. On the one hand, both *Last Resort* and *My Summer of Love* are characterised by deliberate, stylised choices of framing, composition, colour and cinematography that produce a 'poetic' effect: a distinctive blend of the dreamlike, absurdist and super-real. On the other, they are strongly attuned to the *specifics* – as much as the poetics – of both place and human circumstance, and Pawlikowski clearly *understands* the socio-economics of both, while choosing to express these only indirectly (refracted, for example, via character psychology and an eye for absurd detail).

The success of both films in resisting and escaping an *abstracted* poeticism owes much to Pawlikowki's fundamentally performer- and character-led working methods, shaped by a broader commitment to spontaneity originating in his earlier career background in expressive documentary (as Pawlikowki himself puts it, 'I try to ... think on my feet' (quoted in Winter 2005: 25)). This drive to spontaneity extends to minimal scripting and largely improvised dialogue (Calhoun 2005: 14), and even an approach to cinematography in which Ryszard Lenczewski, Pawlikowski's director of photography, has devised technical solutions that enable him 'to be inside the brain of the character I'm photographing ... to be absolutely close to the performers' even when using a long lens (ibid.). In view of this ethos, it is no surprise that both films have brought comparisons with the 1960s New Waves – Czech more than British – while Pawlikowski himself cites not only Milos Forman's *Loves of a Blonde* (1965) but also Italian neo-realism among his key influences (Porton 2005: 38). In their quest to capture spontaneous, nuanced, ' "unrepeatable" moments' (ibid.: 37), the two films could be classified as neo-neo-realist. Both, however, are also distinctive for a subjective realism in which 'external' realities are refracted expressly through the subjectivities of female protagonists. Thus in *Last Resort*, the realities of the grim coastal town of Stonehaven and the asylum-seeker experience – from the disorientation about place to the cultural and legislative incomprehensions and bureaucratic farce – are refracted via the restricted point of view of the Russian Tanya (who is, as Pawlikowski freely points out, a highly atypical asylum seeker). *My Summer of Love*, by contrast, plays with the subjective social realities of two British teenage girls from polarised socio-economic backgrounds via the intense summer friendship and mutual fascination of upper-middle-class Tamsin (Emily Blunt) and quirky, resilient working-class Mona (Natalie Press) – a fascination which, crucially, evolves as both erotic and classed – to build a complex, shaded, very oblique meditation on the nature and truth-value of competing – and socially stratified – 'realities'.

Hyphenated social realisms and the tensions around the 'poetic'

In an astute analysis of *Trainspotting* (1996) – the quintessential 'youth underclass film' of the 1990s (Monk 2000: 276) – as a manifestation of a sensibility that (following Smith 2002) he terms 'black magic realism', Paul Dave argues credibly that, throughout the 1980s and 1990s, an 'aesthetic struggle [that] might be connected to a political one' was being played out across the processes of hybridisation (simultaneously generic, aesthetic and cultural) that transformed British social-realist film during those decades (2006: 96; see also Street 1997: 100). By the 1990s, the 'traditional', once-industrial, *working* class was increasingly represented in British cinema only in elegiac mode, coupled with a marked shift in representational emphasis towards groups understood as lying 'somehow 'outside' the working class' – whether as members of an unemployed 'underclass' or because defined primarily in terms of other sociological attributes such as 'youth' (Dave 2006: 61–2).

For Dave, it is no coincidence that *Trainspotting*–whose 'black magic realism' he characterises partly in terms of an aestheticised celebration of 'degraded, "crappy"' environments–arrives just as 'the working class as an independent political force has vanished' after a decade of 'being busily consigned to the past' (ibid.: 96). On the contrary, he argues, *Trainspotting*'s celebrated aesthetic and representational iconoclasm–even the 'lustre' of its 'aesthetic redemption'–*depended upon* this vanishing: for while 'black magic realism appears to mediate a particular class-inflected exploration of the destructive social consequences of triumphant neo-liberal capitalism–its vividness requires as its background a posthumous or exhausted working-class world' (ibid.). Within the social and political sphere, the 2000s have seen this process completed. The past decade has brought a more complete ideological displacement of the working classes from public and mainstream media discourse (via the incompatible twin myths that we are either 'all middle class now' or that the 'working' class has been superseded by a 'feral underclass'), followed by the rise of anti-working-class misrepresentation and hatred as 'an integral, respectable part of modern British culture' which Owen Jones explores and condemns in his book *Chavs* (2011: 6–7).

It is necessary to revisit this recent history–the social consequences of the destruction of manufacturing industry and working-class identity, on the one hand, and the diverse senses in which British social-realist cinema has hybridised during this period, on the other–as a corrective to a simplifying amnesia evident in some accounts of the 'new' post-2000 British poetic realism. Where critical discussion of social realism in 1990s British cinema often fell back on routinised labels such as 'Brit grit' (see Lay 2002), it at least remained grounded in an understanding that this *realism*, whether social or poetic, was defined by an (ontological) relationship to the (socio-economic) *real*, in which *real* questions of perspective, representation and address remained at stake in the tensions between realism's 'traditional project of subjective incorporation [of] those that traditionally inhabit the margins' and a representational mode that traditionally constructed its subjects as 'all those Others who are not Us' (Hallam with Marshment 2000: 192–3).

Hallam and Marshment, writing in 2000, were able to propose credibly that 'the relationship between place, character and identity' remained social realism's continuing 'distinguishing feature' (ibid.: 192). Crucially, however, they noted too that 'social realism emphasises that characters are inextricably contained within a nexus of social/economic/geographical/historical factors... far beyond the resources of any individual to control or transcend' (ibid.: 194). This general definition also serves as a close fit for the political and structural/narrative logics of the films of Britain's longest-established and most consistent and committed social-realist director, Ken Loach, and Hallam and Marshment explicitly define the guiding principles of Loach's cinema in the following terms: 'Typically, he eschews generic narratives, formal virtuosity and postmodern eclecticism in favour of a plain visual style that emphasises performance, the development of character and the pre-filmic referentiality of situations and events' (ibid.). A striking feature of this description is that – with the exception of the 'plain visual style' and the naturalistic eschewal of 'formal virtuosity' – much of it applies equally to the principles underpinning Pawlikowski's choices and practice in his films, while (clearly) yielding very tonally and stylistically different cinematic results.

To propose such affinities between a 'poetic' realist director such as Pawlikowski and a 'didactic' realist like Loach, however, runs very much counter to the aestheticising discourse around the 'new' post-2000 poetic realism (typified by Forrest 2010) in which a 'poetic' aesthetic is framed as a matter of auteurist 'personal expression' and celebrated *for its own sake* as a *desirable end in itself* – but seemingly also conceived of as binarily opposed to 'an explicit focus on socio-political themes' rather than potentially able to serve the latter (ibid.: 31). In this narrative, 'Loach' not only serves as a shorthand bad object against which the merits of the 'poetic' realists are defined, but is claimed (in conflation with Mike Leigh, despite the evident tonal and methodological differences between the two directors' films) to epitomise 'the' dominant mode of British realist cinema, in which the 'constant emphasis on the relationship between society and the individual' (ibid.: 34) is presented as a hindrance to, and less valuable than, artistic or poetic expression.

Pawlikowski's practice: defining 'resistance'

In what specific senses, then, can *Last Resort* and *My Summer of Love*, and Pawlikowski's principles and practice in making them, be claimed as 'resistant'? The answers span three interrelated areas. First, and centrally, they explicitly resist the reduction of 'characters [to] types', which Pawlikowski has identified as a problem of 'non-commercial' as much as commercial films (quoted in Porton 2005: 39). Both films counter this via his performer- and character-*led* (rather than merely character-*centred*) working methods, in which the building of complex, contradictory central female characters – developed with collaborative, improvisatory input from their actors – generates a 'spontaneity effect' and forms the *starting point* for unpredictable representational outcomes. Character and narrative dynamics thus emerge organically, as opposed to a script-driven construction of instrumental protagonists (whether as social or political ciphers, or solely to serve narrative or genre functions). On this point, Richard Porton suggests that 'like Milos Forman, Pawlikowski is less interested in convoluted narratives than in fablelike character studies' (2005: 37). Perhaps instructively, for *My Summer of Love*, Pawlikowski initially pursued but then abandoned the neo-realist principle of casting local non-actors from the north of England in the two central female roles in favour of using professionals, after finding that the behaviour of the 'working-class girls' he saw 'seemed [too] much shaped by their exposure to television and the media' (ibid.: 40). This anecdote highlights intriguing issues around the impacts of media representation, but may also indicate that Pawlikowki's particular 'performer-led' approach is better suited to professionals.

Second, while both *Last Resort* and *My Summer of Love* are clearly resistant to formulaic social realism – both representational and aesthetic – their specific strategies display an equal resistance both to routinised or solipsistic notions of 'poetic realism' and to genericised hybrids or sub-genres of social realism, be these formulaic forms of committed 'straight' social realism, commercialised hybrid formulae such as the social-realist comedies and underclass films of the 1990s (see Monk 2000), or a reductive treatment of subject matter that might render its representations 'generic'. Pawlikowski's avoidance of generic signposting has not, however, protected either film from interpretative pigeonholing or misrecognitions around their representational intentions and politics. The (near-inevitable) response to *My Summer of Love* as a 'lesbian movie' by some critics caused Pawlikowski considerable irritation – 'are they tone deaf, or what?' (in Porton 2005: 38) – in a film more interested in the psychological and power dynamics of class culture and difference, but articulated via their entanglement with the intensity and erotics of teenage girl/girl fascination. *Last Resort*'s arguably more serious (and widespread) misrecognition – by activists as well as critics – as a campaigning statement on behalf of refugees and asylum seekers seeking to enter and settle in the UK points to a similar 'tone deafness', not least vis-à-vis the extreme atypicality (even inauthenticity) of Tanya as an asylum case (Monk 2001: 42). Yosefa Loshitzky has argued, even, that *Last Resort* 'projects deep ambivalence towards contemporary migrants, sometimes even slightly tainted by covert racist tones' (2010: 33). Third and last, both films

Claire Monk

explicitly resist formulaic notions of a 'political film' in their efforts to eschew a simplistic politics of representation, simplistic 'messages' and socio-political simplifications in general – even while running the risks of misrecognition illustrated above.

Pawlikowksi, politics and the importance of place

Pawlikowski's position on politics and film is more complex and politically engaged than his most forthright statement on the subject – 'If you can't make a good political film, don't' (in Porton 2005: 41) – suggests, making it necessary to gloss this position with some care. As the quotation opening this article attests, his philosophy – as well as the tonal qualities and representational status of his two completed post-2000 British films – departs significantly from a *depoliticised* poetic realism. Pawlikowski notably describes (and indirectly defines) his own films and approach in terms of a set of underlying *principles* and *values*, and the latter in terms of *negatives* but *not* binarisms, with reference to values he resists, rejects or seeks to counter: 'didactic(ism)', 'staple characters', 'media saturation', 'self-limitation', lack of 'autonomy', 'uniformity'. Following on from this, both Pawlikowski's statements about his own position and practice and their actual cinematic outcomes suggest that his aspiration to produce a 'poetry of cinema' (quoted in Winter 2005: 25) is not driven by (abstracted) aesthetic expression as an end in itself, nor by a *formalist* self-distanciation from realism(s) (although he *has* declared that social realism should not be treated as 'a protected species' (Pawlikowski 2007)). Nor does this aspiration entail indifference to larger socio-economic, political and structural questions (whether at the global or local level).

Pawlikowski's actual position is that he is 'obsessed with politics' but is uninterested, himself, in making 'didactic films' and sceptical about their political or analytic effectivity and limitations (asking provocatively: 'What's the point of preaching to the converted and jerking off? It's better to go to a demo or plant a bomb') (Porton 2005: 41). In keeping with his taste for the 'contradictory' as an energising force able to generate productive complexities, however, he has also stated his admiration for the (indisputably polemical, non-'balanced') documentaries of Michael Moore (quoted in Porton 2005: 41). Crucially, then, Pawlikowski's objection is not to political – nor even polemical – film per se, but to what he perceives as 'bad' political films – those which untenably simplify highly complex situations or issues – or 'bad' directors with political pretensions. The name Pawlikowski cites critically in this context is not Loach (with whom, as noted earlier, he shares some common ground) but Michael

488

Winterbottom, including a condemnation of Winterbottom's *Welcome to Sarajevo* (UK/USA, 1997) (which took a conventional liberal-political-thriller approach to the Bosnian war) as 'dishonest... shallow and stupid' (ibid.).

Pawlikowki's statements in interview on matters such as the homogenising effects of 'unstoppable' globalisation in making 'behaviour and choices... uniform' and the formerly distinctive Eastern Bloc/'new EU' countries 'like everywhere else' (quoted in Winter 2005: 27), the equally negative effects of 'enormous media saturation' in the UK (quoted in Porton 2005: 41), the difficulty, in both these contexts, of 'giv[ing] characters autonomy' (ibid.: 39) and the 'cancer' of 'anger and resentment' at the core of British society that he sees as only partly a problem of class (quoted in Winter 2005: 28) all point to a sharp, if primarily diagnostic, socio-political awareness that links back in tangible ways to his film-making approach and the films themselves. In an important distinction from both the form-conscious political debates around realism (and the political thriller) in 1970s film theory and the putatively apolitical or anti-political post-2000 discourse of 'poetic realism', however, Pawlikowki's approach is not merely formally non-prescriptive but aesthetically fluid.

It is logical enough that a director resistant to genre formulae and representational 'types' might be equally resistant – as a matter of principle – to aesthetic formulae ('poetic', 'social-realist' or otherwise) and alert to the potential dead-ends these represent. Moreover, the merits – including political merits – of such aesthetic flexibility have been debated and argued before: initially within Western/Anglophone film theory's late-1980s rediscovery of Third Cinema ideas (Pines and Willemen 1989), but evolving in a direction that is obliquely suggestive in relation to the importance of Pawlikowski's choices and treatments of location in both *Last Resort* and *My Summer of Love*. These are, respectively, Margate/'Stonehaven', the decayed English southern working-class seaside resort transmuted into a 'non-place' or holding place for asylum seekers (for fuller analyses, see Roberts (2002) and Allen (2008)) and the equally liminal and surreal semi-rural topography of a small, ambiguously post-industrial, West Yorkshire mill town. In his essay 'An avant-garde for the 1990s', Paul Willemen both recognises the limitations of rigidly formalist, anti-mainstream modes of counter-cinema as a politically effective 'engaged' film practice, and perceives a way forward in films which activate the 'culturally specific', but do so via a use of landscape and place which:

requires what Raymond Williams, following Brecht, called 'complex seeing': the reading of landscape within the diegesis as itself a layered set of discourses, as a text in its own right... This use of landscape is not to be read according to the habitual 'gestalt' type of image consumption, which is the customary tourist point of view privileged in all dramatic narratives... and not merely as backdrop... [R]ather it is deployed as a site where the dynamics of history can be read... The location not only frames the political dialogue in the film, it also situates that dialogue in a political history. (1994: 141–2)

The cinematic presentation of landscape/townscape in *My Summer of Love* and *Last Resort* does not explicitly foreground its potential for the form of 'layered' reading for histories and cultural specifics envisaged by Willemen (although his form of words suggests that such foregrounding is not a prerequisite for 'complex seeing'). Moreover, Pawlikowski would almost certainly dissociate himself from the kind of 'avant-garde' political project Willemen envisages. Despite these complicating factors, the 'local' British (social, class and industrial) histories 'layered' within Pawlikowski's specific choices of location in both films do, I would argue, contribute vital nuances to the films' socio-political and representational legibility.

The histories and meanings 'layered' or encoded in specifics of place and landscape are, however, precisely what gets detrimentally lost in some of the critical efforts to interpret *Last Resort* and *My Summer of Love* centrally in transnational or European terms, often at the cost of marginalising the films' British socio-economic dynamics and contexts. To take one example, Joanna Rydzewska's reading of *Last Resort* gives interpretative primacy to the post-Communist eastward 2004 and 2007 extensions of the European Union in order to argue that *Last Resort*'s narrative is 'clearly a metaphor for the West/East relationship of power and privilege [which] should be read within the contemporary political debate on... the place of British identity in the "New Europe" (2009: 91).

Last Resort's narrative dynamics between its 'accidental' asylum seeker Tanya – an attractive, emotionally impulsive, archetypal Russian romantic, who arrives in Britain with her son Artiom (Artiom Strelnikov), expecting to be met by a British fiancé who never shows up – and the British men she encounters – her ambiguously drawn saviour, amusement-arcade manager Alfie (Paddy Considine) on the one hand, webcam-porn entrepreneur Les (Lindsey Honey) on the other – certainly offer potential for such a metaphorical reading. However, Rydzewska's gendered East–West analysis (which, curiously, proceeds as if the Russian Federation were part of the EU, and

490

mis-presents Tanya as a mail-order bride in the face of any definite textual evidence) unquestioningly assumes that 'the West's' – and hence Britain's – position of economic and political 'power and privilege' over 'the East' remains unchanged in the post-Communist, post-industrial, neo-liberal world order.

This assumption sits oddly with the epochal twenty-first-century reordering of global economic power relations represented by the emergence of the BRIC countries (Brazil, Russia, India, China) as the world's fasting-growing major economies, and equally with *Last Resort*'s (correlating) portrait of a depressed, economically busted and debased Britain via the microcosm of the fictionalised coastal ex-resort of Stonehaven. Here, global entrepreneurialism is represented solely by Les's Internet sex business ('We've got punters everywhere: Saudi Arabia, Pakistan . . .'), while the local economy ('legitimate' as well as black) consists predominantly of varieties of exploitation of the asylum detainees and gambling (the amusement arcade, the bingo hall). Moreover, Pawlikowski presents a critique of the *values* of this exchange economy via Tanya's efforts (as an applicant for 'political asylum' legally forbidden to work) to monetise her assets. She is a talented artist, but the fantastical picture she has brought with her is unappreciated and unsaleable in the UK, and a fox-fur valuable in Russia is worthless in Stonehaven. Her 'caring' qualities, by contrast, do have an economic value – but only because Les perceives the potential to market her as a nurse or schoolgirl to his webcam punters.

An overly EU-centric or 'migrant cinema' reading of *Last Resort* such as Rydzewska's also illustrates further difficulties that can arise when the British and more local nuances that permit a 'culturally specific' reading are brushed aside – specifically, in this case, salient details of the English regional economic geography of uneven development. Rydzewska's reading of Stonehaven/Margate, the emblematic English resort 'pauperised' by the British taste for overseas package holidays, as 'a [cinematic] sign [for] British working-class relative wealth vis-à-vis Europe' (2009: 95–6) seems not only paradoxically insular (are the British working class still 'relatively wealthy' at the start of the twenty-first century, after a well-documented quarter-century UK trend of increasing social inequality?) but, in view of Margate's East Kent, Isle of Thanet location, even callous. As Steven Allen points out, Margate's decline as a seaside resort dates from the nineteenth century, not the twentieth (2008: 63). And in the more recent post-industrial decades, the whole East Kent region has faced a stubborn history of economic deprivation: at the date of writing, it had UK Regional Growth Fund status, placing it on an economic par with cities such as Sunderland in England's severely de-industrialised North East (Jefferies 2011). Although Rydzewska perceives that 'the relationship between the landscape and the narrative [is] of paramount importance in *Last Resort*' (2009: 94), this 'importance' is understood not in relation to such historical and material specifics but to the more abstract notion – derived from Andrew Higson's earlier analysis of the functioning of landscape in the 1960s British New Wave films – that 'place is used up by the narrative at a metaphorical level, as a "geography of the mind"' (Higson 1984: 8). If understood solely in such a light, 'landscape' and 'place' in *Last Resort* are 'important' only because they perform a metaphorical operation that 'shifts the emphasis of the analysis *from* the *particular*' – which, for Rydzewska, already means the (Russian or ostensibly 'New' European) story of Tanya and Artiom more than British socio-economic-geographical particularities – 'to the *general* level of the investigation of pan-European encounters', so that 'the [film's] representation of place ... becomes the *more general* exploration of the state of a *collective* European identity and the place of particular nationalities within it' (2009: 94, my italics). Ironically, then, this way of reading 'place' may take us *away* from an apprehension of local cultural and socio-economic specifics.

Style, specificity and resistance

Yet both Pawlikowski's specific choices of landscape and location in the two films, and his comments on these, suggest that the culturally and socio-economically grounded specifics of landscape and place *do* have a significance in *Last Resort* and *My Summer of Love* beyond the abstract expression of 'geographies of the mind'. Pawlikowski has commented that '*in landscape as well as actors*, I'm always looking for something contradictory that ... can bring some energy to the process' (in Porton 2005: 38; my italics). More interesting and decisive, however, are his detailed observations about the specific valley on the Yorkshire/Lancashire borders where *My Summer of Love* was set and filmed:

> The whole area is fascinating, because it's where the industrial revolution happened, and yet it left these little patches of idyllic rural life, a post-industrial landscape that overlaps with the farmland. The people are a mix of stubborn Yorkshire farmers and a working class that got stuck there after generations of unemployment with nowhere to go ... There's not much mobility in Britain, especially in valleys like that ... (Quoted in Winter 2005: 26)

Such comments affirm *My Summer of Love*'s choice of location as *knowingly* (in Willemen's terms) 'a site where the dynamics of history can be read': in this case, an industrial-to-post-industrial history. Moreover, this history intersects legibly with the valley's spatial geography and built iconography as presented in the film in ways that are highly suggestive for our reading of the socio-cultural dynamics between Tamsin and Mona and the larger themes suggested through these. Simultaneously, through its cinematographic decisions and other aspects of its precise, dreamlike visual realisation (notably the contributions of its production designer John Stevenson and costume designer Julian Day), *My Summer of Love* plays with – and ultimately subverts – both some of the conventional tropes around character, class and landscape associated with the Northern 1960s British New Wave and the more recent twenty-first-century stereotype of the 'chav'.

Lenczewski's flexible cinematographic style is guided by Pawlikowski's principle of actor-centredness to differing effect in *Last Resort* and *My Summer of Love*. Significantly, however, neither film seeks to produce the Bazinian 'long hard gaze' (Andrew 1990: 122) that we might most expect to encourage a sustained reading of landscape in Willemen's terms. On the contrary, the 'realism' of Lenczewski's cinematography derives from a very short/flat (tele-photo) depth of visual field that brings the viewer intimately close to the actors/characters, so that environment is revealed *through* their responses. Despite a widespread critical emphasis on the importance of landscape in *Last Resort*, in practice its protagonists are almost never shown *within* this wider landscape, a decision that serves the film's construction of restricted point of view (that of Tanya and her son Artiom) as well as Lenczewski's hand-held, close-to-the-actor filming style. In turn, Stonehaven's external environment is often framed – even in what might normally be called establishing shots – in ways that permit neither the protagonists nor the viewer to make coherent sense of the place and its spatiality. Rather, the film alternates between tight, ultra-close, fluidly mobile framing of the actors and action – often obscured, in *vérité* documentary style, by other bodies, notably those of the omnipresent police – and separate, depthless, carefully composed, shots of their environment. Even the film's rarer conventional establishing shots are made strange in ways that retain distance or alienation.

The most memorable shot marking Tanya and Artiom's journey to Stonehaven – in which the convoy of cars, with police escort, carrying the asylum seekers are dwarfed in a shot dominated by two enormous cooling towers – is followed by the *non*-establishment of Stonehaven itself as a coherent place. Thus Margate's most distinctive coastal topographical feature–its curved pier enclosing the old harbour, guarded by the symmetrical 1890s custom house–is glimpsed only in half-obscured fragments via the car's wet windows. A later, more conventional, aerial distance shot of the harbour occurs more than nine minutes into the film, but follows a sequence of static, highly stylised shots of the environment that forms *Last Resort*'s real, degraded iconography: a street-level upward view of the jagged, intimidatingly out-of-scale concrete tower block where Tanya and Artiom are housed on the rundown seafront; the interior of their allocated flat, with its anachronistic tropical-sunset wallpaper left behind by some earlier resident; then, presented in direct contrast, the grey harbour viewed very distantly through the misted window; then Artiom's aerial point of view, in the opposite direction, of Margate's famous Dreamland amusement park, shown as dwarfed, part-dismantled and always deserted. (Later, in a surreal, closer shot, however, the lights still flash on the Scenic Railway rollercoaster.)

Such shots confirm the material existence of Stonehaven/Margate as *a place*–but not one that Artiom and Tanya, nor the 'real' asylum seekers, can truly access or apprehend. In a further strategy, the seafront is most often shown only as close-framed, decontextualised fragments (an isolated phone booth, a shelter, police with dogs), suggesting the asylum seeker's severely restricted, atomised, perspective. Stonehaven is thus understood, experientially, as a 'non-place' not in Augé's (1995) 'supermodern' sense, but as the sum of its police checkpoints, card-operated phone booths and back-alley illegal-blood-donation-for-cash vans.

In a piquant irony, however, *Last Resort* was premature in representing Dreamland as demised, and its half-dismantled appearance in the film, if read with local cultural knowledge as a 'layered discourse', tells another story. Dreamland's closure, and the (then) proposed sale of the site for retail and commercial use were, in fact, not announced until 2003, and the saga of its financial exploitation and asset-stripping by successive owners (up until its 2005 sale to the Margate Town Centre Regeneration Company) is as depressing as anything seen in *Last Resort*. In a detail that, in itself, stands as a grim fable of greed and globalisation (while illustrating how readily EU development funding for a region like East Kent can fall into a black hole), around the time of filming Dreamland's then-owner secured European and regional grant aid to support the site's £3 million redevelopment, while simultaneously selling off its most iconic rides abroad: the Big Wheel to Mexico, the Looping Star to Budapest (Dreamland Margate Trust, n.d.).

Lenczewski's cinematography works differently in *My Summer of Love*, alternating extreme (sonic as well as visual) intimacy with the performers with highly stylised 'establishing' (or other distance) shots that severely flatten the depth of field with the effect of flattening actors/characters *into* the landscape and environment – often with strange or surreal compositional results. For example, in the sequence where Mona's brother Phil (Paddy Considine) and his fellow born-again Christians struggle to carry and erect the huge cross they have built on the top of the Yorkshire hillside in a bid to 'claim this valley back... for Lord Jesus Christ', the flattening of perspective relations first dwarfs the whole town down below relative to the foregrounded crucifix borne on the men's shoulders (ironically recalling the Stations of the Cross), then makes Phil and his helpers loom excessively large above the gardens of the terraced houses below, producing a (spatially false) impression that the men might fall down into them – in both cases, to absurd effect. Once the cross is erected, a similarly flat juxtaposition between the cross high on the hill and the chimney of the old mill down below makes the foregrounded chimney dominate the shot, while the cross looks negligibly tiny from the perspective of the valley. In an ambiguous echo of the lights still flashing in the deserted Dreamland, the town's (presumed and apparent) post-industrial status is thrown into question by white smoke rising out of the mill chimney.

This flattening of depth is also crucial to *My Summer of Love*'s productive messing up (within a wider 'matter-of-fact anarchism' (Winter 2005:2 4)) of both the visual and spatial tropes famously associated with the 1960s British New Wave films, and the conventional representational hierarchies around sex, class and their intersections within social realism. If a central, intensive focus on the feminine (via the film's young, mercurial female protagonists) remains unsettling to social-realist norms, even in the 2000s this is still more true of desire and sexuality – and more so again when these erotics are non-hetero, as in the cross-class girl/girl fascination that germinates between Tamsin and Mona.

Sex, class and place in My Summer of Love

At the meeting point of these destabilising currents, however, it remains fruitful to read *My Summer of Love* as fundamentally a film about class – but class explored experientially, through contrasts in culture, through the transient intensities of teenage female friendship and through erotic desire sparked by difference. In the cultural climate of a contemporary Britain that political rhetoric continued to insist was 'classless' even as the chasms of social, economic and cultural inequality opened ever wider, one might argue that the film's elliptical play with questions of class and opportunity via the idiosyncrasies of character and friendship – even, riskily, a friendship which increasingly slides into a dreamlike, hermetic state of shared solipsism – was one of the more effective approaches Pawlikowski could have taken.

Parentless working-class Mona and boarding-school-educated 'bad influence' Tamsin – who seduces Mona with a blend of pseudo-sophisticated hokum and self-dramatising melancholy – are drawn to one another in a shared spirit of dissent and alienation from family. The parentless Mona lives with her significantly older brother Phil at a disused, part-boarded-up, pub in town, once run by their parents. Phil, a reformed petty criminal who found Jesus in jail, is converting the pub into a 'spiritual centre', but Mona's response is an intense grief, akin to bereavement, at the 'loss' of the brother she knew to Christianity. Tamsin's wealthy parents are much absent, and she tells Mona that her sister Sadie has died of anorexia. When not away at school, she lives in a large house, grand but unmodernised, with definite surreal features: an entire facade is heavily choked in creepers, and its isolated location, high on the moor-top, its lawns and tennis court surrounded by a bleak, pylon-punctuated landscape, presents a visual anachronism. The house looks – and literally is – 'out of place', because it was presumably once the mill-owner's house: the sole property set above, and apart from, the small, isolated mill town.

The class(ed) difference(s) between the two girls are played out, but also questioned, via a telling series of commonalities and contrasts, including an expressly class-coded, but shifting and evolving, iconography of colour and costume. Importantly, class(ed) identities are shown in this process to be part-performative and potentially open to change – perhaps most of all for working-class Mona. Conversely, the (self-)construct of upper-middle-class identity as represented by Tamsin is shown to be unstable in ways that expose both the dubious truth-value of Tamsin's 'reality' and her dubious authenticity (as a person and therefore friend). By implication, bourgeois entitlement and authority themselves – cultural, social and narrational – may be both unreliable and bogus.

Through the semiotics of colour and clothes, the semi-improvised dialogue and other details of Press's performance as Mona, the film plays with working-class, and even 'chav', stereotypes – and with viewers' own potential prejudices – in order to expose and debunk them. Importantly, Mona's and Tamsin's hairstyles, fashions and colour palettes are expressly class-coded throughout, but not statically so. As their friendship evolves, elements of mimicry, exchange and masquerade emerge – in directions that ultimately affirm Mona's potential and Tamsin's inauthenticity. When the two first meet, there is no mistaking the semiotic clash. Mona lies in the moor-top grass next to her engineless scooter, which – in a characteristically wry, self-reflexive line self-foregrounding her own 'chav' status – she claims to have bought 'off some gypos up at the maggot farm'. Tamsin is first glimpsed, surreally, from Mona's point of view, upside-down, mounted on a white horse and haloed in sun-glare. Day's costume design pitches Tamsin's posh-ethnic bohemian chic (hot pinks, deep reds, silk scarves, loose hair, dark denim) against Mona's strawberry-blonde scraped-up ponytail and baby-pink suntop, hoodie and bleached jeans. However, a scene almost immediately after this first meeting shows Mona already with loose hair and already wearing Tamsin's colours – significantly, at the moment when she is dumped, after sex in his car on the moors, by her older, married working-class lover Ricky (Dean Andrews).

In one of the film's two most suggestive sequences in this respect, Tamsin encourages Mona to dress up in a series of rarely-worn formal dresses and admires Mona as she dances (to Gilberto Gil's 'Las Tres Carabelas') in front of Tamsin's long bedroom mirror – a Pygmalion moment that transforms Tamsin's perception of Mona and leads into their first lovemaking, while floating the possibility that class itself is performative. In the second, Tamsin reverses the class masquerade by accessorising her usual outfit with huge gold hoop earrings and a red hoodie – and, pronouncedly and amusingly in Blunt's performance, butching up her body language – to 'dress the part' for the pair's stunt visit to the local council estate (in which Tamsin harangues Ricky's perplexed wife with an exaggerated account of his use of Mona, while Mona feigns catatonia).

The film's cultural references and the erotics of Mona and Tamsin's friendship become two further arenas in which class difference is articulated and classed expectations (or the lack of them) are – sometimes literally – acted out. Where Mona boasts to Tamsin that Ricky is 'all muscle' – 'dead strong, and with a car' – Tamsin simply thinks he looks fat. When Tamsin quizzes Mona about sex with him, Mona responds with a demonstration ('Do you want to be shagged by Ricky?'): a rough, over-in-minutes performance which, to Mona, is 'just normal'. When Mona explains that her nickname is a play on Mona Lisa, Tamsin replies: 'I've studied the original'. Playing the cello barefoot in the bay of her bedroom, Tamsin announces solemnly: 'That was "The Swan" by Saint-Saëns. Mona responds: 'I live at The Swan'. Most strikingly, Tamsin's (drunken) declaration of enthusiasm

497

for Nietzsche both exposes the bogusness of her intellectual authority (she recommends his work to Mona interchangeably with Freud's) and reveals itself as – in class terms – no accident, more an unwittingly brutal declaration of her own presumed destiny: 'He believed, you know, that there are just some people on this planet who are *made* to succeed, or just *made* to blossom, and it doesn't matter how many lesser mortals suffer and get fucked over, it doesn't matter . . .'

On the question of space and place, *My Summer of Love* plays with – but hugely complicates and ultimately messes up – the familiar iconography of 1960s northern British social realism. Its ambiguously post-industrial West Yorkshire mill town location is made strange by a number of unexpected features, then filmed in ways that make it stranger. This place carries the inscribed (or 'layered') social and industrial history and meanings already noted (including by Pawlikowski himself), but surreal (or super-real) compositions and heightened natural sound defamiliarise the moor-and-valley setting, invoking a sense of time slowed down as much as socio-spatial reality. In place of the larger, expansive and expanding industrial cities of the 1960s films, *My Summer of Love*'s establishing shots from the hillside show a monotonous street grid, shrunk to toy-town scale, dwarfed by the surrounding hills: a settlement built solely to house factory workers in an industry that has (probably) gone. The 1960s British New Wave trope of 'That Long Shot of Our Town from That Hill' (Higson 1984: 18–19) survives only vestigially, with its earlier force dislodged and greatly diminished.

However, further complexities arise from Pawlikowski's choice and use of a (small) town sandwiched in a deep cleft between *two* hills – foregrounding the question of which hill and whose viewpoint 'Our Town' is being viewed from – and where the original Victorian street grid in the valley has been joined by two phases of subsequent development. In addition to Tamsin and Mona's escapade to the council estate where Ricky lives, they also visit a new-build, post-industrial, private housing estate – every bit as mechanistically planned as the original Victorian town – where, Tamsin claims, her father is screwing his secretary. The film's first 'Long Shot of Our Town from That Hill' is an objective one. As Mona and Tamsin's friendship deepens, however, it is followed by three variations – taken from different positions and heights on the same hill, but with Tamsin and Mona now present in shot and viewed from their implied perspective(s). Although these shots of 'our' town are taken from (close to) the former mill-owner's house, the patriarch (Tamsin's father) is ever-absent, while working-class Mona, via her relationship with

Tamsin, is permitted to access – or at least try out – the elevated viewing position enjoyed by the middle-class subject/spectator in the original 'That Long Shot of Our Town from That Hill' analyses (see especially Higson (1984: 18–19) and Hill (1986: 134–6)).

This access and the mobility it implies connect directly with Mona's ability to leave the valley – upwards and out – at the end of the film. As Mona comments in the first of these shots, surrounded by pink wild flowers that match her clothing: 'I don't feel like I'm in me own town... I quite like it here, wi' you'. Earlier, on her first visit to Tamsin's house, Mona's comments – made with the town below only hazily visible – explicitly foreground the gap between aspiration on the one hand and 'chav' stereotypes on the other. Asked by Tamsin what she intends to do with her life, Mona initially answers that she's going to be a lawyer – but then pauses and corrects this to give a reply that could be construed either as a self-reflexive commentary on the 'reality' of her options or a satirical deconstruction of class stereotypes:

> I'm gonna get a job in an abattoir, work really 'ard, get a boyfriend who's, like, a *bastard*, and churn out all these kids, right, with mental problems. [Pause.] And then I'm gonna wait for t' menopause. Or cancer.

As Mona's words anticipate, if her brief, intense, part-sexual friendship with Tamsin seems to represent a transcendence of deep social divisions, it is a transcendence which ends with a thud as Mona learns that her seduction has been founded on Tamsin's lies (or what Tamsin herself calls 'poetic licence'). At *My Summer of Love*'s denouement, the transcendence of social chasm is revealed as inevitably temporary – and as both real and unreal. Yet the revelation itself prompts a reinterpretation of the friendship and its erotic trajectory which undermines the (already suspect) position of bourgeois 'authority' Tamsin had occupied within the pairing. What seemed like sophistication and cultural knowledge is unmasked as falsehood and insincerity. The nature of Tamsin's lie further associates her (class/ed) position with delusion and Mona's with authenticity: she proves to have invented a false bereavement – her sister Sadie is in fact alive – to match Mona's genuine emotional bereavement at the 'loss' of Phil to Christianity.

Following Tamsin's mock-seduction of Phil, the friendship's ensuing crisis and Mona's grief-stricken revenge for Tamsin's lies – she chooses to not quite drown Tamsin in a woodland pool – *My Summer of Love* ends with Mona emerging from the woods and striding determinedly away along the moor-top road. Her reaction suggests (analogously) that class deceit and betrayal are no surprise, and that an abrupt end to the 'classless' idyll with Tamsin was inevitable – but also that power relations between them were less unequal than might be assumed. Indeed, these closing moments invert – and even subvert – narrative and class expectation, as Mona – a member of the class condemned (in Pawlikowski's words) to be 'stuck', immobile, in the valley – storms upwards and out, possibly never to return. Affluent Tamsin, born into the class privileged with mobility and opportunity, in the final reckoning serves merely as the catalyst who provokes Mona's departure. Mona may not become a lawyer, but nor will she return to 'her place'.

References
Allen, Steven (2008), 'British cinema at the seaside: the limits of liminality', *Journal of British Cinema and Television*, 5: 1, pp. 53–70.
Andrew, Dudley (1990), *André Bazin*, New York: Columbia University Press.
Augé, Marc (1995), *Non-Places: Introduction to an Anthropology of Supermodernity*, London: Verso.
Barefoot, Guy (2006), 'Pawel Pawlikowski', in Robert Murphy (ed.), *Directors in British and Irish Cinema: A Reference Companion*, London: British Film Institute, p. 481.
Calhoun, John (2005), '*My Summer of Love* warms the English countryside', *American Cinematographer*, 86: 7, pp. 14 and 16.
Carney, Ray and Quart, Leonard (2000), *The Films of Mike Leigh: Embracing the World*, Cambridge: Cambridge University Press.
Dave, Paul (2006), *Visions of England: Class and Culture in Contemporary Cinema*, Oxford: Berg.
Dreamland Margate Trust (no date), 'Timeline: 2000s', *Dreamland Margate* (website), http://www.dreamlandmargate.com/2000s.html (accessed 30 November 2011).
Foley, Jen (2004), 'Pawel Pawlikowski: *My Summer of Love*', November, BBC Movies, http://www.bbc.co.uk/films/2004/10/11/pawel_pawlikowski_my_summer_of_love_ interview.shtml (accessed 1 March 2012).
Forrest, David (2010), '*Better Things* (Duane Hopkins, 2008) and new British realism', *New Cinemas*, 8: 1, pp. 31–43.
Hallam, Julia with Marshment, Margaret (2000), *Realism and Popular Cinema*, Manchester: Manchester University Press.
Higson, Andrew (1984), 'Space, place, spectacle: landscape and townscape in the 'kitchen sink' film', *Screen*, 25: 2, pp. 2–21.
Hill, John (1986), *Sex, Class and Realism: British Cinema, 1956–1963*, London: British Film Institute.
Jefferies, Martin (2011), 'Businesses in east Kent to learn more about £40m Regional Growth Funding', *KentOnline*, 17 November, http://www.kentonline. co.uk/kentonline/news/2011/november/18/regional_growth_fund.aspx (accessed 13 December 2011).
Jones, Owen (2011), *Chavs: The Demonization of the Working Class*, London: Verso.
Lay, Samantha (2002), *British Social Realism: From Documentary to Brit-Grit*, London: Wallflower.
Loshitzky, Yosefa (2010), *Screening Strangers: Migration and Diaspora in Contemporary European Cinema*, Bloomington, IN: Indiana University Press.

Monk, Claire (2000) 'Underbelly UK: the 1990s underclass film, masculinity and the ideologies of "New" Britain', in Justine Ashby and Andrew Higson (eds), *British Cinema, Past and Present*, London: Routledge, pp. 274–87.

Monk, Claire (2001), 'Projecting a 'New Britain", *Cineaste*, 26: 4, pp. 34–7 and 42.

Pawlikowski, Pawel (2007), Comments in general discussion, 'The Realist Impulse: Contemporary Film-Making in Britain' conference, Oxford Brookes University, 12–13 July.

Pines, Jim and Willemen, Paul (eds) (1989) *Questions of Third Cinema*, London: British Film Institute.

Porton, Richard (2005), 'Going against the grain: an interview with Pawel Pawlikowski', *Cineaste*, 30: 3, pp. 37–41.

Roberts, Les (2002), '"Welcome to Dreamland": from place to non-place and back again in Pawel Pawlikowski's *Last Resort*', *New Cinemas*, 1: 2, pp. 78–90.

Rydzewska, Joanna (2009), 'Beyond the nation state: "New Europe" and discourses of British identity in *Last Resort* (2000) by Pawel Pawlikowski', *Journal of Contemporary European Studies*, 17: 1, pp. 91–107.

Smith, Murray (2002), *Trainspotting* (BFI Modern Classics), London: British Film Institute.

Street, Sarah (1997), *British National Cinema*, London: Routledge.

Street, Sarah (2000), *British National Cinema*, London: Routledge.

Watson, Garry (2004), *The Cinema of Mike Leigh: A Sense of the Real*, London: Wallflower.

Willemen, Paul (1994), 'An avant-garde for the 1990s', in *Looks and Frictions: Essays in Cultural Studies and Film Theory*, London: British Film Institute, pp. 141–61.

Winter, Jessica (2005), 'Dreamland welcomes you', *Cinema Scope*, 7: 2 (Issue 23), Summer, pp. 24–8.

Claire Monk is Reader in Film and Film Culture at De Montfort University, Leicester, UK. She has published widely on post-1970 British cinema, from contemporary representations within and beyond the social-realist spectrum to her contributions to the debates around the cultural politics of the heritage film, including her recent work on contemporary period films and their audiences and fans in the monograph *Heritage Film Audiences: Period Films and Contemporary Audiences in the UK* (Edinburgh University Press, 2011) and its sequel 'Heritage Film Audiences 2.0: period film audiences and online fan cultures', *Participations*, 8: 2 (2011). Other key publications include 'London and contemporary Britain in BBC3's *Monkey Dust*', *Journal of British Cinema and Television*, 4: 2 (2007) and 'Underbelly UK: the 1990s underclass film, masculinity and the ideologies of "New" Britain', in Justine Ashby and Andrew Higson (eds), *British Cinema, Past and Present* (Routledge, 2000).

Crossing Borders: Artist Film-Makers in the New Decade

Amy Sargeant

In 1999 the art critic and historian Julian Stallabrass published a polemical attack on the phenomenon then widely known as YBA (Young British Artists). *High Art Lite*'s acute analysis railed not only against the work produced by the artists embraced by the brand, which he found generally vacuous and 'easily digestible', but also the institutions which interpreted, promoted and marketed the phenomenon, including public and private collections, galleries, salerooms and art journalism (1999: 2–4).[1] The response of most critics he found at best inadequate and craven and, at worst, lending the work spurious weight and substance. Echoing his complaints, the literary critic John Carey subsequently pronounced recent exhibitions of conceptual art conceptually weak and declared the puffery of their accompanying catalogues to be often unintelligible and apparently intent upon confounding a general readership (2005: 258–9). The 2006 expanded and nominally revised edition of *High Art Lite* found Stallabrass as trenchant as ever.

Here, responding to the analysis afforded by Stallabrass, I want to examine the migration of a number of gallery artists who came to prominence in the 1990s to feature film production in the last ten years, and the distribution of their work in a more public realm. Some of these artists fall into the category 'YBA' as outlined by Stallabrass in 1999 and 2006, some not: it could even be argued that the publicity generated by the YBAs was allowed to overshadow the work of their contemporaries. The trend is exemplified by such releases as *Who I*

Journal of British Cinema and Television 9.3 (2012): 502–520
DOI: 10.3366/jbctv.2012.0102
© Edinburgh University Press
www.eupjournals.com/jbctv

Am and What I Want (David Shrigley, 2005), *Zidane – A 21st Century Portrait* (Douglas Gordon and Philippe Parreno, 2006), *Nowhere Boy* (Sam Taylor-Wood, 2009), *Exit Through the Gift Shop* (Banksy, 2009), *Elmina* (Doug Fishbone, 2010) and *Self Made* (Gillian Wearing, 2011). I shall contextualise this move with a consideration of various aspects of the art scene in Britain in the 1990s, easing and even abetting the process. I shall suggest that this process can be viewed as a simple extension of practice through time and across space (of materials, methods and formats) and as a decisive crossing of borders, to and fro, with all the territorial anxiety which that activity implies, on either side, for artists and critics alike. The migration of artist film-makers into features is far from novel – Derek Jarman and Isaac Julien are obvious precedents, while Peter Greenaway, commissioned by the BFI for *The Draughtsman's Contract* (1982) and by Channel 4 with artist Tom Phillips for the inspired collaboration *A TV Dante* (1987), has, in recent years, increasingly devoted himself to site-specific installation work outside Britain (Sargeant 2010: 246–8). Andrew Kötting, who received Arts Council co-funding for short films broadcast by the BBC in the early 1990s, secured European funding for his 2009 feature, *Uval*. The current pattern of exchange is, however, marked as much by the movement of content and technique, and exhibition thereof across different sites, as it is by the movement of personnel. Provisionally, I am organising my discussion under the headings of popularity, marketability and celebrity, aspects of the British art scene previously identified by Stallabrass and other commentators. Finally, I shall address Steven McQueen's 2008 *Hunger* as a film meriting substantial engagement.

Popularity

Since the 1990s, contemporary art has become popular in the straightforward sense that looking at art has risen in significance as a leisure activity. In his 2010 Lent Talk for BBC R4, Will Self suggested that a Cult of the Gallery has become a secular substitute for church attendance (although this was not an original observation). This enthusiasm for art has been confirmed by the number of visits to Tate Britain for the Turner Prize (partly prompted by media coverage of proceedings as a routine news item or as the subject of dedicated programming commissioned by its sponsor since 1990, Channel 4, which in 2006 broadcast *The Turner Prize Challenge*), to Tate Liverpool and to the extension of Tate Modern (the most visited museum of modern art in the world, welcoming 45 million visitors in its first

Amy Sargeant

ten years since opening in 2000). Recently inaugurated festivals and galleries include the Folkestone Triennial, and Turner Contemporary in Tracey Emin's Margate. Nottingham Contemporary opened in 2009 with a retrospective show of work by David Hockney (still Britain's favourite artist) and a series of related artists' films in the gallery's cinema, noncommittally called 'The Space', including *Parade*, a 2003 piece directed by Mark Leckey (a Turner Prize winner in 2008). In its first eleven months, Nottingham Contemporary received more than 270,000 visitors and, in 2010, together with the New Art Exchange and the Castle Museum, hosted *British Art Show 7: In the Days of the Comet* (which included work both shot on film and fabricated from archive film and television clips). Meanwhile, more than 300,000 people visited *Banksy versus Bristol Museum* between June and August 2009, some delivered by the busload and waiting up to eight hours to gain entry, with the museum extending its opening hours to accommodate the queues for predictably 'easily digestible' entertainment. Here, an artist previously as well-known for his unlicensed intrusions into, and modifications of, existing displays of art, archaeology and zoology as for his graffiti, was authorised to 'take on' the museum's collection: 'Please be aware that some of the historic relics now on display throughout the museum are fakes', warned a flyer for the exhibition.

Further examples of the use of contemporary artists to encourage audiences to engage anew with public and private institutions might include Marcus Coates' installation for *British Art Show 6*, displayed in Bristol alongside the stuffed specimens common to many a provincial museum. A number of people in different locations were recorded miming to the slowed-down soundtracks of a variety of species of birds and the footage was then subsequently edited at a speed to match the birds' natural delivery. In 2002, Mark Wallinger's ghoulishly compelling 1999 loop-tape, *Prometheus*, supposedly repeatedly presenting the death throes of a man in an electric chair, was selected for 'an intervention of loans' from the nomadic Invisible Museum to Sir John Soane's Museum. This piece not only recalls the fascination of 'primitive' film with such subjects – Edison's 1903 *Electrocuting an Elephant* comes to mind – but also reiterated the self-evident necrophilia of the Soane's founder and his obsessive accumulation of archaic objects. The British Museum's invitation to Damien Hirst, among other artists, to augment its existing collection was perhaps prompted by a fear that the institution was perceived as stale and stuffy. The project was an instance of the Museum's ongoing and ambitious programme of activities designed to promote understanding and expand interpretation of material and visual culture: a genuinely popularising venture. Grayson Perry, Turner Prize winner in 2003, provided expert commentary on pots for BBC R4's 2010 series covering the Museum's collection, *A History of the World in 100 Objects*, while Anthony Gormley commented on Rameses. Tracey Emin has shown work at the Foundling Hospital, and Jeremy Deller at the Women's Library. Contemporary artists, some installing film and time-based media in galleries and museums, have not only added to the catalogue of art currently attracting visitors but have also been employed to re-evaluate an existing stock of art, artefacts and objects for a contemporary audience.

On other occasions over the last decade, art has become popular by involving or emerging from the populace at large. I am thinking here of Gormley's 2009 democratic, living sculpture project for the fourth plinth in Trafalgar Square, *One and Other*, coverage of which extended to BBC R4's *The Archers*. The 2006 exhibition devoted to Jeremy Deller – Turner Prize winner in 2004 – at Bexhill's De La Warr Pavilion demonstrated his consistent interest in working with particular communities. His *The Battle of Orgreave* (2001), a reconstruction of a highly controversial clash between police and striking miners during the 1984–5 coal dispute, used the methods of battle re-enactment (a popular hobby) and cast veterans of the conflict and their relatives. It was filmed, with accompanying interviews, by Mike Figgis for Artangel, and subsequently broadcast by Channel 4 in 2002; it was also shown in the gallery alongside supporting documentation and evidence of Deller's further work at Orgreave. This was communal art as ritual, as memorial, as catharsis.

Stallabrass is disparaging of much of the work produced by the YBAs in the 1990s (among them Hirst and Emin) as overtly populist, 'feeding-off mass culture': in his view, 'this vampiristic art draws life from its already anaemic subject' (1999: 214). In this, as in much else, the nominal group imitated Andy Warhol – a Campbell's soup spray can appearing in *Exit Through the Gift Shop*. However, the nature of this 'feeding' was, and continues to be, diverse. Jane and Louise Wilson (who in 2008 fulfilled an inaugural commission from Quad with a 3D multiple-screen gallery installation, *Spiteful of Dream*, responding to Derby's industrial history) have also produced a series of large, flat photos evoking the anticipation attendant upon closed, illuminated curtains across 'dream palace' cinema screens. Manchester Cornerhouse's 2010 show, *Unspooling*, included the original plates from Wayne Winner's *Arthouse Cinema* (2004) – schematic, iconic, comic strip personal memoranda of such films as *Blow-Up* (1966) ('I'm so bored with my glamorous life', reads a think bubble), *Performance*

(1970) (dubbed 'swinging gangster 1966'), *The Wicker Man* (1973) (Sergeant Howie arrives in a bi-plane emblazoned with a 'Jesus Loves You' sticker), and Andy Warhol's *Empire* (1964). The artist Wayne Lloyd was also commissioned to perform in the gallery an action-packed re-telling from memory of *Hell is a City* (1960), the narrative augmented by his drawing of salient motifs: staring eyes, a black splodge (Manchester by night), a grey splodge (Manchester by day). Lloyd thus appropriately restored the mythical origins of the film's story to an oral rendition in front of an audience in the city in which the film was set. Popular culture as the subject for social commentary in art work, rather than as object of emulation or re-enactment, was appropriated by Phil Collins' 2006 Turner submission *return of the real*, for which he invited a panel of nine people who had appeared on reality television programmes to tell their stories to an audience of journalists. Sarah Thornton reports Collins as saying that he wanted his work to 'sit close to the thing it is critiquing' (2008: 133).

In the 1990s, Douglas Gordon often reworked cinematic materials, methods and formats, equally often mediated, consumed and remembered through a familiar engagement with television, home recording and video re-viewing (Brown 2004: 7–8). This domestic experience was manipulated and defamiliarised in the projection of *24 Hour Psycho* (1992), installed at Modern Art Oxford for Hitchcock's centenary as a vast, double-sided, free-standing screen. At this scale and attenuated speed (the original version running to less than two hours), the film's head shots were rendered monumental and each blink of an eye bore the weight of a heavy burden. In 2010, consistent with the habitual reworking of his own back catalogue, Gordon's *Psycho* was screened forwards and backwards for the Glasgow Biennial. *Between Darkness and Light (After William Blake)* (1997) mounted simultaneous screenings of *The Exorcist* (1973) alongside *The Song of Bernadette* (1943). The bulk of Gordon's effort seems to reside in singularly grand gestures: the staging of self-contained material in uncustomary external circumstances and under novel conditions.

While still employing filmic resources, other artists have been more preoccupied with the imitation and manipulation of existing material. The apotheosis of clever assemblages of popularly accessible material (now via DVD or Internet sources) was achieved by Christian Marclay's *The Clock* (2009), usually screened by Nottingham's New Art Exchange on weekdays from 10.00 till 19.00, which was allowed uniquely to run for its full 24 hour span in December 2010. The piece was selected as a response to the show's comet theme, as a measuring of time and of historical recurrence, and an exploration of the idea of parallel worlds. An international array of clips of clocks, watches and characters reacting to a particular time of day was edited together so as to synchronise with local time. A mere two-hour lunchtime sample (after high noon) delivered an international cross section of sources. Steaks were presented, from the raw to the well-cooked; meals were set out at home, in restaurants or snatched at work. There were kitchen clocks, bedroom clocks, railway station clocks, landmark clocks, electric clocks and digital displays, men's watches, nurses' watches, hourglasses, sundials, metronomes, speaking and striking clocks. There were synchronised and mismatched clocks, intercut or within a single moving frame. There was dialogue about clocks and watches. Appointments were met and missed. Fragments of British material (film and television) were readily identifiable and gamely name-checked. Sometimes a source was used singly, sometimes used several times, sometimes it was repeated out of order. Here could be found: Bond (as incarnated by Sean Connery, Roger Moore and Daniel Craig), Stanley Baker as a policeman (*Hell Is a City* again), *Went the Day Well* (1942), *Whistle Down the Wind* (1961), *Vera Drake* (2004), *Georgy Girl* (1966), *The Office* (BBC, 2001–3), *The Remains of the Day* (1993), *The Cement Garden* (1993), *Sexy Beast* (2000), *In the Loop* (2009), *The League of Gentlemen* (1960), *Sabotage* (1936), plus *Clockwise* (1985) (of course) and Orson Welles' speech in *The Third Man* (1949) about cuckoo clocks – flanked by two clips from elsewhere of a cuckoo clock at different times either side of midday. Over monochrome and colour and different language tracks, diegetic and non-diegetic sound, continuity was eased by standard editing patterns and procedures: 'held' establishing shots, close-ups, cuts on movements, the link of one shot of a foot under a bedcover to another, groupings of sequences from a particular source or on a particular theme. *The Clock* is fiendishly, compulsively, ingeniously accomplished and a glorious celebration of standard continuity editing techniques. Its achievement is that it manages to organise such a disparate mass of material and to sustain its air of both momentum and attraction for so long, foregrounding time-keeping and clock-watching, hitherto the background to, or impetus for, narrative action. It is entirely dependent on the materials and methods of mass culture (cinema and television) and, given what has been observed above, we may no longer say that its exhibition in a gallery contradicts any ambition to reach a popular audience. Apart from its extraordinary length, there is nothing about *The Clock*, separated from its screening environment, which requires its installation in a gallery as opposed to a conventional cinema. Despite the immediate presence of 24-hour television and *The*

Clock's imitation of construction patterns routinely used in television current affairs and documentary broadcasts, exigencies of scheduling and the bother and costs of copyright clearance contrive against its television transmission. Conditions of exhibition and viewing are thus part of its point: *The Clock* continues, like many clocks, even while a potential viewer is elsewhere and not looking. *The Clock* may thereby also be compared to (and distinguished from) Marclay's *Pianorama*, a site-specific and contained piece commissioned (alongside David Shrigley's *Walker*) for Ron Arad's programme *Curtain Call* at the London's Roundhouse in 2011. Meanwhile, Duncan Campbell's 2008 *Bernadette*, a 37-minute television portrait of the Northern Irish campaigner Bernadette Devlin, which also used archive material, was lifted to run under gallery conditions at the *British Art Show 7*.

The use of found footage to produce new work has been assisted in the last ten years by enhanced access to, and the dissemination of, newly digitised public and private archives – from the popular to the *recherché*. This tendency is shared by work produced for theatrical release (Terence Davies' *Of Time and the City* (2008)) with work intended for gallery exhibition (*The Clock*).

Marketability

The most conspicuous obsessive-compulsive private collector of art in the 1990s was former adman Charles Saatchi, purchasing en masse the work of a generation. Despite the mixed fortunes of his speculative shopping spree, he is not yet cured. Having bought cheap in the recession of the early 1990s in the hope of selling high later, in the current recession he has launched, with his friend Alan Yentob, BBC TV's *School of Saatchi* (2009), a talent show for the current crop of art school graduates, fronted by erstwhile protégée, Tracy Emin. Saatchi's Newspeak gallery was launched in the wake of the show. To the question: 'Are you trying to educate or entertain?' Saatchi has replied: 'If the programme is a dull flop, I'll pretend it was intended to educate. But obviously it would be nicer if it were entertaining enough to draw people to contemporary art'; to the question: 'Who is the next big artist?' he has answered: 'That's what the TV show will discover, we're hoping' (2009: 128, 133). Unremarkably, submissions included video work, although Saatchi confessed that 'even video god Matthew Barney looks a bit MTV to me' (ibid.: 154). In 1995, Saatchi used his gallery to promote advertising art; to her chagrin, Gillian Wearing (Turner Prize winner in 1997), saw a video work, in which children's voices were dubbed over adults, bought and subsequently imitated by a Saatchi & Saatchi subsidiary in ads for Volkswagen.

Saatchi is, of course, not the only link between advertising and the current British art scene. London Underground, a prominent site of fixed and time-based advertising, in 2011 launched its first film festival, *Smile*, including work by the sculptor Anish Kapoor. Shell has sponsored awards at the National Portrait Gallery, the annual Wildlife Photography award and Classic Drama at the National Theatre, while Mobil has sponsored the BFI's film restoration programme. Unilever sponsors a series at Tate Modern (including Tacita Dean's 2011 *Film*) while BP sponsors exhibitions at Tate Britain – prompting demonstrations against 'corporate imaging' in the summer of 2010 as a consequence of oil spills off the Gulf of Mexico. After the Turner Prize, one of the most prestigious accolades in British art, Beck's Futures, is sponsored by the makers of an imported lager. Conversely, British art has proved itself an exportable and desirable commodity elsewhere in Europe. The 2002–3 programme of the Musée d'Art Moderne de la Ville de Paris scheduled Steve McQueen (sponsored by agnès b. and Artangel) after Matthew Barney's *Cremaster Cycle* (1994–2002) and Philippe Parreno; in Berlin's Hamburger Bahnhof, Hirst's fancifully arranged decorative rubbish (fast-food and confectionery wrappers caught in a hedgerow) is installed alongside Joseph Beuys' rubbish, commemorative of specific historical and political events.

Meanwhile, the output of various artists has continued to lend itself to readily identifiable 'branding' across various media – including film and video – via certain themes, strategies, preoccupations and motifs. Mark Wallinger's interest in the British tradition of sporting art has extended from greyhound racing (an interminable loop-tape shown at the ICA) to boxing (the 2000 gallery piece, *Cave*) to horses: immaculate life-size paintings, in the manner of Stubbs, in Saatchi's 1997 *Sensation* show at the Royal Academy; an actual racehorse; and a larger-than-life, chalk-white horse sculpture intended to 'brand' the South of England as Gormley's *Angel* has done for the North. Even Wallinger's 2008 curated touring exhibition from the Hayward – *The Russian Linesman* – referenced competitive football and its place in popular memory via the 1966 World Cup. *State Britain*, a reconstruction of a long-running anti-war demonstration in London's Parliament Square, proudly celebrated the campaigner Brian Haw and the freedom to protest, securing the Turner Prize for Wallinger in 2007.

Deploying his familiar tactics of rumour, stealth and surprise, the artist known as Banksy was originally hailed as something of a romantic rebel and urban guerrilla, thanks partly to sentiments such as: 'The greatest crimes in the world are not committed by people breaking the rules but by people following the rules... As a precaution to ever committing major acts of evil it is our solemn duty never to do what we're told, this is the only way we can be sure.' Best known for his graffiti, he stated that 'a wall has always been the best place to publish your work... the most honest artform available' (2005: 8). His graffiti has now been catalogued as a tourist attraction, and in his home town of Bristol, 'The Mild Mild West' has been appropriated as the attractively autographed backdrop to Canteen, a trendy bar housed in a redundant office block in the self-appointed cultural quarter of the People's Republic of Stokes Croft.

Perhaps as a comment on the move of other artists into film and theatrical distribution, early in 2010 Banksy announced his own Sundance debut, *Exit Through the Gift Shop* ('the incredible true story of how the world's greatest Street Art movie was never made'), which is also the title of one of the exhibits in the 2009 Bristol Museum show. Despite his loudly proclaimed resistance to 'Brandalism', Banksy's promotional campaign was characterised by signature rat stencils appearing on walls in Utah, home to the festival, and announcements of a 'Spotlight Surprise', matched by the equally predictable photo-opportunity manifestations in Los Angeles in February 2011 which greeted the film's subsequent Oscar nomination. In February 2010, 'mystery' screenings in a disused vault in Waterloo converted into a 'pop-up cinema' complete with a painted red carpet and popcorn stall, along the lines of Banksy's 'pop-up' Christmas shops in Oxford Street and elsewhere, were predictably sold out. Publicity material and a jokey trailer freely viewable online (in the manner of music downloads) were fronted by a figure in a familiar monkey mask. A mysterious rat-backdropped 'hero' Banksy in black hood with mask at his side performed dubbed on-screen commentary ('it's not a film about me but I'm in there somewhere') while Rhys Ifans provided credited, off-screen, disgruntled commentary on the film's hired cameraman/anti-hero, the self-styled 'Mr Brainwash'–who is reported in the final credits (thus sustaining the film's mockumentary mode to the end) as being engaged on the artwork for *Madonna's Greatest Hits* album. Theatrical distribution of *Exit* was secured with art-house cinemas and, in Bristol at least, the Odeon chain. Long before 2009, Banksy had become corporate, not only in that the elaborate animatronics displayed in Bristol Museum obviously necessitated the enrolment of additional personnel, but also in that Banksy, as a brand, had sold out to the market–via estate agents and the saleroom (as indeed is acknowledged by *Exit* itself). *Exit*'s video archive of Banksy's site-specific installations and stunts thus complements and augments the lavish photographic catalogues, already published, of this often logistically ephemeral work. Official interest in authenticity, affirming Banksy's passage from transgression to incorporation, paralleled the concerns of *Exit Through the Gift Shop* with artistic credentials, attribution, usurpation and selling out: released on DVD by Paranoid Pictures it simultaneously, gesturally and redundantly, disclaimed itself 'not *Gone With the Wind*' (an archaic reference matching Banksy's pun on Judy Garland in *The Wizard of Oz* in his Bristol show: 'I don't think we're on canvas anymore').

Celebrity

For some artists of the 1990s, in particular Tracy Emin, manufactured celebrity was a vehicle by which they extended themselves into common and commodity culture (Merck and Townsend 2002: 6–7). The title of Grayson Perry's 2009 touring (and thereby accessible) show, *Unpopular Art*, was something of a misnomer, indicating work of itself not necessarily unpopular but rather of a preceding period in which artists were less well-known, their names less the topic of household conversation. Perry drew his exhibits from the Arts Council collection of work produced from the end of the Second World War to 1980. A dim John Bratby interior sat alongside a contorted bronze head of Francis Bacon, alongside early Martin Parr monochrome photographs which, typically, took the grubbiness of everyday life in Britain as their subject. A selection from the BFI National Archive, collectively titled *Nostalgia for the Bad Times*, ran concurrently with the exhibition through the BFI Mediatheque.

Much was made, prior to Perry's Turner Prize, of the fact that much of Tracy Emin's output was based in domestic handicraft. Paradoxically, perhaps, one of the most simplistic criticisms simultaneously levelled at Hirst was that his work was produced assembly-line style. For anyone with a basic knowledge of art history (from Renaissance workshops to Rodin to Warhol's Factory), this failed to disqualify the work from recognition as art (Krauss 1986: 151–70; Stallabrass 1999: 30). However, what interests me here is the procedure entailed in enrolling assistants and skilled professionals, often from the audio-visual media. Hirst's 2007 patronage of royally appointed Bond Street jewellers Bentley and Skinner (for *For the Love of God*) seems to me to sit comfortably alongside Douglas Gordon and Philippe Parreno's enlistment of Oscar-winning cinematographer Darius Khondji for *Zidane* (partly sponsored by the agnès b.

foundation, partly by Canal+). Both Hirst and Gordon/Parreno were beholden to the technical skills of master craftsmen. Furthermore, while Sally Potter seemingly refers tacitly to contemporary Julian Opie portraits in the flat colour backgrounds of her mobile-phone release *Rage* (2009), Gordon and Parreno explicitly directed their cinematographer's attention to art historical material for *Zidane* (most obviously Uccello's *The Rout of San Romano* and Goya's *The Third of May*) (Sargeant 2008: 94). For the chromatic range of *Hunger*, McQueen and his regular cinematographer, Sean Bobbitt (similarly photographer for the *Giardini* project), turned to Velázquez (Ciment 2008: 16; McQueen 2009: n.p.). In other words, artists now moving into films intended for theatrical distribution have not only made short films (albeit for gallery installation) – a familiar route for features directors – but certain artists have also already become accustomed to a directorial role in other work produced for the gallery.

Sam Taylor-Wood, like Hirst and Emin one of the original YBA's identified by Stallabrass, through her marriage to dealer Jay Jopling, enjoyed the doubly extraordinary privilege of a one-woman retrospective at the Hayward in 2002 (again, partly sponsored by agnès b.). Composite photographs exhibited evoked Warhol's short film, *Couch* (1964). *Third Party* (1999), also shown, cast Gina McKee, Ray Winstone and Adrian Dunbar with Marianne Faithfull (a characteristic nod to 1960s British pop celebrity) and Gillian Wearing solo dancing (a typical YBA in-joke, referring to Wearing's 1994 *Dancing in Peckham*). Filmically, the piece achieved little more than to deconstruct a formal device of conventional film editing – close-ups and eye-line matches across an imagined space – reconstructed in the actual space of the gallery. On film, Michelangelo Antonioni had achieved as much in *Blow-Up*. However, it did establish Taylor-Wood's social interests.

Philip French in the *Observer*, 27 December 2009, reviewing Taylor-Wood's Film4/UKFC-funded debut feature, *Nowhere Boy* (2009), commented:

> One would have expected a stark or experimental biopic from an avant-garde artist like Taylor-Wood, something comparable, say, with Julian Schnabel's film about the French writer Jean Dominique Bauby, *The Diving Bell and the Butterfly* or Steve McQueen's study of Bobby Sands, *Hunger*. Instead, she has truly surprised us by making a highly conventional film that most closely resembles *That'll Be the Day* (1973), starring David Essex as a composite character partly modelled on John Lennon, who drops out of grammar school to pursue a musical career. It ends as he's on the threshold of success and a sequel, *Stardust*, examines his rapid rise and fall.

The reference to Claude Whatham's *That'll Be the Day* struck me as apposite, not least in its comparable dullness. Not entirely coincidentally, a newly remastered issue of Beatles hits was the highest-selling CD of 2009. I was more surprised that the *Independent* could find the film **** 'Remarkable' and the *Evening Standard* **** 'Fresh and original'. Given that Taylor-Wood's recent oeuvre spans forgettable window-dressings for Selfridges flagship department store in Oxford Street (which also sponsored Gillian Wearing's 2000 show at the Serpentine), a numbing 2004 video portrait of David Beckham sleeping, photos of the couple referred to by David Furnish as 'myself and Elton' for the *Observer Music Monthly*'s 'Art Issue' in April 2009 and celebrity endorsements for Yves Saint Laurent, I wondered why French should expect anything 'stark' or 'experimental'. Press coverage in general, from the broadsheets (the front cover of *The Times* in May 2010) to *Hello!* (January 2010), has meanwhile evinced more interest in Taylor-Wood's pregnancy with her juvenile lead, Aaron Johnson, than in the film itself. The move of former YBA Taylor-Wood into film may once have been indebted to Warhol, but is now more comparable to that of fashion photographer Bruce Weber (into documentary – with *A Letter to True* (2003)) and of fashion designer Tom Ford (into features – with *A Single Man* (2009)) in the calculated use of celebrity to carry her from one area of activity to another.

'Better to be a celebrity because people talk about your art', said Saatchi in 2009, 'rather than your wedding photos in *Hello!*' (116). However, the popularity, marketability and celebrity achieved in general for contemporary art and artists in the 1990s and since – remarkable but by no means new – can and has been deployed usefully, and its currency can result in worthwhile things. While eased by these aspects of the art scene, the turn of artists to films made for distribution outside the gallery can be more than just a stunt.

Hunger

Steve McQueen was not one of the group tagged with the label YBA. However, he was one of only three black artists in Britain in the 1990s to have a gallery deal. This, together with his quietly expressed concerns with identity politics, eased his reception in America where, noted Stallabrass, the YBAs were often thought parochial: 'His themes took in issues of race but not too specifically, giving them a universal resonance – a convenient and dignified figure for the US art world' and elsewhere (1999: 232). In 1996 he contributed to the Hayward Gallery group show, *Spellbound*; in 1999 he won the Turner Prize; in 2003–4 his work was included in Tate Britain's retrospective screenings of artists' films, alongside work by Wearing and Emin; in 2009 he represented Britain at the Venice Biennale. In its first week of UK distribution in February 2008, *Hunger* was released on DVD through some 70 cinemas. Its theatrical release was assisted by UKFC post-production funding; *Hunger* was subsequently broadcast by Channel 4 (with Film4 being one of its original funders).

McQueen has used the public profile attained by the award of a Cannes film prize and the release of *Hunger* to promote a previous work, *Queen and Country* (2007), which toured regional galleries, culminating in its display at the National Portrait Gallery in 2010 (Pill 2008: 23). Commissioned by the Imperial War Museum and the Manchester International Festival, the film is the product of a collaboration with families of Britain's war dead in Iraq in order to produce a set of commemorative stamps. These have yet to be printed by the Royal Mail. Simon Poulter (1998) and Banksy have also produced mock stamps and currency, including 'Banksy of England' £10 notes bearing the head of Princess Diana (2005), duly promoted in passing in *Exit Through the Gift Shop*. But there was nothing frivolous in McQueen's stamps.

Hunger covers a specific period in the 1980s of the conflict euphemistically known as 'The Troubles'. *Hunger* is a political film but has not provoked the furore or controversy surrounding, say, London Weekend Television's *Death on the Rock* (1988), Jim Sheridan's *In the Name of the Father* (1993) or Paul Greengrass' *Bloody Sunday* (2000). *Bloody Sunday* was distributed and broadcast while the Saville Inquiry into the events depicted was still sitting, the Inquiry's final report, running to enormous length and cost, appearing only in March 2010. The reasons for a shift in reception are, to some degree, themselves political: investment by various parties in the 1998 Good Friday Agreement and the consequent power-sharing initiative; and the restoration of legislative powers to Stormont. However, the murder of two unarmed soldiers at Massereene Barracks in March 2009 and a car bomb planted outside the headquarters of MI5 in Northern Ireland in April 2010 served as reminders of a long history of violence and continuing in-fighting between opposing factions. But also, I suggest, film critics have been disposed to discuss *Hunger* narrowly as an 'artist's' film – as if McQueen's sole interest was to put together artfully composed images – despite the concurrence of Deller, Wallinger, Parker and Perry as artists who also demonstrate an investment in contemporary and historical political issues, and despite the concerns presented in McQueen's preceding projects. Like the prison orderly who stands back in awe at the perfect symmetry of a circle daubed in excrement on a cell wall, before hosing it down to erase the protest which its dirt represents, there has been a distancing on the part of certain critics from the intimately political content of McQueen's film. However, broadcast statements by Margaret Thatcher on the soundtrack and an opening title establish a context for the action which follows: 2,187 people have been killed in 'The Troubles' since 1969.

As the opening and closing titles of *Hunger* remind us, all the interests involved suffered casualties: sixteen prison officers were killed by paramilitaries during the 'blanket' and 'no wash' protests. Bobby Sands (here played by the Irish/German actor, Michael Fassbender) was only one of a number of hunger strikers, although the best-known by dint of his election to Westminster as MP for Fermanagh and South Tyrone during the course of his sacrifice. The introduction of Sands some way into the film serves to focus attention on starvation as a strategic political act within a longer war of attrition rather than as the prerogative of a single individual. I disagree entirely with Tony Rayns' estimation of *Hunger* as 'chaotically put-together' and 'from an aesthetic point of view... a mess'. If it lacks 'characterisation' and 'maintains no coherent point-of-view', the film is served all the better as an exposition of a battle of wills (2008: 63).

Much has been made of *Hunger*'s silences, the soundtrack only sparsely augmented by David Holmes' backing music, diegetic sound and exchanges of dialogue. Certainly, these allow the images to speak all the more volubly. But the silence can also be understood as resistance, the power of the powerless, equivalent in its oppressive volume and duration to the protesting clattering of canteen cans which underscores the title sequence and the subsequent, equally aggressive, battering of riot shields. A similar staccato-shot outburst of noise occurs when the nonconforming prisoners demolish their cells in protest at the humiliation represented by the civilian clothes with which they have been issued in the course of 'the circus of negotiation' as a substitute for standard, criminalising uniforms. 'Penal institutions', explains Juliet Ash, 'under the authority of particular states, use dress strategically to diminish the imprisoned... Sartorial punishment denies basic rights [and] diminishes self-esteem' (2010: 3). The notorious H-block of the newly built Maze prison was opened in 1976 on the site of the 'Nissen-hut dormitories' of Long Kesh internment camp. It was a formidable architectural structure designed to punish those incarcerated within its walls through constant surveillance. The denial of political status was one of the prison regulations wielded by prison authorities as a punitive measure in line with the prison's 'fortifications [that] show the toughness of the prison regime and the seriousness of those responsible for running it' (ibid.: 126). Not only can the men not be allowed to wear their own clothes, but are also deliberately insulted by the issue of clothes in which they would not be seen dead.

In its austerity and measured tone, *Hunger* has been justifiably compared with Robert Bresson's *Un Condamné à mort s'est echappé* (1956), likewise a film based on a 'true story'. The same punctilious preparation and rigorous self-control that have made a member of the French Resistance effective as a saboteur are applied to Fontaine's laborious planning of his escape, narrated in retrospect in measured and calm voice-over. The tedium of solitary confinement is interspersed with communal activity, dramatic incident set against the banality of everyday routine (in *Hunger*, a tea trolley is trundled down a corridor). The timing of Fontaine's bid for escape is prompted by his condemnation to death by his German captors. In *Hunger*, Sands achieves an escape, of sorts, by condemning himself to death.

McQueen, like Bresson, organises time as well as he composes shots – within single segments (an orderly laboriously hosing down a prison corridor) – and across the duration of the film as a whole. However, McQueen parts company with Bresson in the choice of structure for the presentation of his material. Dramatically, the action of *Hunger* is staged as a four-act play. The first act is marked by the prisoners' ability to communicate with the outside world (a radio smuggled into the prison and notes exchanged during visiting hours) and with one another – only the newest inmate seems interested in taking Holy Communion. Time spans across the opening acts are indicated by the healing of wounds brutally inflicted on Sands and his fellow prisoners by warders and riot guards beating the life out of their adversaries. Scars and bruises are worn as badges of honour. While the summary punishments exhilarate Sands, the pain reminding him that he is still alive and, in the denial of basic rights, asserting that the protest is being taken seriously in its ability to provoke such extreme retribution, reinvigorating his sense of self-esteem and purpose, they are too much for one of the policemen, who breaks down in tears. This figure is the 'boy-faced policeman' of Padraic Fiacc's 'Station/An Ordo' or the 'lonely little winter robin' of 'Enemy Encounter'. Outside the prison, the IRA takes yet more violent revenge on the warders. The final act is marked by Sands' turning inwards, in isolation, to his own resources, and the diligent attempts of warders and carers to keep their captive alive, to prevent him from wilfully wasting away. When nothing else is left to him, however dire the consequences for his body, turning away from food is Sands' last assertion of spiritual agency and resistance.

The prison interiors of the first two acts are generally characterised by bilious greens, fetid browns and the acrid, dark dampness of men's sweat on uniform shirts; Sands' withdrawal in the last act is shot in ethereal whites and cool blues, reminiscent of the warder's preceding ritualistic self-purgation in smoke, snow and water. The earth made flesh is set against the spirit; hardness against softness. Sands is laid gently on the sheepskin underlay which protects his bedsores – here, scars do not heal, and he recoils at the gentlest application of a salve. The UDA nurse (the tattoo across his knuckles echoing a warder's Union Jack key fob at the beginning of the film) sent to oversee Sands in the bath carries his stumbling charge back to bed in the manner already of a pietà. Sands' breath is by now so weak that it fails to disturb even the fall of a feather. Plates of food are delivered and removed, untouched. A distanced, anonymous voice-over flatly and authoritatively inventories a clinical prognosis and a litany of physical collapse as Sands' body closes down.

The most intense episode of Enda Walsh's screenplay decisively dominates the pivotal third act, introduced in a long, unrelentingly locked, formal two-shot of Sands and his priest confessor. Sands receives the only sort of priest to whom he might, just perhaps, listen – 'You're respected: you know that' – one who has seen life on the street, a smoking, 'whisky' priest, of the type characterised by Raoul Walsh's *Regeneration* (1915), Elia Kazan's *On the Waterfront* (1954) or Padre José in Graham Greene's 1940 novel *The Power and the Glory*. When I first saw *Hunger* I was also reminded, in the exchange between Sands and the priest, of Jean Anouilh's 1959 play *Becket*, and of the religious and political conundrum there voiced direct to God: is it saintly conduct to choose martyrdom for oneself? While Sands, in introspective close-up and flashback, recollects a boyhood experience of his preparedness to release a suffering animal from pain through death, Anouilh casts a little Saxon monk as token observer to the now mighty Becket's breach with his Norman master, the King of England. Both Sands and Becket are wrung by contending allegiances: Sands to his family and to Irish Republicanism, Becket to his former fraternal friendship with the King and his sworn duty to the Church of Rome. The priest appeals to Sands on behalf of his child; Sands' mother blesses his war wounds ('You're looking well, ma', 'So are you son, so are you') and his sacrifice, rushing to his bedside with a rosary as soon as she and her husband are admitted to the prison. But it is too late, nor will she try, to make this resiliently stubborn child eat. What McQueen gives us, therefore, is not a partisan endorsement of any position within the political conflict but a picture of a man, among other men, in crisis, left with nothing more than a hope that, by resolving that crisis, his political goals will be achieved and witnessed by others. It may even give us a man who is prepared to take the most drastic measures available to him in order to secure his own release from conflict.

Conclusion

In the ongoing debate concerning the transfer of White Cube artists to Black Box distribution, critics have adopted a number of positions. In the *Observer*, 24 September 2006, Mark Kermode, in alarmist, panicky mode, dismissed *Zidane* as unfit for cinematic purpose, while Jason Solomons in the same paper on 28 May 2006 had niftily dubbed it 'the greatest film about football ever made'. In turn, I would say that Isaac Julien's *Derek* (2008), mostly assembled from a previously broadcast television profile, often duplicating the self-same archival material alongside which it was shown, was out of place in the Serpentine (though, actually, I'm not sure where I *would* place it). What can be said, for sure, is that different gallery artists have used film and video differently, across a variety of exhibition spaces. Cornelia Parker (Turner shortlisted in 1997) contextualised her 2007 show, *Never Endings*, at Birmingham's Ikon (including flat gun blanks and metal bullets drawn down to fine coiled threads, alongside timber planking burnt to a shard in arms tests) with a frontally framed, head-shot interview with Noam Chomsky, reproduced as text in the accompanying catalogue. In the gallery, Chomsky's interlocutor was silenced. Tacita Dean has variously installed film and sound pieces at Tate Britain (in 2001) and with *Berlin Works* at Tate St Ives (in 2005). Her 2004 documentary *The Uncles* (devoted to Michael Balcon and Basil Dean) readily lent itself to theatrical screening. With the letterbox format, feature-length, anamorphic 16mm film study of the choreographer Merce Cunningham, *Craneway Event*, scheduled throughout May and June 2010, Frith Street was, to all intents and purposes, cast as a space for cinematic exhibition. However, as Dean's agent, the gallery offered for outright sale the four editions of the film thus far produced. While making work materially and technically susceptible to reproduction, Dean has thus exercised her right to restrict the distribution of her work and to control the conditions of exhibition. Distribution and exhibition are constrained by considerations apart from material and subject content.

518

Furthermore, in a culture where art and artists have become the subject of common currency and widespread popular commentary, the 'art film' can no longer be understood generally to designate an object of arcane or rarefied interest. Categorical boundaries have been not just crossed but have become blurred, not least through the availability of selections of 'artists' films', contemporary and retrospective, in formats shared with regular features and television. *Hunger* seems to me to demonstrate that certain artists have adapted not only readily but purposefully to various sites of exhibition and distribution – both in the content of the work and its form – and that audiences are more relaxed and better prepared to accept the transfer than are some critics. What is needed now, I suggest, is a reappraisal of the fields and methods of criticism – in particular instances and in general.

A version of this article was first given as an invited paper at the conference 'British Film 2000–2010: Crossing Borders, Transferring Cultures', Mainz, Germany, 2010.

Note

1. Significantly, Stallabrass was denied the right to reproduce material of which he was critical by galleries representing the artists, including Steve McQueen (*Bear*, 1993) and Richard Billingham (*Ray's a Laugh*, 1996). Mandy Merck and Chris Townsend, on the other hand, were fully supported by White Cube (London) and Lehmann Maupin (New York) for their sympathetic appraisal of the artist in *The Art of Tracey Emin* (2002).

References

Ash, J. (2010), *Dress Behind Bars*, London: I. B. Tauris.

Banksy (2005), *Wall and Piece*, London: Century.

Brown, K. M. (2004), *Douglas Gordon*, London: Tate Publishing.

Carey, J. (2005), *What Good are the Arts?*, London: Faber & Faber.

Ciment, M. (2008), 'La soif avant *Hunger*' and 'Entretien avec Steve McQueen: les raisons de vivre et les raisons de mourir', *Positif*, 573, pp. 9–16.

Fiacc, P. (1994), *Ruined Pages: Selected Poems*, Belfast: Blackstaff Press.

Krauss, R. (1986), *The Originality of the Avant-Garde and Other Modernist Myths*, Cambridge, MA: MIT Press.

McQueen, S. (2009), *Giardini Notebook*, London: British Council.

Merck, M. and Townsend, C. (eds) (2002), *The Art of Tracey Emin*, London: Thames & Hudson.

Pill, S. (2008), 'A starkly striking debut', *Metro*, 28 October.

Rayns, T. (2008), '*Hunger*', *Sight and Sound*, November, p. 63.

Saatchi, C. (2009), *My Name is Charles Saatchi and I am an Artoholic*, London: Phaidon.

Sargeant, A. (2008), 'Reading the grain: *Zidane*', *Bianco e Nero*, 561–2, pp. 87–98.

Sargeant, A. (2010), 'Combustible materials, general anxiety disorder and too much information', in F. Casetti, J. Gaines and V. Re (eds), *In the Beginning, at the Very End*, Udine: Forum, pp. 243–50.

Stallabrass, J. (1999), *High Art Lite: British Art in the 1990s*, London: Verso.

Amy Sargeant

Thornton, S. (2008), *Seven Days in the Art World*, London: Granta Books.

Thorpe, V. (2010), 'Fight to save Hirst and Banksy graffiti building', *Observer*, 31 January.

Amy Sargeant has written extensively on British silent and sound cinema, being co-editor (with Claire Monk) of *British Historical Cinema: History, Heritage and the Costume Film* (Routledge, 2002) and a previous contributor to this *journal*. She is author of *British Cinema: A Critical History* (BFI, 2005) and *The Servant* (BFI/Palgrave, 2011) and teaches film for Tisch School of the Arts, NYU.

Printed and bound by CPI Group (UK) Ltd, Croydon, CR0 4YY

14/03/2025

01833346-0003